LEWIS CARROLL

Self-portrait.

LEWIS
CARROLL

Fragments of a Looking-Glass
From Alice to Zeno

JEAN GATTÉGNO

Professor of English Literature at the University of Vincennes

Translated by Rosemary Sheed

London
GEORGE ALLEN & UNWIN
Boston   Sydney

Printed in Great Britain
by Biddles Ltd, Guildford, Surrey

Acknowledgements

I wish to thank the authorities of Christ Church, Oxford, for kindly allowing me to consult and reproduce various Lewis Carroll manuscripts in their possession; I am especially grateful to J. F. A. Mason, the college librarian, who read and corrected the sections on Christ Church and the Liddells, and to Denis Crutch for checking the text of the English translation so carefully.

I would also like to thank A. P. Watt & Son for allowing me to reproduce numerous extracts from Lewis Carroll's letters, diaries, and posthumous papers.

Roger Lancelyn Green has once again been of tremendous help, and I should like to express my gratitude to him. The number of references I make both to his work and that of Derek Hudson shows clearly enough how much I owe to these two important biographers of Lewis Carroll.

Finally, it was Denis Roche who believed I could write this book, and was its first thoughtful reader, after myself. My thanks to him for the heavy responsibility he thereby undertook.

J.G.

Contents

OVERTURE

Foreword

Is this a biography?

That is not just a rhetorical question; I have felt considerable hesitation in writing *Lewis Carroll*. Who am I, in
fact, talking about? The man who answered to the name
of Charles Lutwidge Dodgson? Or the man known only as
Lewis Carroll? The life of Charles Dodgson was written by
his nephew in the year he died. To write a life of Carroll,
one would have to be able to draw a line between his life and
his books. Is the author of *Alice* a different person from the
Reverend mathematical lecturer of Christ Church?

I am afraid I don't know the answer to that. In Carroll's
case, the pseudonym represented far more than just a pen
name: it transformed Dodgson's entire life. But it did not
split it in two, as many people have suggested. You cannot
look at either the writer or (for want of a better term) the
English citizen without considering the other: they are
inseparable. His nephew Collingwood, aware of the difficulty,
endeavoured to resolve it by writing *The Life and Letters of
"Lewis Carroll"* (*Rev. C. L. Dodgson*). To use a parenthesis in
juxtaposing the names was clever: it avoids both the duality
and the kind of equality that would have been suggested by
the word *and*. But Collingwood evaded the central problem;
indeed he probably could not help evading it: what sort of
"life" would produce the author of *Alice*? Since his day, two
fairly recent biographers have attempted to provide an

3

answer. First, Florence Becker Lennon in 1945[1] with the help
of psychoanalysis opened some genuinely new avenues of
vision. But her book, with its wealth of ideas, is rather like
one of those Chinese dishes in which the various ingredients
don't really mix together, and keep turning up on your fork
again and again, in a manner confusing and disconcerting to
the Western palate. In this book, there is a bit of life, a bit of
literature, a bit of history, a bit of psychoanalysis, and a great
deal of interpretation. Then, Derek Hudson, in 1954,[2] took
the occasion of the first publication of Carroll's diaries to give
us the essence of both Dodgson and Carroll; he does seem to
have produced a good likeness of his author. But, though putting out feelers in all directions, he does not risk extrapolating
from Carroll's writings, with the result that his biography
leaves certain areas in shadow which you need not be a confirmed Freudian to illuminate further.

The appearance of Hudson's book, in any case, made it
superfluous to write another "life" of Lewis Carroll, even
with additional material. But one could still try to re-create
—with as much coherence and unification as possible—"the
world of Lewis Carroll," and this I tried to do a few years
ago.[3] But since I eschewed biography, and felt that apart
from *Alice* and *The Game of Logic* Carroll's writings were
virtually unknown in France, it was on the unknown writings that I concentrated my major effort. Since then, there
has been an incredible advance in French studies of Carroll.

It became time to try once again to make an assessment
of Carroll who, though he may have been a double person,
was a single writer.

So I am writing once again about Lewis Carroll—but
there is a difference. Carroll is not at the centre of this work,
any more than the speaker is at the centre of his own discourse. By looking and discussing we may hope gradually to
discover him—and the two approaches sometimes coincide
and sometimes diverge with huge shadowy areas between—

[1] F. B. Lennon, *Victoria through the Looking-Glass*, New York,
1945; revised edn., as *The Life of Lewis Carroll,* New York, Dover, 1972.
[2] Derek Hudson, *Lewis Carroll*, London and New York, 1954.
[3] Jean Gattégno, *Lewis Carroll*, Paris, J. Corti, 1970.

and so re-create him (or perhaps create him?). The numerous short sections into which this book is divided reflect the nature of this endeavour. They also reflect Carroll's conviction that there are as many *worlds* (universes) as there are problems, and that these different worlds do not all fit together to form one world that embraces them all—or at least not within the range of our vision. Whatever exists can be classified; and every "thing," of whatever kind, belongs to its own world; that world determines it but is, in turn, determined by it. We cannot produce any "unity" that will totally encompass Lewis Carroll; but we can try to get near him by bringing together these various worlds, though in no kind of hierarchy of importance. This is what I have tried to do, without any suggestion (even to myself) that fitting the last piece of the puzzle into place is the end of the story.

One final, more personal, comment. It would be hard for me to behave as if I had not already written a book on Lewis Carroll, even though it was from such a totally different standpoint. And it is also hard to believe that what I then said was not of some value. I therefore trust that my readers will not mind my referring to it from time to time. In my journey through the world of Lewis Carroll, what I wrote in 1970 represented a particular stage. One need not, of course, stop at every staging post, but let me also say, to complete the metaphor, that I do not believe in short cuts either.

A Note on References

Six works to which repeated references are made will, for convenience, be abbreviated in the footnotes as follows:

Abbreviation	*Full Title of Work*
Collingwood	*The Life and Letters of Lewis Carroll (Rev. C. L. Dodgson)*, by Stuart Dodgson Collingwood, London and New York, 1898; Gale Research Company, Detroit, reissue 1967.
Diaries	*The Diaries of Lewis Carroll*, edited and supplemented by Roger Lancelyn Green (two volumes, but paginated as one), London and New York, 1953; Greenwood Press, Westport, Conn., reissue 1971.
Handbook	*The Lewis Carroll Handbook*, by S. H. Williams, F. Madan, and R. L. Green, London, 1962; Barnes & Noble, New York, 1970.
Hudson	*Lewis Carroll*, by Derek Hudson, Constable, London, 1954; The Macmillan Company, New York, 1954.
LCPB	*The Lewis Carroll Picture Book*, by S. D. Collingwood, London, 1899; Dover, New York, augmented reissue under the title *Diversions and Digressions of Lewis Carroll*, 1961, and later as *The Unknown Lewis Carroll*.
Works	Except where Roger Lancelyn Green's edition of the *Works* is specified, all references are to *The Complete Works of Lewis Carroll*, with an introduction by Alexander Woollcott, Modern Library, New York, 1936; Nonesuch Press, London, 1939; new edn., 1949.

A Carroll Chronology

———◆———

1832   January 27: Birth of Charles Lutwidge Dodgson, third child of Charles Dodgson, Perpetual Curate of the parish of Daresbury (in Cheshire).

1843   Mr. Dodgson becomes Rector of Croft, in Yorkshire. All of Charles's education up to now has taken place at home.

1844   Charles goes to nearby Richmond Grammar School, to prepare for entry to public school. He gets high marks and good reports.

1846   Charles goes to Rugby, one of the major public schools. His memories of this are to be most unhappy. During this period, he begins to write things for his brothers and sisters, in particular some of the parodies we later find in *Alice in Wonderland* and *Through the Looking-Glass*. He also organizes successful marionette shows.

1850   Charles matriculates.

1851   He enters Christ Church, Oxford on January 24, where he is to reside till his death. His mother dies a few days later.

1852   He passes the first part of his examinations, and gains a Studentship,[1] thus becoming a life member of the college. His mathematical success is assured.

---

[1] At Christ Church "Fellows" were called "Students"; they were teachers attached to a college, elected and paid by the college itself.

1854   Charles takes his B.A. and starts to prepare for ordi-
        nation.

1855   Liddell is elected Dean of Christ Church. His daugh-
        ter Alice is three years old. Charles makes contact
        with Edmund Yates, editor of the *Comic Times*, and
        offers him some poems (mostly parodies) and a few
        short stories.

1856   Yates opts for the pseudonym "Lewis Carroll." Charles
        meets little Alice Liddell for the first time.

1856-   Uneventful life in Oxford. Charles becomes a keen
61   photographer, and often uses Alice for a model.

1861   He is ordained Deacon on December 22, but intends
        to go no further.

1862   July 4: Rowing expedition on the Isis, when the story
        of Alice is told for the first time.

1863   His friends the MacDonalds strongly encourage him
        to publish the manuscript of *Alice*. John Tenniel
        agrees to illustrate it, and Macmillan's to publish it.

1865   Publication of *Alice's Adventures in Wonderland*.
        Charles's first satirical pamphlet, *The Dynamics of a
        Parti-cle*, published anonymously in Oxford. He falls
        out with the Liddells.

1867   Charles begins work on *Through the Looking-Glass*.
        He spends July–September travelling with his friend
        Liddon through Europe (as far as Russia).

1868   Death of Charles's father, now Archdeacon of Ripon.
        ("It was the greatest blow that has ever fallen on my
        life," he was to write thirty years later.) He continues
        to look after his family, especially his sisters, whom he
        establishes at Guildford (in Surrey).

1869   Appearance of *Phantasmagoria and Other Poems*. The
        first chapter of *Through the Looking-Glass* reaches
        Macmillan's.

1871   He completes the manuscript of *Through the
        Looking-Glass*, and Tenniel reluctantly agrees to illus-
        trate it. The book appears in time for Christmas.

1872   Charles publishes (anonymously) a pamphlet, *The
        New Belfry of Christ Church, Oxford*, making a
        forceful attack on Liddell's architectural plans. The

following year he returns to the charge with *Vision of the Three T's.*

1873 He starts working seriously on *Sylvie and Bruno*, one chapter of which, "Bruno's Revenge," has appeared earlier in a magazine in 1867.

1874 Charles publishes several mathematical works under his own name, and, anonymously, *Notes by an Oxford Chiel*, containing his Oxford pamphlets. Begins *The Hunting of the Snark.*

1875 He meets Gertrude Chataway, who is to be one of his most faithful "child-friends."

1876 March: Publication of the *Snark*, illustrated by Henry Holiday. Charles begins immersing himself in logic.

1877 He spends his summer holiday by the sea at Eastbourne, where he spends every August from then on.

1878 He starts inventing word games.

1879 Under his real name he publishes *Euclid and His Modern Rivals* and another word game. Influenced by the artist Gertrude Thomson, he starts to enjoy drawing child nudes.

1880 He suddenly gives up his beloved photography.

1881 He decides to give up lecturing at Christ Church which, though he has been doing it for twenty-six years, seems never to have been very successful.

1882 Charles is elected Curator of the Common Room by his colleagues, a post he is to retain for nine years. He publishes a work of mathematics.

1883 He publishes some verses (most of them old ones) as *Rhyme? and Reason?* He works on a stage adaptation of *Alice.*

1884 He publishes several articles on proportional representation, and several more appear the following year.

1885 *A Tangled Tale,* which appeared in *The Monthly Packet* between 1880 and 1884, is published in book form. He works on *The Nursery "Alice,"* and begins writing a treatise on logic.

1886 He gives some lectures at Lady Margaret Hall (one of the women's colleges in the university). The facsimile of the original manuscript of *Alice, Alice's Ad-*

ventures Under Ground, is published; also several articles on logic. Charles agrees to an adaption of *Alice* for the stage, under the title of *Alice in Wonderland*.

1887   He writes an article, "Alice on the Stage," for *The Theatre*, a magazine. *The Game of Logic* is published. He teaches logic in a girls' senior school in Oxford. Meets Isa Bowman, another of his favourite "child-friends."

1888   He publishes (under his own name) two mathematical works, one being *Curiosa Mathematica, Part I.*

1889   Publication of *Sylvie and Bruno* (begun in 1867), with illustrations by Harry Furniss.

1890   Publication of *The Nursery "Alice."*

1891   He sees Alice Liddell again (now Mrs. Hargreaves) after a long separation, and makes his peace with her mother, Mrs. Liddell.

1892   He resigns his post as Curator, and publishes several short texts on logic.

1893   Publication of *Sylvie and Bruno Concluded*; a collection of word games, *Syzygies and Lanrick*; and *Curosia Mathematica, Part II: Pillow Problems* (signed C. L. Dodgson).

1894   He completes *Symbolic Logic*, and publishes two logical paradoxes—one being "What the Tortoise Said to Achilles."

1896   Appearance of *Symbolic Logic, Part I: Elementary* (signed Lewis Carroll). Part II never, in fact, materializes.

1897   He gives several sermons to a congregation of children. Also, he discovers a number of rules for rapid division and multiplication. On November 8, he decides to send back all letters addressed to "Lewis Carroll, Christ Church," with the words "not known" written on them.

1898   At the beginning of January, a mild chill develops into bronchitis; Charles Lutwidge Dodgson dies peacefully January 14.

VARIATIONS

The last photograph of Alice Liddell taken by Lewis Carroll
(1870).

Alice

Though there were a great many Alices in Carroll's life, only two of them really mattered: the daughter of the Dean of Christ Church, and the heroine of the first two stories. Luckily, they have enough in common to be brought together under one chapter heading.

Alice Liddell

When Liddell's appointment as Dean of Christ Church was announced in June 1855, it was not well received in the college, and Carroll gave expression to this general feeling in his diaries (p. 51). Nor did he ever have cause to change his mind on the point, though the fact that the Dean was accompanied by his four children—Harry, Lorina, Alice, and Edith —led Carroll personally to see things in a rather different light.

Alice was three years old in 1855, but he met her first in 1856. In the meantime, he had met two of her cousins on the beach: little Frederika—"One of the most lovely children I have ever seen. . . . One of the nicest children I have ever seen, as well as the prettiest: dear, sweet, pretty little Frederika!" (*Diaries*, pp. 62–63); and then Gertrude, Frederika's sister, "even prettier than my little favorite Freddie; indeed she has quite the most lovely face I ever saw in a child" (p. 65). In March 1856, he "made friends with little Harry Liddell,"

then aged nine ("certainly the handsomest boy I ever saw");
two days later he saw him again with his sister Lorina, the
eldest of the girls, aged seven. His first meeting with Alice
was a month and a half later, April 25, 1856, on one of Carroll's first photographic sorties into the college. He marked
this day "with a white stone"—an undeniable sign for him of
great emotion; and since of the three little girls present he
already knew Lorina, and Edith, the youngest, was only
two, it seems clear that it was Alice who affected him so profoundly. It was to be some time, however, before they became
friends. In June, Carroll went on a rowing expedition with
Harry and Lorina ("the latter, much to my surprise, having
got permission from the Dean to come"). In the many photographs he was to take of the Dean's children, Alice was
obviously always included, but there is no mention of her in
the diaries before May 5, 1857, the day after her fifth birthday. In the meantime, though, Carroll had visited the Dean's
home so frequently that he began to feel, from November
1856, that Mrs. Liddell found him a nuisance. And, in May,
when he brought Alice a "small birthday present," he found
to his astonishment that it was believed in the college that he
was in love with the children's governess. He immediately
decided:

> I shall avoid taking any public notice of the [Liddell] children
> in future, unless any occasion should arise when such an inter-
> pretation is impossible. (p. 111)

For all that, his visits to them remained just as constant. In
November, the Dean needed a rest, and the whole family set
off for Madeira; Carroll took leave of "the dear loving little
children, . . ." (p. 130). They stayed away for several
months, and Carroll's diaries are missing from April 18, 1858
(before the Liddells' return) to May 9, 1862, barely two
months before he first told the story of "Alice's adventures."

So for this lengthy, and possibly decisive, period we have
no precise information, not even the subjective comments of
the diaries. However, a letter from Carroll to his sister Mary,
dated February 1861, mentions one detail:

My small friends the Liddells are all in the measles just now. I
met them yesterday. Alice had been pronounced as commencing,
and looked *awfully* melancholy.[1]

Apart from that, we are indebted to Alice's own account (as
Mrs. Hargreaves), which was published in 1932,[2] but, given
that seventy years had elapsed since the recorded events, her
account could hardly be expected to contain anything surprisingly new. We do find in it an interesting, though probably idealized, picture of the atmosphere during those after-
noons the Liddell children spent with Carroll.

We used to go to his rooms. . . . escorted by our nurse. When we got
there, we used to sit on the big sofa on each side of him, while
he told us stories, illustrating them by pencil or ink drawings as
he went along. When we were thoroughly happy and amused at
his stories, he used to pose us, and expose the plates before the
right mood had passed. He seemed to have an endless store of
these fantastical tales, which he made up as he told them, drawing busily on a large sheet of paper. . . . When we went on the
river for the afternoon with Mr. Dodgson—which happened at
most four or five times every summer term—he always brought
out with him a large basket full of cakes, and a kettle which we
used to boil under a haycock, if we could find one. . . . The party
usually consisted of five: one of Mr. Dodgson's men friends as
well as himself, and us three [Lorina, Edith and Alice]. . . . Mr.
Dodgson always wore black clergyman's clothes in Oxford, but
when he took us out on the river, he used to wear white flannel
trousers. He also replaced his black top-hat by a hard white straw
hat on these occasions, but of course he retained his black boots,
for in those days white tennis shoes had never been heard
of. He always carried himself upright—almost more than
upright—as if he had swallowed a poker.

In 1932, Alice, recalling that period of her life, always
speaks of "us," and Carroll in his diaries almost never mentions Alice apart from her sisters. There is one interesting
exception: on March 12, 1863, during the celebrations in

[1] Hudson, p. 124.
[2] Captain Caryl Hargreaves, "Alice's Recollections of Carrollian
Days," *The Cornhill Magazine*, July 1932.

honour of the Prince of Wales's marriage, Carroll writes: "It was delightful to see the thorough abandonment with which Alice enjoyed the whole thing"; and: "The Wedding Day of the Prince of Wales I mark with a white stone" (*Diaries*, 193–94). Something must have happened to him that day, for three days later we read:

> I began a poem the other day in which I mean to embody something about Alice (if I can at all please myself by any description of her) and which I mean to call 'Life's Pleasance'. (p. 194)

This is a pun, since Pleasance was Alice's second name. In May he sent her a birthday present—probably a traditional gesture. But the boat trips in the spring of 1863 were the last. Mrs. Liddell seems to have disliked Carroll's assiduity more and more; in 1864 she categorically refused to permit any further outings. In March 1865, he met Lorina in the street in Oxford, and notes: "It is long since we interchanged a word, but we met as if it had been yesterday" (*Diaries*, p. 228). And three weeks later, by one of those ironies which seem almost too good to be true, he came upon the three Liddell sisters in a museum—in a painting by W. B. Richmond:

> A very pretty picture on the whole: Ina [Lorina] looking a little too severe and melancholy—much as, I am sure, she would have looked sitting to a stranger [!]; Alice very lovely, but not *quite* natural . . . (*ibid.*)

The whole thing was now over. A month later, Carroll ran into Alice in one of the college quadrangles, and notes: "Alice seems changed a good deal, and hardly for the better —probably going through that awkward stage of transition" (pp. 230–31). She was twelve. He saw her again, of course; on July 4, for instance (the third anniversary of the "famous expedition" on the Isis), in another museum, this time in the flesh, escorted by her father. But it is significant that he does not even bother to note down the day when he sent an inscribed copy of *Alice* to the Liddells; he merely says, on July 15, 1865: "Went to Macmillan's and wrote in twenty or more copies of *Alice* to go as presents to various friends . . ." (p. 233). Even though Alice came to be photographed in

1870 (accompanied by her mother), and even though Carroll sent her a signed, leather-bound copy of the *Looking-Glass* in 1871 (he sent three in all to the family), and then in 1873 an Italian translation of *Alice*, there was no longer any deeper relationship between them. And by 1885, she had become "Mrs. Hargreaves" in his diaries. Carroll wrote to ask her permission to print the manuscript of the first version of *Alice*; in 1888 he met Mr. Hargreaves, and notes:

> It was not easy to link in one's mind the new face with the olden memory—the stranger with the once-so-intimately known and loved 'Alice' [the quotation marks are significant indeed].
> (p. 465)

Late in 1891, kept at home by a "synovitic knee," he says:

> As Mrs. Hargreaves, the original 'Alice', is now at the Deanery, I invited her also over to tea. She could not do this, but very kindly came over, with Rhoda, for a short time in the afternoon.
> (p. 488)

This was the end of the friendship between Carroll and Alice Liddell.

The Two Alices

Clearly, we cannot just leave it at that. But we cannot take it further without making a long detour by way of the other Alice. There is good reason for this: biographically speaking, we have absolutely no basis for any hypothesis that Carroll was passionately attached to Alice Liddell—but neither have we any evidence, objectively, against it. Some critics, as we know,[3] have suggested that he went so far as to ask Mrs. Liddell for Alice's hand in marriage; that hypothesis should, I am sure, be rejected out of hand. But apart from that, almost any supposition remains possible, for Carroll himself never said or wrote anything, and his letters to Alice (which might have been as revealing as some of those he later sent to various of his other young friends) were burnt by Mrs. Liddell's orders.

[3] See also "Celibacy."

If, then, we seek the answer to the inevitable question—
just what was the nature of Carroll's attachment to Alice
Liddell?—we must go by way of the literary *Alice*.

The origins of the story deserve a brief glance.

On July 4, 1862, Carroll set off on one of his favourite
expeditions, with the three little girls and his friend Duckworth:

> We had tea on the bank there [at Godstow], and did not reach
> Christ Church again till quarter past eight [in the evening] when
> we took them on to my rooms to see my collection of micro-pho-
> tographs, and restored them to the Deanery just before nine.
> (*Diaries*, p. 181)

And on February 10, 1863, Carroll added opposite this a
note: "On which occasion I told them the fairy-tale of
Alice's Adventures Under Ground."[4] We have three other
versions of this event. First, Carroll's own:[5]

> Many a day had we rowed together on the quiet stream—the
> three little maidens and I,—and many a fairy tale had been
> extemporised for their benefit ... yet none of these many tales
> got written down; they lived and died like summer-midges, each
> in its own golden afternoon, until there came a day when, as it
> chanced, one of my little listeners petitioned that the tale might
> be written out for her. That was many a year ago, but I distinctly
> remember, now, as I write, how, in a desperate attempt to strike
> out some new line of fairy-lore, I had sent my heroine straight
> down a rabbit-hole, to begin with, without the least idea what
> was to happen afterwards. ...

Alice's version,[6] though obviously less precise, corrob-
orates Carroll's in essentials:

> Nearly all of *Alice's Adventures Underground* was told on that
> blazing summer afternoon, with the heat-haze shimmering over
> the meadows where the party had landed to shelter for a while
> in the shadow cast by the haycocks near Godstow. I think the
> stories he told us that afternoon must have been better than

[4] This was the title Carroll first gave his story.
[5] From "Alice on the Stage," *The Theatre*, April 1887. Reproduced
in *LCPB*, pp. 163–74.
[6] Hargreaves, "Alice's Recollections."

usual, because I have such a distinct recollection of the expedition, and also, on the next day, I started to pester him to write down the story for me, which I had never done before. It was due to my 'going on, going on' and importunity that, after saying he would think it over, he eventually gave the hesitating promise which started him writing it down at all.

But the third version, Duckworth's,[7] gives more detail about the circumstances of the actual narration:

> I rowed *stroke* and he rowed *bow* in the famous Long Vacation voyage to Godstow, when the three Miss Liddells were our passengers, and the story was actually composed and spoken *over my shoulder* for the benefit of Alice Liddell, who was acting as 'cox' of our gig. I remember turning round and saying, 'Dodgson, is this an extempore romance of yours?' And he replied: 'Yes, I'm inventing as we go along'. I also well remember how, when we had conducted the three children back to the Deanery, Alice said, as she bade us good-night, 'Oh, Mr. Dodgson, I wish you would write out Alice's adventures for me'. He said he should try, and he afterwards told me that he sat up nearly the whole night, committing to a MS. book his recollections of the drolleries with which he had enlivened the afternoon.

If we bring together the physical details reported in all these versions, we get a fine picture: the heat[8] and the haze shimmering over the meadows; the peaceful afternoon on the river which appears to have been almost deserted (the summer vacation had begun, so that most of the students had left, and in those days tourists scarcely existed), water so calm as to be almost like a mirror; the three little girls, his favourites of the moment. In the boat, Duckworth was in the position that demanded the major physical effort, while Carroll, facing Alice, with Duckworth between them, rowed in time to Duckworth and told his story, no doubt in leisurely fashion. Everything combined to make this one of those special moments when "inspiration" can be given free reign.

[7] *The Lewis Carroll Picture Book*, pp. 358, 360.
[8] Despite the fact that when a check was made with the London Meteorological Office in 1950, it was found that Oxford was "cool and rather wet" on July 4, 1862.

Carroll's memories, in the article I have already quoted,
express this vividly:

> In writing it out, I added many fresh ideas, which seemed to
> grow of themselves upon the original stock; and many more
> added themselves when, years afterwards, I wrote it all over
> again for publication; but . . . every such idea, and nearly every
> word of the dialogue, *came of itself.*

This "inspiration" was quite different from that which
marked the origins of *The Hunting of the Snark*, described
by Carroll in the same article:

> I was walking on a hillside, alone, one bright summer's day,
> when suddenly there came into my head one line of verse—one
> solitary line: 'For the Snark *was* a Boojum, you see'.

No sudden thunder clap in a clear sky this time; it was the
whole atmosphere that combined to produce the "inspiration"; physically, the heat, the stillness, and slight bodily
exercise; and emotionally, the adored little girls, an adult
friend engaged with something else who could not even see
the face of the storyteller. These are the ideal conditions for
daydreaming, and also (perhaps it is the same thing) for the
confessions of the analyst's couch. Though it may not have
been the Unconscious itself talking, certainly the major bar-
riers were removed. But if they were, it can only have been
during the actual time Carroll was talking, the afternoon of
July 4. Just as when one tries to recount a dream afterwards,
the moment he tried to write down the story he had told, all
the old blocks reappeared; thus the manuscript version, completed eight months later, must inevitably have been far
removed from the original. How much more so the text of
Alice in Wonderland, almost twice as long and with considerable additions—notably the episodes of the Cheshire Cat and
the Mad Hatter's tea party. And in both something is left out
that concerns us directly here: the presence of Alice in the
flesh. In fact, the first manuscript includes, though we cannot
know whether the original did, a whole series of references to
the actual situation. Alice's main companions in the pool of
tears, to start with: "There was a Duck [Duckworth] and a

Dodo [Dodgson—who stammered], a Lory [her sister Lorina][9] and an Eaglet [Edith]." They were to be preserved in the final version, but allusions that were too patent were omitted—such as Alice's saying, after all the animals have left: "Really, the Lory and I were almost like sisters! and so was the dear little Eaglet![10] In the same way, details that were too true to history were left out, like the two following:

> How nicely the Duck sang to us as we came along through the water; and if the Dodo hadn't known the way to that nice little cottage, I don't know when we should have got dry again. . . . (*ibid.*)

> 'I only meant to say,' said the Dodo in rather an offended tone, 'that I know of a house near here, where we could get the young lady and the rest of the party dried.' . . . (p. 26)

Both these, as indeed the whole episode of the pool of tears, clearly hark back to the preceding expedition (June 17), which Carroll describes in his diary (p. 178):

> About a mile above Nuneham, heavy rain came on, and after bearing it for a short time I settled that we had better leave the boat and walk: three miles of this drenched us all pretty well. I went on first with the children . . . and took them to the only house I knew in Sandford, Mrs Broughton's. . . . I left them with her to get their clothes dried.

The connection could hardly be clearer.

The first manuscript also preserved, though at the cost of a certain disorganization of structure, references to the river on which the tale was told, which were afterward omitted. For instance, when the party all emerge from the water: "The pool had by this time begun to flow out of the hall, and the edge of it was fringed with rushes and forget-me-nots" (p. 33). Also the reference to Carroll himself, abundantly clear to the Liddell children, in the guise of the White Rabbit, when Alice hunts for the pair of gloves he wants:

[9] Hence the argument between Alice and the Lory about their respective ages.
[10] *Alice's Adventures Under Ground,* New York, Dover, 1965, p. 32.

She knew he had lost a pair in the hall, but, of course, she said
to herself, he has plenty more at home. (p. 34)

—an allusion to Carroll's insistence upon always wearing
gloves;[11] and the vision of the end of the story, when Alice's
sister, after listening to her account of her dream, "saw a very
old town, and a river winding gently not far off along the
plain" (p. 89) is far too direct a reference to Oxford.

Not all these omissions are equally significant, but the
overall result—and no doubt the reason they were made—is
to separate the story from the situation that brought it into
being (thus actually drawing more attention to the expeditions on the Isis in June and July 1862) and from an atmosphere whose most vital component was Alice's presence.

The content of the first version of *Alice* provides further proof, in at least two ways. First, the episodes added to
the 1865 *Alice* introduce a totally new factor: playing with
words. Only one play on words appears in the earlier text: the
pun on *tortoise* and *taught us*,[12] during Alice's meeting with
the Mock Turtle (whose name we are never told, inciden-
tally). But the play on syntax when the Mouse uses the
phrase "found it advisable,"[13] though it was made possible by
the fact that the expression figured in the first text, was not
Carroll's own. In other words, a major facet of Carroll's
world had not, at that time and in those circumstances, yet
appeared. Second, and more significant still, the narrative
structure of the story changes: the first *Alice* recounts, in a
more or less linear way, the adventures that *happened to*
Alice, whereas the second takes Alice through a world where
things happen *outside* her. That is natural enough in the
added episodes, the Mad Hatter's tea party, for instance, or
the meetings (which are simply dialogues) with the Cheshire
Cat. But even in some of the scenes preserved from the first
version, like the trial of the Knave of Hearts, or the meeting

[11] Isa Bowman says that "in all seasons he wore black and grey cotton
gloves"; *The Story of Lewis Carroll*, London, 1899, p. 9.
[12] *Alice in Wonderland*, Chap. IX.
[13] *Ibid.*, Chap. III.

with the Mock Turtle and the Gryphon, the part not concerning Alice directly is minimal as compared with the final
version. In short,[14] I would say that where the first manuscript told the story of an *adventure*, the final text is more
the story of a *journey*.

It is easy to see how simple that adventure was, in
fact, the moment one tries to tell the story in brief (and
oddly enough, the same is also true of the second *Alice*):
Alice follows a rabbit, goes down a rabbit hole with him,
keeps changing her height, almost drowns in her own tears, is
then half-suffocated, recovers her normal height, gets into the
longed-for garden, and finally emerges triumphantly from a
confrontation with the woman who is in charge there. Summed
up thus (and one could no doubt shorten it still further
without changing it in essentials), the story is so obviously
open to a Freudian interpretation that it is not surprising that it
should have been precisely this thread in the final version that
William Empson seized upon, as long ago as 1935.[15] But
we can see its elemental, basic character even more clearly if
we note that the episodes added afterward—apart from the
wordplay which, though essential, is different in kind—are in
most cases simply a recapitulation of Alice's adventure: at the
Mad Hatter's tea party,[16] for instance, the Dormouse is in
the same relation to the March Hare and the Mad Hatter as
Alice herself is to the various creatures she meets who behave
so aggressively toward her. And its position in the teapot is
the precise equivalent of hers in the White Rabbit's house.
The Duchess's baby is Alice again ("I know who I *was* when
I got up this morning, but I think I must have been changed
several times since then," she says to the Caterpillar); and the
Knave of Hearts's trial, when he is accused of a crime of
which there is no proof at all, is Alice's own trial: her crime

[14] Cf. my *Lewis Carroll*, Part II, Chap. 3.
[15] "Alice in Wonderland: the Child as Swain," *Some Versions of Pastoral*, London, Chatto & Windus, 1935. Reprinted in *Art and Psychoanalysis*, New York, Criterion Books, 1957.
[16] According to Green (*Diaries*, p. 172), this episode was, in fact, a
separate story, which Carroll told the Liddell girls on another occasion.

is being a child, and she emerges triumphant. The sympathy
she feels for the baby, the Dormouse, and the Knave is due
not merely to her sense of justice, but also to her feeling of
affinity with them all. It is clear from the way these episodes
keep covering the same ground again and again that Alice's
position is central; and in the earlier version that position and
its meaning is even clearer.

This is just the first step. We are still left with the question, not whether "Alice" is the centre of the story of which
she is heroine, but of the nature of her relationship with Alice
Liddell. As to this, I think we must dismiss all the "biographical" interpretations; they really cannot help us. Of course, the
Liddells' cat was called Dinah; of course the poems Alice parodies are poems the Dean's children must have recited many
times and had many opportunities to maltreat; of course the
children's formidable governess may well have figured as the
Queen of Hearts or the Duchess; and of course the lovely
garden must have been reminiscent of the college gardens,
especially those reserved for the use of the Students and the
Dean himself. But these are only superficial details. In spite of
them—perhaps, indeed, because of them, since they tend to
conceal the essential point—it is not Alice Liddell whom Carroll brings alive in his story, it is an idealized image of himself. That image was obviously in part the result of his
devoted contemplation of a flesh-and-blood child—in the
same way as each of us sometimes thinks to read his own features and destiny in the features and destiny of someone else.
But what Carroll is seeing in this story is Carroll; what he is
talking about is himself and not anyone else. As he made up
the original version of *Alice* in the boat, Carroll could only
just see Alice Liddell, half-hidden behind Duckworth's back;
in terms of the somewhat facile analogy outlined above, it
was Alice who was the analyst, and at that stage, the object of
a powerful transference.

That this is so is proved by comparing *Alice in Wonderland* with *Through the Looking-Glass*; the latter not only
intellectualizes "Alice's" fundamental situation, but deliberately establishes a gulf between the heroine and the author,

thus concealing still further what he really wants to say.[17]
The function of the White Knight is, in fact, to present a
Carroll who is recognizable—the absent-minded, pathetic old
bachelor-inventor—but has *aged* (he was to do the same
thing in *Sylvie and Bruno*) and is made to seem even older,
since the author flouts all "biographical probability" by
giving Alice a definite age: seven and a half. Her age was not
stated in *Alice in Wonderland*. Here it has the added advantage of allaying suspicion, since by the time the second story
was published, the "real" Alice was twenty. So Carroll is
definitely separated from his heroine, yet still present in his
book. But the adventure that is recounted is fundamentally
the same: it is death, resurrection, and victory, but this time,
as I have said, it is intellectualized. Alice's death, here, is the
loss of her name, and doubts as to her "reality," rather than
any threat to her physical integrity; the Red King's dream
takes over from the Queen of Hearts' "Off with her head!"
And it is no mere chance that it is the White Knight who
shows Alice the way to her reconciliation with the world of
other people (in this case grown-ups):[18] the subject becomes
divided, speaking with two voices, and it is in this split that
the solution is to be found.[19]

Is Alice Himself?

Though there is this infinite distance between Alice Liddell and the Alice of the books, there are still some points of
contact. But they are little more than coincidences. The age
Carroll attributes to his heroine in the *Looking-Glass*, for

[17] "Carroll wanted to tell a story to a little girl; the story wanders, the
little girl changes, and the Wish remains in sole control of a space undeter-
mined by any time, while, alongside the text, the person who gave the
starting signal grieves, and confides the sufferings of an aging and maso-
chistic adolescent in tearstained verse," writes H. Cixous (introduction to
the bilingual edition of *Through the Looking-Glass*, Paris, Aubier-Flam-
marion, 1971, p. 17).

[18] See my *Lewis Carroll*, Part II, Chap. 3.

[19] At the risk of schematizing, we may note that all emotion and
action is reserved to Alice, while the White Knight only thinks and talks.

instance, was not Alice's age when she first read or heard the story: it presents her *sub specie aeternitatis*, as in a snapshot, a film still (and remember that, in painting, a still-life depicts inanimate nature!) of a child and of childhood; Sylvie was to be rather older in *Sylvie and Bruno*. Alice Liddell was seven and a half in 1859; hence it seems probable that there was at that time some intensely passionate feeling for her on Carroll's part. But, if so, it was not a passion for Alice; it was for Carroll no more than the best, perhaps the only, occasion he had of coming face to face with himself as he wished to be. Humpty-Dumpty's statement ("An uncomfortable sort of age. Now, if you'd asked *my* advice, I'd have said 'Leave off at seven'—but it's too late now") applied to him quite as much as to Alice Liddell. It was not that that precise age held any special magic for him, but it evoked a phase supposedly idyllic because prepubertal; further, in Carroll's own life, it evoked a period before he went to school—a time of which all his memories seem to be happy ones. The conjunction of these two closely interlinked factors resulted logically in an idealization of that age. And since what he depicts is a nature in which sexuality, though present, is as yet barely differentiated (at least to pre-Freudian eyes), the metamorphosis whereby Charles becomes Alice can take place without regard to any other personal factors, and without any great effort.

To identify "Alice" positively with Carroll would call for more rigorous proof. But she must certainly be dissociated from Alice Liddell. In the first place, because, contrary to what Collingwood says[20]—though cautiously, it must be admitted—Alice Liddell was not the first of his uncle's little-girl friends: in 1855, the first year of his diaries to survive, we find him becoming attached to Florence Crawshay (p. 60), and then to Alice's two cousins whom he met before he met her, Frederika and Gertrude Liddell (pp. 62–65). In the second place, because Carroll, as we have seen, made a highly significant change over the years in introducing quotation marks when referring to his heroine in the diaries (pp. 465 and

[20] "His first child-friend, to my knowledge, was Miss Alice Liddell." Collingwood, p. 385.

488). (He refers to her nowhere else: she remains out of sight of an indiscreet public who might take all too much interest in the original "Alice" of the book.) This is proof enough of the distance he himself set between the two, proof above all that though the fictional child was made possible by a unique encounter with a unique little girl, she could not be explained, by Carroll or anyone else,[21] in terms of a single person. In the triangle Carroll–Alice Liddell–"Alice," no single identification can possibly account for the reality. Carroll is not "Alice" any more than he is Alice Liddell; and Alice Liddell is not the character in the books. At most we can say that some kind of current passed through Alice Liddell and brought to life a picture waiting to become animated. But as in Poe's "Oval Portrait," the life drawn away from Alice Liddell for "Alice" was taken at the expense of the real little girl. That Carroll's fondness for her did not survive the writing of *Alice* (a fact not often enough stressed) was not coincidence, nor was it due to Alice's growing up suddenly; it was for the reason Poe gives at the end of his story, when the painter, looking at his picture, discovers the truth: "and crying with a loud voice, 'This is indeed *Life* itself!' turned suddenly to regard his beloved:—*She was dead!*"

[21] See, for instance, what Proust has to say about literary heroines in *Time Regained* (translated by Stephen Hudson), London, 1957, pp. 256–62.

Assets and Expenditure

————◆————

The Dodgsons were not rich. The benefice he had in the parish of Daresbury, where Charles was born, provided Mr. Dodgson with a very small stipend, which he supplemented by private tutoring. Even so, it did not go far. Derek Hudson quotes a letter Mr. Dodgson sent to the Christ Church authorities, the patrons of his benefice, just before Charles's birth in 1832. Christ Church wanted to establish a potato tithe which would have brought Dodgson "nearly £200 a year," and with this he expresses his warmest satisfaction; he also points out that he has spent nearly £30 on manure for the ground attaching to his living, which they might perhaps "take into consideration." His letter concludes:

> . . . For myself, I am going on as well as a man can be supposed to do, without prospects, living upon a precarious Income, and subject to constant drawback on his domestic comforts. I already begin to experience the anxieties incidental to my situation, having at this moment two Vacancies for Pupils unfilled.[1]

Eleven years later, when he received a benefice at Croft, he wrote to his brother Hassard:[2]

> In the first place you will be gratified at having the exact value of the living:

[1] Hudson, pp. 28–29.
[2] *Diaries*, p. 7.

	£	s	d
Rent Charge	923	0	0
Advantage on Dc. for 1843			
something above	53	0	0
19 Acres of Land at £3.10.0d per acre	66	10	0
Fees and Easter Dues (average)	8	0	0
	1050	10	0

In the above value I have not included 3½ Acres of land close to the House (the rest is a mile distant) wh. I mean to keep in my own hands for the pasture of two Cows, and whatever more can be got out of it—and this in point of fact is also *Income* though I know not precisely how to calculate it. The outgoings to be deducted are:

	£	s	d
Tenths to Q. Anne's Bounty	21	8	10
Rates (average)	110	0	0
Old Rent (of wh. I can get			
no explanation)	9	3	0
	140	11	10

It needs therefore but little Arithmetic to conclude that the Income for this year will be about £910 clear of all deduction except the Income Tax, and, taking the *standard* Rent Charge as the average, that the *net* average Income will exceed £850. Comparing myself therefore with persons who have to pay their House Rent, I may fairly consider my Income as equivalent to a life estate in Land worth £1100 a year, exclusive of my private resources. . . .

This letter is interesting to a historian of the Church of England; but it is interesting also in showing that money worries were an everyday fact in the Dodgson family. Clearly, concern for his "career" prospects must have affected the kind of future Mr. Dodgson would trace out for young Charles. We find evidence that it did in the following letter, sent to Charles by his father in August 1855, when he had just been appointed mathematical lecturer at Christ Church:[3]

[3] Collingwood, p. 61.

I will just sketch for you a supposed case, applicable to your own circumstances, of a young man of twenty-three, making up his mind to work for ten years, and living to do it, on an Income enabling him to save £150 a year—supposing him to appropriate it thus:—

	£	s	d
Invested at 4 per cent	100	0	0
Life Insurance of £1,500	29	15	0
Books, besides those bought in ordinary course	20	5	0
	150	0	0

Suppose him at the end of ten years to get a Living enabling him to settle [i.e. marry], what will be the result of his savings;—

  1. A nest egg of £1,220 ready money, for furnishings and other expenses.

  2. A sum of £1,500 secured at his death on payment of a *very much* smaller annual Premium than if he had then begun to ensure it.

  3. A useful Library worth more than £200, besides the books bought out of his current Income during the period.

As we know, Charles remained unconvinced by his father's arguments; he taught for much more than ten years, and rejected both marriage and the parochial ministry. Nonetheless, at the end of 1855 he had come to a point when his spiritual life and his financial life were thoroughly in harmony:

> It has been the most eventful year of my life; I began it a poor bachelor student, with no definite plans or expectations; I end it a master and tutor in Christ Church, with an income of more than £300 a year, and the course of mathematical tuition marked out by God's providence for at least some years to come.[4]

The Son's Affairs

Naturally enough, it was with the ending of his career as an undergraduate that young Dodgson began talking about

[4] *Diaries*, p. 70.

money. That same year, 1855 (when he was twenty-three),
he was paid his first salary:

> This day [February 14] I was made Sub-Librarian, in place of
> Bayne who has just taken his M.A. This will add £35 to my
> income—not much towards independence. (*Diaries*, p. 41)

Four months later, good news comes:

> The Dean and Canons have been pleased to give me one of the
> 'Bostock' Scholarships—said to be worth £20 per year. This very
> nearly raises my income this year to independence—Courage!
> (p. 50)

And, in the summer, the independence was to become complete, his career secured.

Thenceforth we hear no further lamentations about
money. For ten years, these were his sole sources of revenue;
and so adequate were they that *Alice* was first published at
the author's expense. Yet his university income remained
modest: in 1882 as a Student of Christ Church he got about
£200 a year; to this was added £40 for his work as Curator of
the Common Room. The sum total would be roughly equivalent to £3,000 today. But one must bear in mind the considerable advantage conferred then—and indeed still—by the
status of Student: free rooms, and free dinner each day. And
soon, his earnings as a writer were to free him from all
anxiety; so much so that in 1870 he suggested to the Dean
that he might both teach less and be paid less:

> Wrote to the Dean proposing (now that Sampson is to be a Lec-
> turer) that in future I shall take Pass-work only, and he Class,
> and that, as this will fairly equalize the work the £500 shall be
> divided evenly between us instead of £350 to me and £150 to
> the assistant lecturer. I want some spare time very much, for
> other reading, etc., and am quite willing thus to buy it. (*Diaries*,
> p. 290)[5]

We do not know how many of his books were printed,

[5] Carroll gave up tutoring Honours work (or Class work) as it was
more arduous than merely tutoring those working for Pass degrees, and he
really did want more time.

nor can we study his tax returns, which would tell us what
he earned from them. On the other hand, what we do know is
that money was of no importance to him in comparison with
typographical or aesthetic considerations; thus, he had the
first printing of *Alice* withdrawn and sold at a loss (in the
United States). Nor did he mind reducing the price in order
to sell more copies. For instance, we read in his diary for 1894
(pp. 514–15):

> [As] the booksellers do not seem to think them worth keeping
> on view at the present price, we [he and his publisher] agreed to
> offer them special terms for *The Nursery Alice* and the two vol-
> umes of *Sylvie and Bruno*. We have about eight thousand of
> each of these three. Of course this required the lowering of the
> 'royalties' to be paid to me: the new prices being as follows:
> *Nursery Alice* to be offered 13 as 12 at 2/6 net; and my royalty
> reduced from 3/- to 2/3 . . . *Sylvie and Bruno* to be offered, 13
> as 12, at 5/-, and my royalty reduced from 5/7½ to 4/6.

Sometimes his calculations are less certain. Thus, when
publishing his *Eight or Nine Wise Words about Letter-writing*, he
writes in his diary (p. 478):

> The case, *Wise Words,* and the envelope will cost about
> 5¾d. So I must either get Emberlin [the publisher] to allow me
> more than 6d, or we must charge for *Wise Words.* The case costs
> 4½d. and the envelope ½d. Charging for *Wise Words* might
> check sales.

On the other hand, Derek Hudson quotes a letter from
Carroll to his publisher, written in June 1890, in which he
demands "slightly better terms for myself. I am obliged to
look to L.S.D. a little, as the calls on me, relatively to my
income are enormous."[6] It seems, too, that the main part of
his expenditure in fact consisted of gifts of all kinds—not
just to members of his family, but to numbers of good causes
as well. Collingwood, admittedly concerned to demonstrate
his uncle's moral excellence, waxes enthusiastic on this count:

> My own experience of him was that of a man always ready to do
> one a kindness, even though it put him to great expense and

[6] Hudson, p. 293.

inconvenience. . . . The income from his books and other sources [what other sources?], which might have been spent in a life of luxury and selfishness, he distributed lavishly where he saw it was needed, and in order to do this he always lived in the most simple way. . . . In several instances, when friends in needy circumstances have written to him for loans of money, he has answered them: 'I will not *lend*, but I will *give* you the £100 you ask for.'[7]

After his father's death, as we know, it was Charles who enabled his family to settle at Guildford; he also gave constant help to his sisters, and paid considerable sums toward the education of his nephews and nieces. One would hardly expect him to boast about this in his diary. But we do read on October 1, 1894:

> Wrote to Fanny, Mary, Henrietta and Wilfred, to warn them that, as my receipts from Macmillan next January will be about £500 less than I had hoped, I don't see how I can give my usual family gifts next year. (p. 515)

And in *Sylvie and Bruno*, Arthur, who is often a kind of mouthpiece for Carroll himself, states very clearly the principle he was to adopt:[8]

> I would say, *generally*, that a man who gratifies every fancy that occurs to him—denying himself in *nothing*—and merely gives to the poor some part, or even *all*, of his *superfluous* wealth, is only deceiving himself if he calls it *charity*.

Carroll maintained a total reserve about his literary earnings, and Charles Morgan in *The House of Macmillan* (London, 1943) has nothing to say on the matter. But in view of the fact that *Alice* was first published at the author's expense, we can understand how, when he decided that the illustrations were such a failure as to make it necessary to withdraw it and reprint, his calculations were not markedly optimistic:

> The total cost [of reprinting] will be . . . £600, i.e. 6/- a copy on the 2000. If I make £500 by sale, this will be a loss of £100,

[7] Collingwood, pp. 324–25.
[8] *Sylvie and Bruno Concluded*, Chap. III.

and the loss on the first 2000 will probably be £100, leaving me £200 out of pocket. But if a second 2000 could be sold, it would cost £300, and bring in £500, thus squaring accounts; and any further sale would be a gain—but that I can hardly hope for. (*Diaries*, pp. 234–35)

To this, written in 1865, we may add the following lines, dating from 1868:

The first 2,000 copies brought no profit, and the next 2000 only about £80, so that the rate—adding £185 for pictures . . . is about 55 per 1,000; i.e., a sales of 9,000 copies gave £500 profit. (p. 273)

According to Green, from unofficial calculations (since Macmillan refused to give the precise figures), *Alice* sold 180,000 copies *in Carroll's lifetime*!

From reading his books, it does not seem that money was ever a problem, let alone an obsession with him. He was well aware of its importance, at least for other people; so much so that in 1876 he wrote a short pamphlet protesting against the university's avarice in refusing to pay an adequate salary to a deputy Professor of Comparative Philology. But as far as he himself was concerned, a regular and apparently fairly large income,[9] for which he made amends by equally regular and equally large gifts, protected him both from anxiety and from remorse. We may perhaps conclude this section with an anecdote taken from his Russian journal,[10] which illustrates his business sense:

I took a *drojky* to the house [of some friends], having first bargained with the driver for thirty *kopecks*; he wanted forty to

---

[9] The disappointment Carroll complains of in the letter I quoted above represented a considerable sum (in the region of £6,000 or more today). But it is very difficult to get any idea, even with this figure to base it on, of just how much money Macmillan's actually paid him all told.

[10] Collingwood, p. 123; the complete journal was published in the United States in 1935 in *The Russian Journal and Other Selections from the Works of Lewis Carroll*, edited by John Francis McDermott, New York, E. P. Dutton. It did not appear in England until 1965, when it was included in *The Complete Works of Lewis Carroll*, edited by Roger Lancelyn Green, London, Hamlyn.

begin with. When we got there we had a little scene, rather a novelty in my experience of *drojky*-driving. The driver began by saying, '*Sorok*' (forty) as I got out: this was a warning of the coming storm, but I took no notice of it, but quietly handed over the thirty. He received them with scorn, and indignation, and holding them out in his open hand, delivered an eloquent discourse in Russian, of which '*sorok*' was the leading idea. A woman, who stood by with a look of amusement and curiosity, perhaps understood him. *I* didn't, but simply held out my hand for the thirty, returned them to the purse and counted out twenty-five instead. In doing this I felt something like a man pulling the string of a shower-bath—and the effect was like it—his fury boiled over directly, and quite eclipsed all the former row. I told him in very bad Russian that I had offered him thirty once, but wouldn't again; but this, oddly enough, did not pacify him. . . . Some people are very hard to please.

Celibacy

At twenty-five, after a conversation with his father in which the latter urged him to take out life insurance, Charles wrote in his diary (p. 117):

> My present opinion is this: that it will be best not to effect any insurance at present, but simply to save as much as I reasonably can from year to year. If at any future period I contemplate marriage (of which I see no present likelihood), it will be quite time enough to begin paying the premiums then.

(This explicit connection between money and marriage must not lead us along what would at this stage be a false trail.)

At fifty-two, he writes to one of his former Oxford contemporaries:

> So you have been a married man for twelve years, while I am still a lonely old bachelor! And mean to keep so, for the matter of that. College life is by no means unmixed misery, though married life has no doubt many charms to which I am a stranger.[1]

We may take these two declarations as our basis for considering the problem of Carroll's celibacy. This is not the same as the problem of his emotional life, for it must be seen in terms of *social likelihood*: Carroll could not even remotely have envisaged marrying a child. The theory of a supposed

---

[1] Collingwood, p. 231.

36

(or possible) proposal to Alice Liddell[2] is *ipso facto* ruled
out. In 1855, when Carroll was twenty-three, Alice Liddell
was three, and relations between Carroll and Alice's parents
had become strained by 1862, at which time Alice was only
ten. This is amply proved by the fact that in 1867 (when
Alice was fifteen), Carroll writes in his diary (p. 260):

> . . . paid a visit to Mrs. Liddell, and had a long chat with her,
> walking about the Deanery garden—a thing I have not done for
> years.

It is possible, of course, that some such occasion as that would
have provided Carroll with the opportunity of asking permission to marry Alice; but there is absolutely nothing to justify
so unlikely a supposition, especially given Carroll's view of
what the Liddell parents felt about him.

The same must be said of a proposal he is supposed to
have made to Ellen Terry, the actress. Unfortunately, Collingwood himself first broached this idea in 1932:

> When Ellen Terry was just growing up—perhaps seventeen—
> she was lovely beyond description . . . and it is highly probable
> that he fell in love with her; he may even have proposed to her.[3]

Mrs. Lennon is quite right when she insists on the absurdity
of this suggestion, since Ellen Terry remained married,
although separated from her husband, from 1863 to 1877
(from the age of fifteen to twenty-nine), and it would have
been out of the question for Carroll to have considered
marrying a divorced woman.

We can, then, only reject these baseless hypotheses, while
noting that in Carroll's works, as in Charles Dodgson's life,
the marriage bond was extraordinarily unobtrusive or fragile,
and widowhood a commonplace. The Duchess in *Alice* seems,
certainly, to have been widowed; the Warden, Muriel's
father, and for a time Muriel herself are so in *Sylvie and
Bruno*. A number of men are also bachelors, as for instance
the White Knight, the White Rabbit (though we may

[2] Possibility mentioned by F. B. Lennon, *The Life of Lewis Carroll*,
pp. 191–93.
[3] Quoted in Hudson, p. 191.

wonder), and the two professors in *Sylvie and Bruno*, to say nothing of the narrator himself. Finally, those couples who do appear together seem to be in such a state of eccentricity or tension that it would be hard to find a clearer condemnation of marriage: the Vice-Warden and his wife, Willie and Polly, in *Sylvie and Bruno*; the King and Queen of Hearts in Wonderland; and the kings and queens in the *Looking-Glass*. And significantly, it is usually the husbands who are weak and the wives shrews or viragoes; the cleverest is the Red King, who escapes into sleep and dreams, rather than be persecuted like the King of Hearts.

If we remember that, of Carroll's brothers and sisters, only three married, and none of these did so before their parents were both dead, it seems probable that the family's history helped to reinforce the personal blocks that obliged him to remain a bachelor—the fact that it was his only possible course in view of the peculiarities of his emotional life combined with the ethical standards he set himself.

Christic Church

————◆————

As his father had been there, it was to Christ Church that young Charles went for his university studies. It was the largest, and also the most celebrated of all the Oxford colleges. In fact, the existence of the university, apart from the colleges, was in those days so nebulous that, to an undergraduate, his college in practice represented the whole of university life. You had only to become a permanent member of your college —and it was less common than it is today for the members of one college to be elected by another—for it truly to become your home; especially since the celibacy customary among Fellows in the mid-nineteenth century meant, above all, that you needed no other place of residence.

This is what happened to Carroll. Having entered Christ Church on January 24, 1851, he lived there till his death in January 1898. As was usual, he spent all his vacations out of Oxford, but it was in Christ Church that he essentially lived. He had four successive lodgings, and his last move was in November 1868. From then on, for almost thirty years, he lived in an extremely spacious apartment. According to his nephew, it was "one of the finest lodgings" in the college, consisting of "four sitting rooms and about an equal number of bedrooms, besides rooms for lumber, etc." (Collingwood, p. 133). It was there, shortly after moving in, that he established his photographic studio.

Christ Church was his home for forty-seven years,

and he seems to have been genuinely attached to it. In 1881 he wrote a letter in defence of the college to *The Observer*, which had attacked it following some student upheavals:

> . . . The truth is that Christ Church stands convicted of two unpardonable crimes—being great and having a name. Such a place must always expect to find itself 'a wide mark for scorns and jeers'—a target where the little and the nameless may display their skill. . . .
>
> However, as general statements can only be met by general statements, permit me, as one who has lived here for thirty years and has taught for five-and-twenty, to say that in my experience order has been the rule, disorder the rare exception, and that, if the writer of your leading article has had an equal amount of experience in any similar place of education, and has found a set of young men more gentlemanly, more orderly, and more pleasant in every way to deal with, than I have found here, I cannot but think him an exceptionally favoured mortal.[1]

Living in a college involves experiencing the tensions of the college community. And there must be many. Some are inherent in its very existence; others are imposed on it by its historical context. This was especially the case in the nineteenth century. Carroll felt both, and though he may appear to have played an unobtrusive part, this impression does not necessarily accord with the reality. Certainly, as we shall see, he was unable to assume the responsibilities that would have forced him into a direct confrontation with the problems of the time. But at least, as his controversies with Dean Liddell make clear, he never evaded the real issues.

Some Significant Points

Almost all the permanent university jobs in Oxford were reserved for clergymen, who were of course Anglican. This ecclesiastical stamp was especially marked at Christ Church, since the college was an educational establishment—in which it was on the same footing as the other Oxford colleges—and served as a cathedral: a function of its Dean and

[1] Collingwood, pp. 215–16.

Chapter was to elect the Bishop of Oxford, and they were therefore appointed by the sovereign, never co-opted, and only very rarely elected.[2] And in the functioning of the college, the Canons, who did not necessarily do any teaching, had precedence over the teaching staff. But the Chapter also had certain non-ecclesiastical functions; it was they who administered and distributed the college's considerable income (most of which came from the property it owned); it was also upon them that the gift of the college's ninety benefices depended—and a benefice meant an assured income. The Dean was undisputed head of the Chapter, with permanent and extensive powers of action which he exercised, as far as the undergraduates were concerned, in collaboration with the two censors; it was he who accepted the undergraduates, appointed the tutors (tutors in Oxford being teachers who were also responsible for the overall intellectual and moral well-being of a certain number of students each, acting almost *in loco parentis*) and the non-academic staff. And it was he who supervised the granting of teaching posts—known in all other colleges as *Fellowships*, but in Christ Church as *Studentships*. One is irresistibly reminded of a slightly laicized Father Abbot—an Abbot in the days when the abbeys wielded power over a far wider sphere than the purely spiritual.

Besides the Dean and Canons, the Students—of whom Carroll was to be one—had no right to any views of their own, and had to obey the Chapter. They, even more than the undergraduates, were subject to the administration. They were recruited in a most undemocratic fashion. The 101 posts were divided into three groups or categories: *theologi, philosophi*, and *discipuli*. The twenty Senior Students must already have been ordained. Below them were forty who had either their B.A. or their M.A., and might or might not have been ordained. At the very bottom were forty undergraduate Students, all of whom were paid. The "election" was in fact a nomination made in rotation by the Dean and Chapter—the

[2] See E. G. W. Bill and J. F. A. Mason, *Christ Church and Reform, 1850–1867*, Oxford, 1970, to which I am indebted for a great deal of this section.

Dean having two turns and each Canon one.[3] This procedure
led to the establishment of long waiting lists, so that a young
man might gain a Studentship before even being enrolled in
the university. Worst of all, it opened the way to all possible
forms of nepotism, and at times to the abandonment of intellectual criteria altogether.

Once elected, provided only that he remained unmar-
ried, a Student could always keep his place; he had, however,
to gain his B.A. and M.A. within the prescribed time, and
then either take Holy Orders, which would enable him to
remain at Christ Church, or, in the case of only four Students, practice a liberal profession (law or medicine), which
would oblige the Student to live out of Oxford. He who
remained in residence did not have to teach—and "research"
had not yet become recognized as a way of life at Oxford. So he
was paid, whatever his actual job, but only modestly—between
£25 and £80 a year, whereas a Canon received over £1,000—
and he could retain his salary even if he took a benefice. But
Students who remained in residence could be given teaching
jobs as tutors, which would raise their incomes slightly. They
usually ended by joining the university examining boards
which had been set up in the eighteenth century. Carroll held
the post of Public Examiner in Mathematics until 1864.

Conflicts

A great deal of this system was the proposed subject of
reform by a Royal Commission in 1852. At Christ Church, in
particular, the commission dwelled on the way Students were
chosen, their ridiculously low salaries (from which the
Canons were the gainers), and the need to reduce their
number. In 1854, a bill (introduced by Gladstone, then
Member of Parliament for the university) proposed the gradual introduction of a series of "reformist" measures, directed
to Oxford as a whole, but in consequence affecting each of
the colleges. Unfortunately, nothing was specified as to the

[3] Thus Carroll owed his nomination to Pusey; but Pusey did assure
Archdeacon Dodgson that he had judged his son solely on academic merit.

respective powers of the Chapter and Students at Christ
Church. The result was that a major conflict broke out in
1865. When Liddell was nominated, he came heralded by an
aura of reformism, but in fact he never sided with the Students in their battle with the Chapter. In 1857, they had
asked, collectively, for what was basically a sharing of power,
and had implied that the Chapter had far less right to power
than they; they even went so far as—verbally—to reject an
increase in salary that would mean in practice a reduction of
power.

At the end of 1864 and beginning of 1865, the Students
took united action. Carroll, who was involved in it, wrote on
February 11, 1865:

> A meeting of Students was invited by Prout in his rooms on the
> subject of our position. We agreed on the necessity of Students
> being raised to the position of Fellows. (*Diaries*, p. 227)

It was vital—and on this point Carroll was militant—that
the Students be associated in the financial, and not just the
academic, administration of the college, as the Fellows were
in all other Oxford colleges.

This agitation, furthermore, coincided with a dispute
over the payment of the Professor of Greek—a layman—on
which Carroll wrote a pamphlet, "The New Method of Evaluation as Applied to π," and two letters. For the Dean and
Canons, any adjustment of salaries (whether of Professors or
Students) would mean that their own incomes were reduced.
Carroll also commented in his "American Telegrams" (the
title and style of which were suggested by the Civil War and
the dispatches arriving from it) on the conflict as a whole,
but unhappily these are rather obscure for the modern reader.[4]

Faced with a refusal by the Dean and Chapter to do
anything, the Students contemplated appealing to Parliament. This would have meant publicizing another scandal,
which also affected the undergraduates: the matter of the
college dining hall, which apparently was used to line the pock-
ets of certain of the staff who, being agents rather than salaried

---

[4] See Bill and Mason, *Christ Church and Reform*, pp. 110–13.

workers, could gain a lot by inflating the prices of what they sold. Indeed, Carroll had been one of the first to suggest that this system be abolished and fixed wages paid. The publicity the affair received in the newspapers led to a victory for the reformers in December 1865, and a Bursar (a friend of Carroll's) was made responsible for the economic administration of the college.

In January 1866, it was decided by common consent that a commission of arbitration would try to resolve the dispute, and both sides would abide by its verdict. It gave its decision in December of that year, wholly in favor of the Students' demands. A law was passed in Parliament in 1867, on the basis of that decision, which settled the matter once and for all.

As we have seen, Carroll made no public comment on the various phases of the dispute, and his diary (as it has come to us) says very little about it. But some years later, he refers in his diary (p. 299) to an occasion when he offered his services in synthesizing various plans for institutional reform, and did so, apparently to everyone's satisfaction. Evidence from other quarters, however, shows that he was actively involved, and absolutely of one mind with his colleagues, even though there were certain critical moments when he seems to have urged compromise as the only way to preserve any kind of harmony. It may well be that his strained relations with Liddell (though as far as the Students were concerned, he was a lesser enemy than the Canons) helped to strengthen his nerve. But he also had a strict concept of the value of services rendered and the need for the rules of the game to be clearly laid down as a protection against arbitrariness and authoritarianism. It was only tolerable to be a pawn if one could be certain of eventually becoming a queen.

Period of Responsibility

At the end of 1881, Carroll gave up the Mathematical Lectureship and for the first time in his life found himself "without any *fixed* occupation" (*Diaries*, p. 401). But the year 1882 was to see him taking a more active part in the

institutional life of the college. After the 1867 reform, as one
of the Senior Students, he had become part of the Governing
Body of the college. And, in 1882, we find several references
in his diary to occasions when he made suggestions—sometimes successfully—at meetings. On October 25, for instance,
he writes:

> Governing Body Meeting for four hours—a very stormy one. I
> was surprised to find that a motion of mine was carried by 13 to
> 12. I am usually in a small minority. (p. 410)

Was this a sign that he was gaining in moral authority among
his colleagues? Maybe. Certainly, in December, they seized
the opportunity offered them to propose him to a post of
responsibility which, they may have hoped, would stop his
criticizing other people quite so much. Little did they know
what they were getting!

Every college had a kind of club, the Senior Common
Room (S.C.R.), where the teaching staff could relax, read
newspapers, have snacks, and buy wine and spirits. Given the
fact that at that time they were virtually all bachelors, the
Common Room played a considerable part in their life as a
community. It was traditional that one of the Fellows should
be responsible for it, as Curator. In November 1881, Thomas
Vere Bayne, one of Carroll's few friends, resigned from the
Curatorship of the Christ Church S.C.R., having held it for
twenty-one years. On December 8, Carroll writes:

> A Common Room Meeting. Barclay Thompson had (at the
> meeting of Nov. 30) brought (by implication) charges of
> obstinacy and extravagance against the Curator. These I now
> attempted to rebut. Fresh powers were given to the Wine Com-
> mittee, and then a new Curator elected. I was proposed by Hol-
> land, and seconded by Harcourt, and accepted office with no
> light heart: there will be much trouble and thought needed to
> work it satisfactorily: but it will take me out of myself a little,
> and so may be a real good. My life was tending to become too
> much that of a selfish recluse. (pp. 411–12)

I believe this to have been said in all seriousness. But,
whether or no, it was a clear forecast of what were to be nine
years of immense activity on Carroll's part. Nine years that

could have been cut short, for he threatened to resign at least
twice—a delicate form of blackmail that brought him an increase of power, or at least made it harder to criticize him.

The Curator's functions consisted in keeping the
Common Room accounts (expenditures for wine, tea, candles, oil, etc.), seeing to the upkeep of the premises and the
efficiency of the service, supervising the domestic staff, seeing
that the place was heated, being responsible for the Common
Room library, ordering newspapers, and also making sure
that all members paid their subscriptions regularly. Carroll did
all this most zealously, and with a strong sense of the moral
responsibility it entailed. Thus, after two unsuccessful
attempts, he managed to get the staff paid overtime when
they stayed until 10.30 p.m.; he also succeeded in raising the
subscription paid by those members who did not live in the
college and who, up to then, had enjoyed all the facilities of
the Common Room for a ludicrously small sum.

Two aspects of his activity seem to me peculiarly significant: his management of the Wine Committee, and his concern with technical progress.

As to the Wine Committee, Carroll's biographers have
often been dismayed to see how much time he devoted to
anything so frivolous. They fail to understand both its seriousness and the English taste for good wine—mainly meaning
claret, port, sherry, and champagne—which Carroll shared.
His two major considerations were that the wine should be
good, and should not cost too much.

If it was to be good, it must be properly looked after. So
Carroll—who did, in fact, have to have an extra cellar built—
sent each of his suppliers an extremely clear little form to fill
out, making clear for each type of wine and liqueur:

- cellar temperature for wine being stored
- cellar temperature for wine to be drunk soon
- temperature of wine at time of serving
- how long the wine should be decanted prior to
  drinking
- any further points to be specially noted

- should the cellar be dry or humid? light or dark? ventilated?

From information sent in reply to this by the suppliers, Carroll produced a table collating it all, having worked out the averages! And, armed with that table, he then proceeded to inspect the temperature of the cellar each week, and to note that on another table. All this, of course, he wrote out himself.

Then, too, the wine must not cost either the Common Room or individual members too much. There was considerable correspondence with the suppliers about this, and a number of rules were passed by the Wine Committee, which his colleagues had to abide by. Here, for instance, is the motion proposed on February 16, 1888, with Carroll's comments:[5]

> Motion: 'That some measure of relief be devised for wine-drinkers, at Common Room dessert, who do not require more than a single glass'.
>   The present charge, both for Port and Claret, is 4/8 a bottle, while the amounts consumed are very different, a Claret drinker very frequently consuming half a bottle or more, i.e. fully twice the amount that a Port-drinker would take. Moreover, the average consumption has increased of late years. During the last two years, the average charge, per head, was 1/5; in Christmas Quarter 1887 it was 1/7; this year, it has reached 1/8. The number of times that it has been as much as 2/— was, during the last 2 years, 8%; in Midsummer Quarter 1887 it was 10%; in Christmas Quarter 14%; this year it has reached 36%, being on one occasion 2/8.

And here are two further extracts which further illustrate how Carroll's anxiety over accounts was at times hard to reconcile with his wish to do what was satisfactory to his colleagues:

> A desire having been expressed that a better *quality* of wine should be supplied as 'Champagne A' (though not accompanied

[5] This and the following are extracts from documents contained in the archives of Christ Church.

by any expression of willingness to pay a higher *price*) the Curator has procured samples, which Members are invited to taste, in,
C.R. at 1.30 p.m. Sandwiches &c will be provided.

We have a stand of three Liqueur-decanters, which can be had
for dinners given in C.R. or (when not wanted there) in private
rooms. Arrangements have been made, by which the quantity in
a decanter can be estimated. The giver of a dinner will be
charged the values of the Liqueurs in the decanters at the time
they are sent to him, and from this will be deducted the values
of the remainders, if large enough to be worth rebottling: but if
the remainders be less than 3/- worth in the case of 'Green Char-
treuse' or less than 2/- worth in the case of the other two
Liqueurs [Curaçao and Maraschino] they will be sent to the
giver of the dinner, and no deduction will be made.

At the end of his first year as Curator, Carroll also drew
the attention of his colleagues to:

A curious phenomenon. The consumption of Madeira (B) has
been during the past year, zero. After careful calculation I esti-
mate that, if this rate of consumption be steadily maintained,
our present stock will last us an infinite number of years. And
although there may be something monotonous and dreary in the
prospect of such vast cycles spent in drinking second-class Madeira, we may yet cheer ourselves with the thought of how eco-
nomically it can be done. . . .[6]

And there I will leave the Wine Committee, noting only
that it was in connection with it that Carroll had his sharpest
interchanges with his colleagues, having decided that he must
be given absolute discretion once and for all in this domain.
He made it clear that he would resign if he met with too
much opposition:

Any attempt to dictate [to the Curator] the exact method, in
which he shall perform this service for C.R. would be a clear
infringement of existing rights. . . . The writer [of the motion]
is obviously unaware what the present limits are of the [Wine]
Committee's control over their Chairman. In a bygone age, no
doubt, their powers were all but unlimited, and all but intoler-

[6] Collingwood, p. 306.

able: mais *nous avons changé tout cela.* . . . To alter this rule in
the direction of curtailing the Curator's right 'to exercise his
own discretion', would require the occurrence, not only of a new
Wine Committee, but also of a new Curator.

Then there were the technical innovations. Carroll's passion for new devices of all kinds meant that his colleagues
benefited to the full from the progress of Victorian civiliza-
tion. Not only was it he who introduced Afternoon Tea to
Christ Church (with a choice of tea, coffee, or chocolate), but
he was also concerned with making life more comfortable.
Hence, the following circular in 1889, accompanied by a motion of his own:

Motion: 'That the Curator be authorised to place, in the Drawing Room a five-light gas chandelier with "incandescent" burners'.
        The present method of lighting it, by candles placed in
brackets attached to the walls, is troublesome, costly, and not
nearly so effective as the proposed method, which would give, if
all 5 burners were turned on 'full', the light of 100 candles, at a
cost of a penny an hour. . . .
        The objections, that exist against the use of *ordinary* gas-
burners in a sitting room—viz. great heat, a vitiated atmosphere,
the formation of soot, and the injury done, by the sulphur
evolved, to the binding of books—are, all of them, almost entirely
obviated by the new 'incandescent' burners, which have the additional merit of only consuming about *half* the gas required by
ordinary burners.
        The Curator has a 2-light chandelier, of this kind, in his
own rooms, and will be happy to show it, any night, to any
Member of C.R.
        To enable Members to judge what the effect would be in
the Drawing Room he has had gas laid on, and an old chandelier
put up. The costs of this he will pay himself, should his proposal be rejected.ˌ. . .

Two years later, for progress never ceases, he came up
with a new idea:

The Curator (with the hope of improving the lighting of C.R.,
which is hardly sufficient, at present, for reading the Evening
Paper comfortably), has borrowed a new kind of oil-lamp, called

the 'Sunlight', and is trying the effect of it in various places and
at various heights. The room is lighted at present by 4 'Duplex'
lamps, each of which is supposed to give the light of about 30
candles ('40' is about the maximum power claimed for such
lamps): whereas it is claimed, for the 'Sunlight' lamp, that its
illuminatory power, when it is turned 'full on' is equal to 100
candles. . . .

Are we to dismiss the care he took over these documents
—never, of course, intended for publication—as sheer waste
of time on Carroll's part? Certainly to him, as a man, the
matters they dealt with were all very important. It becomes
clear from reading them how much of a "family man" he
was,[7] as witness this notice he put up in the Common Room
for the benefit of his colleagues:

To all Lovers of Orange Marmalade

The Curator's brother (who has a large family and several
pupils) makes it on a large scale, and could supply some for the
use of Members of C.R., if any let the Curator know that they
desire it. He finds it very good, and it can also be guaranteed as
absolutely genuine, and not, as is the case with much that is supplied in shops, largely composed of Vegetable-Marrow. C.R.
would probably be able to supply it at 10d. (possibly 9d.) for a
1 lb. jar.

We also find his concern with a "fair price" and a "fair
wage" coming into play in his exercise of these supposedly
"trivial" functions.

Here, for instance, is an excerpt from a letter to an
Oxford newsagent:

As Mr. Dodgson has to account to the Common Room for all
money spent on their account, he is obliged to trouble Messrs
Slatter & Rose with further questions.

He would be glad to have any explanations they have to

---

[7] In this connection, it is worth remembering that, in those days, university teachers were more in touch with the outside world than we tend to
think, since they generally spent their vacations with their families rather
than in Oxford.

give for the fact that although the above periodicals were
fetched, ever since March 21, 1890, the charge for delivery has
remained the same. . . .

And here is an account of a dispute with his colleagues in
1892:

The Curator, having asked permission, at the meeting of May 9,
to give to the C.R. servants what he considered to be reasonable
remuneration for the additional trouble entailed on them by the
new Smoking-Room, and having been refused that permission,
summoned this meeting to receive his resignation. It was thereupon resolved (*nem. con.*) to leave the whole matter in his hands.
The Curator did not tender his resignation.

Though, as I have said, all this concerned Carroll the
man, Carroll the writer is never wholly absent. Of course
none of these documents suggests the wide perspectives of
Alice, or the complex ones of *Sylvie and Bruno*. But they are
in the same tone—apparently joking yet profoundly serious;
there is the same precision of form, the same clarity of demonstration. Of course, too, these peculiar talents are here
directed to small matters. But surely Carroll the writer, as
well as Carroll the Christian, would have made his own the
parable of the steward: "He who is faithful in a very little is
faithful also in much." The very uselessness, as literature, of
all this mass of writing, is a sign of the identity of Carroll and
Dodgson which it has been traditional to deny. When writing
about the functions of the Curator he is precisely the same
man as the author of *Alice*: the note about "Madeira (B)" is
like something from *Sylvie and Bruno*; and the description of
the various lighting systems is reminiscent of the White
Knight. They are only hints—and if there were no *Sylvie and
Bruno*, no *Looking-Glass*, these documents would not be
worth a second glance. But seen in conjunction with his mas-
terpieces, they indicate something more durable.

One final point: the nature of Carroll's position. As
compared with the major battles raging around Christ
Church, the microcosm of the Common Room was insignifi-
cant. To a man who has just quit the service of education, the

serving of wine can hardly appear of the same importance.[8]
And, as compared with the problems of the age, what can one
possibly say about one person's attempt to deal with the prac-
ticalities of one situation? Actually, we can probably say the
same thing as we would say about marriage and the Lectureship. Carroll always wanted to do great things, but always
recognized in time that it would be better to do less. A "social
role"—a notion that had come to be very much in vogue even
in the Victorian era—presupposes fitting into society, and for
this one must be a well-balanced individual. Carroll never
refused any of society's demands, but he always had to adapt
them to the restraints imposed by his personality. To be
Curator of a Common Room may not be the antechamber of
power, but at least it indicates a willingness not to become
totally isolated. A detail of a larger canvas—just as Christ
Church was in Oxford, or Oxford in England. When Icarus
fell, he was so tiny and so solitary that no one noticed him—
but he knew himself that he was falling. Carroll at Christ
Church was the individual who, while the body of society
might smother or reject him, did what lay in his power to
protect himself. He was not precisely well-adjusted, but neither was he maladjusted: people doubted his practical capa-
bility, and he proved them wrong, but he chose the criteria
himself.

[8] Though it was richly symbolic of the welcome given to college
guests, the very sign of hospitality.

Correspondence

The Wonderland

Postage-Stamp Case

One of the chapters of the second book Collingwood produced about Lewis Carroll is entitled "An irresponsible correspondent." This is fully borne out by the facts. Three quotations will give ample indication of it. The first, from Harry Furniss, who illustrated *Sylvie and Bruno*:[1]

> I sent him drawings as they were finished, and each parcel brought back a budget of letter-writing, each page being carefully numbered. This [reproduced in the text] is the top of page 5 in his 49,874th letter. I am not sure if I received all the remaining 49,873 letters in the seven years.

The second is from one of the directors of Macmillan's publishing house, who replied to one of his letters with immense politeness:[2]

> It does add very largely to our labour to discuss wordy detail in writing. I notice that the letters written by you touching on the arrangement concluded in our last agreement covered thirty

[1] H. Furniss, *Confessions of a Caricaturist*, vol. I, p. 112.
[2] Hudson, p. 239n.

pages of your writing. Just think how impossible it would be to carry on any business at this rate.

The third is from Derek Hudson himself, in his biography (p. 122):

Mr. Warren Weaver has shown by careful study of the numbers he inscribed on his correspondence[3]—the last is 98,721—that from 1861 until about 1870 he registered approximately 460 items a year, from 1872 until about 1881 approximately 2,315 items a year, and from 1881 until his death approximately 3,760 items a year. [And Hudson adds in a footnote] his correspondence as Curator of the Common Room at Christ Church (1882–92) was additional to this, and has more than five thousand items.

Register of Correspondence

This vast mass of letters was made more manageable for their author (and possible future readers) by a register of correspondence which Carroll kept from January 1, 1861, until his death; had it not disappeared, we would have in it a description of every letter sent or received by Carroll during the latter thirty-seven years of his life.

Despite the fact that very few letters have been published,[4] we luckily have access, in a wonderfully Carrollian way, not to the content of that register, but to its *form*. In 1888, in fact, Carroll decided to publish a special little folder to hold stamps, which he thought would sell well under the name "The Wonderland Postage-Stamp Case"—this splendid title being justified by the fact that when one pulled the folder out of its cover (it was made of cardboard), the picture of Alice holding the Duchess's baby turned into Alice holding a pig, and the Cheshire Cat into merely its smile. This

---

[3] The term also covers things like proofs of his pamphlets, which Carroll also numbered.

[4] And which are almost all in Collingwood and *LCPB*; in Hudson (who made considerable use of Carroll's letters to Macmillan's, the publishers, and certain family correspondence); and *A Selection from the Letters of Lewis Carroll to his Child-Friends*, edited by Evelyn M. Hatch, London, 1933. The *Correspondence* now in preparation, edited by Morton H. Cohen and Roger Lancelyn Green, will supply us with more.

folder he offered to an Oxford printer, who accepted and produced it, and Carroll decided to accompany it with a short text: "Eight or Nine Wise Words about Letter-Writing."[5] They are well worth reproducing.

He begins by recommending his stamp case, not for emergency use (though, as he points out, it is always a good thing to have a little of the sticky edges of stamps upon one, "for cut fingers (it makes capital sticking-plaster and will stand three or four washings, cautiously conducted)" but for letters written at leisure, at home:

> Since I have possessed a 'Wonderland Stamp-Case', life has been bright and peaceful, and I have used no other. I believe the Queen's Laundress uses no other.

Then come the "wise words" about letter writing, under four headings: "How to begin a letter"; "How to go on with a letter"; "How to end a letter"; and "On registering correspondence." Finally, there is a specimen "Letter-Register."

Under the first heading, he has several very sensible bits of advice to give: address and stamp the envelope before writing the letter, put your own address on the letter, and write the *full* date.

Under the second, there are nine rules:

1. Write legibly.

2. Don't begin with long excuses for not having written sooner, but go straight to the point, referring to the contents of the letter to which you are replying, and preferably quoting it word for word, so as to avoid any misunderstanding.

3. Don't repeat yourself.

> To repeat your arguments, all over again, will simply lead to his doing the same; and so you will go on, like a Circulating Decimal. *Did you ever know a Circulating Decimal come to an end?*

4. Always put off sending an unpleasant letter until the next day,

> then read it over again and fancy it addressed to yourself. This will

[5] *Works*, p. 1211.

often lead to your writing it all over again . . . if, when you have done your best to write inoffensively, you still feel that it will probably lead to further controversy, *keep a copy of it.*

5. Always be more friendly than your correspondent:

If, in picking a quarrel, each party declined to go more than *three-eighths* of the way, and if, in making friends, each was ready to go five-eighths of the way—why there would certainly be more reconciliations than quarrels!

6. Never try to have the last word.

7. If you want to make a joke, 'be sure you exaggerate enough to make the jesting *obvious*'.

8. When you say you are enclosing something, put the thing in question into the envelope there and then.

9. Never cross out!

The third head is briefer, dealing chiefly with post-scripts:

The post-script is a very useful invention; but it is *not* meant (as many ladies suppose) to contain the real *gist* of the letter; it serves rather to throw into the shade any little matter we do *not* wish to make a fuss about.

And he concludes with the advice:

When you take your letters to the post, *carry them in your hand.* If you put them in your pocket, you will take a long country walk (I speak from experience), passing the post office twice, going and returning, and when you get home, you will find them *still* in your pocket.

The fourth section is the vital one:

Let me recommend you to keep a record of Letters Received and Sent. I have kept one for many years, and have found it of the greatest possible service, in many ways: it secures my *answering* Letters, however long they have to wait; it enables me to refer, for my own guidance, to the details of previous correspondence, though the actual letters may have been destroyed long ago; and, most valuable feature of all, if any difficulty arises, years after-wards, in connection with a half-forgotten correspondence, it enables me to say, with confidence, 'I did *not* tell you that he was "an *invaluable* servant in *every* way", and that you *couldn't* "trust him too much". . . . So, if he's cheated you, you really must not hold *me* responsible for it!'

Then, in this last section, there follows some practical advice on how to keep your letter register. It is tremendously detailed, and when put into effect, produces a very odd result, and one that is quite incomprehensible without the explanations that precede it. Here is an extract from the specimen invented by Carroll, in which, by numbering letters sent and received, we find a double story; and once again, details are added that lighten up what might be a rather arid demonstration:

29217	/90.	
(217) sendg, J., a	Ap. 1. (Tu) *Jones, Mrs.* am as present from self and Mr. white elephant.	27518 225
(218) grand	do. *Wilkins & Co.* bill, for piano, £175 10s. 6d. [pd	28743 221, 2
(219) "Grand to borr	do. *Scareham, H.* [writes from Hotel, Monte Carlo"] asking ow £50 for a few weeks (!)	
	(220) do. *Scareham, H.* would know *object*, for wh loan is and *security* offered.	like to asked,
218 246	(221) Ap. 3. *Wilkins & Co.* vious letter, now before me, undertook to supply one for decling to pay more.	in pre- you £120:
23514 218 228	(222) do. *Cheetham & Sharp.* written 221 — enclosing previo ter — is law on my side?	have us let- [

(223) G. N. dressed 'very	Ap. 4. *Manager, Goods Statn, R.* White Elephant arrived, ad- to you — send for it at once — savage.'	226
29225	/90.	
217 230	(225) Ap. 4 (F) *Jones, Mrs.* th but no room for it at present, am ing it to Zoological Gardens.	anks, send-
223	(226) do. *Manager, Goods Sta N. R.* please deliver, to bearer note, case containing White Ele- addressed to me.	tn, G. of this phant
223 229	(227) do. *Director Zool. Garde* closing above note to R. W. Ma call for valuable animal, prese Gardens.	ns. (en- nager) nted to
(228) misquot is £18	Ap. 8. *Cheetham & Sharp.* you e enclosed letter, limit named o.	222 237
(229) case de Port— quet—	Ap. 9. *Director, Zoo. Gardens.* livered to us contained 1 doz. consumed at Directors' Ban- many thanks.	229 230
225 .	(230) do. T *Jones, Mrs.* why doz. of Port a 'White Elephant'?	call a
(231) joke.'	do. T *Jones, Mrs.* 'it was a	.

The various signs Carroll uses all have a particular emphasis. It is important to know that the right-hand margin[6] is used for internal references, the number in parentheses is the number by which he records the letter being received or sent, and when it reappears without any parenthesis, it is being used to refer back to.

As Carroll says in conclusion:

> All this looks very complicated when stated at full length: but you will find it perfectly simple, when you have had a little practise, and will come to regard the 'making-up' as a pleasant occupation for a rainy day, or at any time that you feel disinclined for more severe mental work. In the Game of Whist, Hoyle gives us one golden Rule, 'When in doubt, win the trick'—I find that rule admirable for real life: when in doubt what to do, I 'make-up' my Letter-Register!

The Letter Writer

Armed with this method of classification, Carroll could freely indulge his taste for letter writing without danger. (The order of the various elements is significant: as always with Carroll, the form seems to come before the content, and this letter register made him tend to write more, rather than less; there was a marked increase in the number of letters recorded over the years). He wrote to an extraordinary number of people on a very wide range of subjects: to his little-girl friends, of course; to his brothers and sisters, at least when he was young; to his publisher; to his illustrators—and though Tenniel has not bequeathed to us any information about such a correspondence, it seems unlikely that he was less favoured than Furniss; to the college suppliers. As for the steward of Christ Church, in his last years he positively persecuted the poor man with complaints and suggestions: he proposed, for instance, that in snowy weather the college messengers be provided "first, for their own health & comfort in such weather, [with] a set of waterproof capes with high col-

---

6 In the Register itself, he uses the colours red and blue on the two sides.

lars—secondly for the security of our letters & parcels, a set of
deep baskets (as more easily carried when loaded than square
ones) with waterproof covers";[7] in 1888 he once again found
occasion to display his methodical and classifying bent, in
regard to an electric bell he wanted installed in his rooms: the
steward suggested a bell that would ring continuously until
stopped in the porter's room, to which Carroll replied:[8]

(1) If it didn't wake him at first going off, it wouldn't do
so by *continuity* of sound, which is as somniferous as silence: it
is the sudden *change,* from sound to silence, or from silence to
sound, that *wakes.* A miller will sleep sound while the mill is
going: but wakes if it stops.

(2) It would limit our power to *one* kind of signal. Now
it might be very desirable to institute a *code* of signals (by different numbers of rings in) for various purposes (e.g. one kind
to mean 'Fire!').

Another letter to the steward goes into greater detail
still:[9]

Ch. Ch.
5 May '93

Dear Steward
A short time ago there was a London Mail for which the
P.O. closed at 11.20 a.m.; and letters were taken across, from
Tom Gate, at 11 a.m.; and I understood that letters, put into the
Messenger's box by 11, were at once taken to the Gate to be
posted, or, if too late for that, were taken across to the Post. So,
Haithwaite used to come to my room, just before 11, and carry
off the morning's letters.

They have now altered the P.O. hours, closing, for an early
mail (delivered in London early that afternoon) at 10.20; and,
for the next mail, at 11.45. But the *Gate* arrangements are unal-
tered. So, if I want letters to go by the 10.20, I have to post
them myself; if by the 11.45, I must either get them ready ¾ of
an hour before the time, or post them myself (I always prefer
the *latter*).

Could not the present 11 o'clock posting, which is too late

[7] Hudson, p. 254.
[8] *Ibid.*, pp. 256–67.
[9] Senior Common Room Papers, Christ Church.

for one mail and too soon for the next, be shifted so as to suit one mail or the other? Sending across at 10.15 would be of use, or at 11.40. The present sending is useless.

Also would you tell me what happens to letters for the post, put into Messengers' boxes, when there is a mail going out *before* the next sending across from the Gate? e.g. if a Messenger clears this box at 11.15, and finds a letter for the post, does he post it in time for the 11.45 Mail, or simply leave it at the Gate, to be taken across at 3, in time for the 3.20 Mail (thus missing *two* London Mails, the 11.45 and the 1.20)?

Again, if I want a letter to go by the 1.20 London Mail, is my alternative to either put it into the Messengers' box by *11*, or else post it myself?

Yours bewilderedly

C. L. Dodgson

We may suspect that the steward, too, may have felt somewhat "bewildered."

This type of letter—which we might call the "explanatory"—is the one of which we have the most examples, apart from the "diverting"—the best instances of which are his letters to children.[10] There are more serious types: the "offended," as in the case of his quarrel with Tennyson; the "indignant," like the letter to a theatrical manager protesting over a play that offended his religious sense; and then the innumerable letters to newspapers which, when signed "Lewis Carroll," were very likely to be published. In them he declaims against vivisection, urges the establishment of proportional representation, or defends his college. He was indeed an indefatigable correspondent—exasperating, extravagant, enchanting—a man for whom writing became more and more the only conceivable method of communication, especially after he had decided to refuse almost all invitations (and, of course, he had to write to refuse them!). We can easily picture him, as his life drew to an end, "making up" and remaking his register of correspondence, like a kind of giant and complex spider's web in which he tried to hold together all the many threads of his life.

[10] See E. M. Hatch, *Letters*.

Dodo

———◆———

Carroll's biographers—and Carroll himself—have little to say about his stammer. Green says, in his edition of the *Diaries*:

> Dodgson's stammer was with him all his life; an affliction which other members of his family shared, notably his sister Henrietta, and to a lesser degree, his youngest brother Edwin. (p. 153)

Collingwood, before Green, mentioned it, but only in reference to the problem of ordination. We know, then, that Charles stammered, but no more.

Actually he himself makes some allusions to it in his diaries. On October 31, 1862, he writes:

> Went to the new Church both morning and afternoon, and read service in the afternoon. I got through it all with great success, till I came to read out the first verse of the hymn before the sermon, where the two words 'strife, strengthened', coming together were too much for me, and I had to leave the verse unfinished. (p. 186)

A similar situation—involving the same kind of effort on his part—is mentioned on April 28, 1867: "Read the first lesson in the afternoon, with a good deal of hesitation. I must try what more practice can do" (p. 258). And, in 1872, he tried some treatment:

> A day whose consequences may be of the greatest importance to me. I went to Nottingham, by the advice of my friend Hine, and heard Dr. Lewin lecture on his system for the cure of stammering. . . . The lecture lasted until after midnight, having begun about 9.

The next day, he writes: "Tried Dr. Lewin's system by reading to Hine and Mrs. Hine, and was well pleased with the result." Three weeks later, we have his last mention of this attempt at a cure: "Taught Dr. Lewin's system to [a friend's] cousin Tollemache, and so earned £10 for Dr. Lewin" (p. 311). But there is nothing to suggest that he was himself cured by then, and indeed what Green says suggests the contrary. Furthermore, in a sermon he preached later we find him still troubled by his speech impediment.

This stammer represents a problem. Obviously it must have originated in Carroll's early childhood, but the question is at what point, and in what circumstances, it first manifested itself. Of this we know absolutely nothing. Phyllis Greenacre[1] hazards the hypothesis—as likely as any other—that he was naturally left-handed but trained into right-handedness, which would help to account for his fascination with the mirror as well as for his stammer. But Green objects, with some justification, that this amounts in effect to making two wholly gratuitous suggestions, and that being able to find a causal relationship between them is not the same thing as proving them true. I certainly make no claim to resolve the twofold problem here.

On the other hand, it is important to remember that Carroll did not stammer all the time. We have excellent evidence of this from Isa Bowman:[2]

> Thus encouraged [by Isa] Mr Carroll added other absurd details about the dog, how, if we waited long enough, we would see an attendant bring him a bone . . . and how this badly-behaved animal on one occasion jumped right out of the panorama

---

[1] P. Greenacre, *Swift and Carroll: A psychoanalytic study of two lives*, New York, 1955, p. 124.

[2] Langford Reed, *Lewis Carroll*, London, 1932, p. 75.

among the onlookers, attracted by the sight of a little girl's sand-
wich, and so on. Suddenly he began to stammer, and turning
round in some alarm, I saw that a dozen grown-ups and children
had gathered around, and were listening with every appearance
of amused interest. And it was not Mr. Carroll but a very confused Mr. Dodgson who took me by the hand and led me
quickly from the scene.

Certainly Green's more modest conclusion seems quite as
acceptable as the hypotheses of Dr. Greenacre or Mrs. Lennon:

> Added to his genuine love of children, and the retention of
> some at least of the child's outlook resulting from the mental
> aloofness which accompanies shyness, this fact [that he could
> talk naturally with children, but stammered with adults] must
> have encouraged him more and more to make child-friendships
> and to seek the society of children.[3]

However, it is clear that children did sometimes witness
his speech difficulties; there can be no other explanation for
his having introduced himself into *Alice*, in the earliest version, as the Dodo—Dodgson with a stammer.

In other words, since there is no incontestable cause we
can attach to it, the stammering—which is not something
Carroll makes any of his characters do—can be of interest
only as the symptom of a general state, a symptom of malad-
justment, or perhaps, rather, of a refusal to "adjust." Stammering seems to be connected primarily with a *rejection*: in
his case most obviously that of the clerical state for which he
had been destined, indeed predestined. It was also a weapon,
used to affirm his own will as against that of others (his
father? his teachers? society?), and then to determine the
surroundings in which he himself wanted to live: the company of children. It was not just chance that, after 1880, he
was prepared to go back on his earlier refusal, but this time it
was of his own volition: from then on he preached, and
though his speech impediment did not totally disappear, it
clearly was not an insurmountable handicap.

It would seem that we might even turn Green's hy-

[3] *Diaries*, p. 154.

pothesis the other way round: it was not his stammer that led him to seek out the company of children. It was because he rejected the adult world—though not, of course, totally —that he set himself apart from it by stammering, and thus made his fondness for the world of children appear natural. His stammer was a weapon not of defence but of attack: it was one of the keys to Wonderland.

Early Years[1]

There is no point in concealing the fact that we know virtually nothing of Carroll's childhood; nothing, that is, that has not been handed on to us by, and filtered through, his nephew Stuart Dodgson Collingwood. Collingwood's biography of Carroll certainly has plenty to say about the period, but neither he nor his uncle would have been inclined to see childhood as the most important time in a person's life. However, nobody else ever stepped forward to give evidence about the first years of Charles L. Dodgson's life. So let us read Collingwood.

Childhood According to Collingwood

It was spent, up to the age of eleven, at Daresbury, in Cheshire. They were years of "complete seclusion from the world," since the parsonage was a mile and a half from the village, and "even the passing of a cart was a matter of great interest to the children." Collingwood stresses the solitary nature of Charles's pastimes at that stage:

> In this quiet home the boy invented the strangest diversions for himself; he made pets of the most odd and unlikely animals, and numbered certain snails and toads among his intimate

[1] See also "Family," "Papa and Mama," "Profession: Teaching," and "Rugby."

friends. He tried also to encourage civilised warfare among earthworms, by supplying them with small pieces of pipe, with which they might fight if so disposed.[2]

And he sums up the period in these terms:

He seems at this time to have actually lived in that charming 'Wonderland' which he afterwards described so vividly; but for all that he was a thorough boy, and loved to climb the trees and to scramble about in the old marl-pits.

The phrase "a thorough boy" might cause a raised eyebrow—if only for the reason that, up to the age of five, Carroll's only playmates were his four sisters; do we sense a wish not to see the small Charles as a dreamer, cut off from the world and its problems? Hard to say. But certainly the framework in which Charles spent his early childhood—a rural world on which industrialization barely impinged, a harmonious family unit dedicated to a Christian ideal in which "love" (filial and parental) was believed to be the mainspring of education, yet not devoid of intellectual interests—that framework must have represented for Charles both a factor of stability, and perhaps also, by its very stability, the cause of the strong rejection in his later years.

In 1843, Mr. Dodgson left Daresbury for Croft—a move from Cheshire to Yorkshire. The scene changed: there was a river close by, the rectory stood "in the middle of a beautiful garden" (containing "a specimen of that fantastic cactus, the night-blowing Cereus, whose flowers, after an existence of but a few hours, fade with the waning sun") and the village very near. All this was to offer Charles a social life far wider than anything at Daresbury, but the following year he was sent to boarding school at Richmond, some miles away. However, it was at Croft that his gifts as an entertainer, an inventor, and an author first became apparent. It was there that he made his marionette theatre, constructed his "railway," and put together several family magazines.

The school, where he stayed only for two years, does not seem to have presented any dreadful shock:

[2] Collingwood, p. 11.

The discomforts which he, as a 'new boy', had to put up with from his school-mates affected him as they do not, unfortunately, affect most boys, for in later school days he was famous as a champion of the weak and small, while every bully had good reason to fear him.

And Collingwood, labouring the point, continues:

Though it is hard for those who have only known him as the gentle and retiring don to believe it, it is nevertheless true that long after he left school his name was remembered as that of a boy who knew well how to use his fists in defence of a righteous cause. (p. 23)

A letter from Carroll to his family would seem to corroborate this double statement, for after describing two tricks the other boys had played on him, he adds, "The boys play me no tricks now."

The boys have played two tricks upon me which were these— they first proposed to play at 'King of the Cobblers' and asked if I would like to be king, to which I agreed. Then they made me sit down and sat (on the ground) in a circle round me, and told me to say 'Go to work' which I said, and they immediately began kicking me and knocking me on all sides. The next game they proposed was 'Peter, the red lion', and they made a mark on a tombstone (for we were playing in the churchyard) and one of the boys walked with his eyes shut, holding out his finger, trying to touch the mark; then a little boy came forward to lead the rest and led a good many very near the mark; at last it was my turn; they told me to shut my eyes well, and the next minute I had my finger in the mouth of one of the boys, who had stood (I believe) before the tombstone with his mouth open.

It is true that the picture, not of Carroll as champion of the oppressed, but of Carroll as David against the Goliath of bigger boys, is a little surprising. However, since all the evidence we have comes from Collingwood, we can only accept it. At Rugby, he does not seem to have been enthusiastic about games, and (according to a quotation reproduced by Green in *Diaries*, p. 18) he made the sacrilegious statement that "cricket was a game in which he never took the slightest interest." Collingwood seems to suggest that he played football, which was probably compulsory. As I say, we have generally to accept Collingwood's evidence albeit reluctantly, for lack of any other source of information.

His academic work seems to have gone without a hitch. Charles had studied earlier with his father, and the only thing that presented problems at Richmond was Latin. Only when he got to Rugby did the routine of work, combined with the school's own particular form of community living, manage to make a strong, and disagreeable, impression on him.

Intellectually, then, his childhood seems to have gone very smoothly. Though Charles was not painfully precocious, his intelligence was lively, and the letters reproduced by Collingwood are evidence of this. This one was written from Rugby (at seventeen years of age):

> I have read the first number of Dickens' new tale, 'Davy Copperfield'. It purports to be his life, and begins with his birth and childhood; it seems a poor plot, but some of the characters and scenes are good. One of the persons that amused me was a Mrs. Gummidge, a wretched melancholy person, who is always crying, happen what will, and whenever the fire smokes, or other trifling accident occurs, makes the remark with great bitterness, and many tears, that she is a 'lone lorn creetur, and everything goes contrairy with her.' (pp. 28–29)

That same letter—written to his sister Elizabeth, and the only one we have from that period[3]—also gives a description of a visit to a Roman camp not far from Rugby, some historical-cum-moral comments arising out of his reading of Macaulay, and an account of some purchases he has made:

> I have got a new hat which I suppose Papa will not object to, as my old one was getting very shabby which I have had ever since the beginning of last holidays. I have also got a pair of gloves, as I found I had not *one* pair of summer gloves, as I thought I had.[4]

[3] The whole of it is reproduced in the *Diaries*, pp. 15–18.

[4] He appears to have been obsessed with gloves. On August 4, 1888, he writes in his diary (p. 463): "I record, as a curious piece of Eastbourne statistics, that I have just been to fourteen shops, trying to get a pair of ordinary thread gloves, and have failed!"

and then a series of twenty-three questions, followed by a twenty-fourth: "Will you condense all these questions into one or answer each separately?"

Childhood According to Carroll

In later years, the thing Carroll spoke about most directly was his time at Rugby. From his literary writings I can only give one quotation that could relate to his childhood; it comes from a poem he wrote in 1860, "Faces in the Fire":[5]

> An island-farm—broad seas of corn
> Stirred by the wandering breath of morn—
> The happy spot where I was born.

This recollection of Daresbury is the only one anywhere in his works. On the other hand, it is quite possible to read into some of his imaginary writings indirect references to his own childhood: for instance, the image of the garden (to be found in both *Alices*, and in *Sylvie and Bruno*) must surely reflect the wonderful garden at Croft as well as the college gardens of Oxford. But to reduce the canvas of Carroll's work to a representation of Charles's childhood memories would certainly be a grave misconception; his vision is very much broader than that.[6]

What, then, can we say? Only what I said at the beginning of this section: we have a few highlights, but no picture —even a distorted one—of the total reality. An uneventful childhood in which, naturally enough, there were already traces of what were to be the outstanding interests in Carroll's later personality. Derek Hudson (p. 38) gives considerable importance to an inscription in what is undoubtedly Charles's handwriting, found in 1950 on a block of wood in the Croft rectory. It runs:

> And we'll wander through
> the wide world
> and chase the buffalo.

[5] *Works*, p. 975.
[6] On this point, see my *Lewis Carroll*, Part II, Chap. 3.

Hudson sees this as perhaps the sign of an early longing to
escape, a hankering for Wonderland.[7] And Collingwood, too,
as we have seen, viewed the solitary little boy as already an
inhabitant of that country. But, at the risk of being accused
of wilful blindness, I would reject this tidy hypothesis of
hindsight. Though Charles was no doubt a boy with many
and varied talents, I do not believe his many brothers and sisters left him with enough time to cherish longings for escape.
Wonderland was a shock that was to come later on.

[7] He later reported that it was more probably misquoted from an
early eighteenth-century song, "The Buffalo." See Hudson, *Lewis
Carroll* ("Writers and Their Work" Series), London, 1958, p. 9, note.

Family[1]

The Dodgsons were a north of England family, with connections in Yorkshire and Cheshire. They had a strong ecclesiastical tradition—Charles's great-great-grandfather, great-grandfather, and father all being clergymen, and one of them, the great-grandfather, a Bishop. They were an upper-middle-class family who had had aristocratic connections in the seventeenth century. Dodgson's middle name, Lutwidge, came from his maternal grandfather (who had married Elizabeth Dodgson, daughter of the Bishop). It also came from his mother, Frances Jane Lutwidge, who was her husband's cousin; the husband himself came from Ireland, where his family had settled in the thirteenth century. Green, who gives these details in the *Diaries* (pp. 2-3), adds that the slightly strange spelling was a corruption of "de Ledwich," passing by way of "Luitwick," "Lutwyche," or "Lutwich," till it finally became Lutwidge. When Charles Lutwidge married Elizabeth, he owned an estate in Cumberland, and was Collector of Customs at Hull. All in all, a ramifying family of solid landed or clerical gentry—the two types were generally found together—without a great deal of money, but, their sons usually going either into the army or into Holy Orders, living pretty comfortably nonetheless. But Carroll's own parents found themselves at once the possessors of a large

[1] See also "Papa and Mama."

The six sisters of Lewis Carroll and young Edwin.

family and a small income: in fact they had eleven children, ten of whom were born at Daresbury in Cheshire, Mr. Dodgson's first living. Young Charles—the eldest son seems to have been given this name in every generation—was the first boy, but two daughters, Frances and Elizabeth, had come before him. Eight more children were to follow—and survive: five girls and three boys. In all, a family of seven girls and four boys, produced in fifteen of the twenty-four years of their marriage.

Everything we are told by Collingwood and Carroll's nieces indicates that he was always intensely aware of his responsibilities as the eldest son. After his father's death in 1868, it was he who took charge of getting his sisters moved and settled in at Guildford (in Surrey). From his father's death on he was regularly to spend part of his vacations in the family home (where he assumed the responsibilities of head of the family); Christmas in particular he always spent there. This is clear from an entry in his diary on January 1, 1892 (p. 489): "The year begins, for the first time in my life, at Christ Church, instead of with my own family"—but it was only because he was kept in bed by a "synovitic knee." He also took charge of the education of several of his nephews —including his future biographer, Stuart—helping them both financially and personally, especially on their arrival in Oxford. As for the younger nieces and nephews, he would have them to stay, take them for walks, and entertain them as a good uncle should; nor did he forget to compliment their parents on the excellence of their offspring, as we see from this letter to his brother Wilfred in 1887:

> Now that I have known scores, almost hundreds of children, I am perhaps abnormally critical of them: but I must in candour say I *never* met with children of more perfect behaviour, or more sweetly fascinating, than your Nella and Violet. Alice [his sister-in-law] . . . has somehow managed to make these children combine the high spirits of children with the good manners of grown-up people.[2]

Though he certainly had more than a merely dutiful affection for his family, he does not seem to have had a really

[2] *Diaries*, p. 450.

Edwin Dodgson, the youngest brother of Lewis Carroll.

close relationship with any of them. We have letters to several
of his sisters, especially one to his sister Mary, who must have
passed on to him comments she had heard made about the
little girls he invited to his rooms:[3]

> I think all you say about my girl-guests is most kind and sisterly.
> . . . But I don't think it is at all advisable to enter into any con-
> troversy about it. There is no reasonable probability that it would
> modify the views either of you or of me. I will say a few words
> to explain my views: but I have no wish whatever to have 'the
> last word', so please say anything you like afterwards. . . .
> Another result of my experience is that the opinion of 'people'
> in general is absolutely worthless as a test of right and wrong.
> The only two tests I now apply to such a question as having
> some particular girl-friend as a guest are, first, my own con-
> science, to settle whether I feel it to be entirely innocent and
> right, in the sight of God; secondly, the parents of my friend, to
> settle whether I have their *full* approval of what I do.

It seems likely that the polite but absolutely firm tone of
this letter was enough to make it clear to Mary that her
brother's private life, including any insinuations she might
hear about it, was not a matter for family concern.

But do we, in this connection, accept the possibility that
some form of "censorship" was exercised by his family on the
manuscripts he left? If four years of his diary were not missing (though Collingwood had them in his possession in 1898,
when writing his biography), and they did not happen to be
the years of his youth at Oxford—1858 to 1862—the question would probably not have arisen. Green, the first to consult them after Collingwood himself and Helmut Gernsheim,
says categorically:

> The fact that the Diaries have been inaccessible to the general
> critic, biographer, and research student has led to the suggestion
> that they contain information about Lewis Carroll which his
> pious relatives wish to keep from the world. That rumour can
> now be set at rest once and for all: they contain nothing what-
> soever about Lewis Carroll that the world at large could not
> read.[4]

[3] *Diaries*, pp. 501–02. See also "Girl-Friendships."
[4] *Diaries*, p. ix.

Wilfred Dodgson, another brother of Lewis Carroll.

Green adds (p. 143) that the missing volumes were lost before 1930, together with the Letter Register Carroll kept, but finds absolutely no evidence of any bad faith on the part of the Dodgson family.

We can surely go no further than the most tentative hypotheses. The letter I have quoted certainly proves that his sisters found some aspects of Carroll's life disquieting. We know, too, that Carroll had the negatives of a number of photographs which he had preserved destroyed after his death.[5] It is tempting to decide that two and two make four, and to deduce that Carroll—like a latter-day Rousseau—must have put into his diary descriptions or statements that would be distasteful to the moral notions of his family or of society.

But one can hardly take such a hypothesis seriously. It would be justified only on the supposition that Carroll, like certain of his contemporaries, had dwelled amorously on the charms of the little girls he photographed. Yet this would have gone against everything else he wrote, and indeed everything we know of him. Above all, it would mean that he could at one point in his life have put down in black and white the "impure thoughts" (to use his own phrase) arising out of some of his friendships—and still go on steadfastly giving the kind of assurances he gave, not only to his sister but also, no doubt, to his friends as well, and to himself in his diary. Nothing could be more improbable.

(The reader will realize that, for reasons I have explained further in the section "Celibacy," it seems to me quite impossible that he should have suffered from a broken heart, or the kind of disappointment that would have called forth comment and sympathy from his relatives.)

What seems to me most likely—though obviously fresh discoveries may alter matters—is that his family's disapproval of some aspects of his life went no further than a tactful comment now and then punctuating an eloquent silence. It is probable, on the other hand, that Carroll felt his brothers and sisters did not understand him. For this reason, it would seem that no one in his family—least of all Collingwood!—can be taken as a reliable guide to understanding Lewis Carroll.

5 Hudson, p. 270.

Henrietta Dodgson, sister of Lewis Carroll.

Girl-Friendships

There is obviously a misunderstanding between British students of Lewis Carroll and their counterparts from other countries regarding the problem this chapter tries to examine. French and American critics in particular are often felt to be motivated by a taste for cheap sensationalism or by sheer nastiness when they write that Carroll's "friendships" with young girls, or Carroll's photographs of young girls, cannot be overlooked or explained away by Mr. Dodgson's "eccentric" nature. I sincerely hope that this chapter will dispel part of the misunderstanding and also shed some light on a matter which undoubtedly represents, for Carroll's biographers, one of the most sensitive problems they have to tackle.

Collingwood, writing in the very year his uncle died, devotes his last two chapters to it. The reason he gives is, first, to throw light on "that beautiful side of Lewis Carroll's character which afterwards was to be, next to his fame as an author, the one for which he was best known—his attitude towards children, and the strong attraction they had for him." And then to explain it:

> I shall attempt to point out the various influences which led him in this direction; but if I were asked for one comprehensive

word wide enough to explain this tendency of his nature, I would answer unhesitatingly—Love.[1]

Once that word has been used, the trouble starts. In fact, all historians of the Victorian era have stressed how, apparently under the influence of the "evangelical" tendency in English religious life (a tendency closely linked with Methodism), a tendency whose literary form is linked in turn with certain aspects of romanticism, the latter half of the nineteenth century in England was absolutely saturated with "love," both with the word itself, and with all the outward manifestations of the sentiment. Men and women alike would weep at the slightest provocation, for joy as well as for sorrow; people were continually kissing each other, men kissing men as well as women kissing women, and the most natural expression of affection between parents and children was a kiss on the lips; strangest of all, in moments of great emotion, we find master and servant, teacher and student, suddenly turning to embrace one another. And all this is described by the one word—"love." Love of one's neighbour, of one's enemy, love of all mankind; love of children, love of animals—there was no getting away from it.

So, when Collingwood used the word "love" to explain Carroll's fondness for little girls, we can say that though he fully believed he had explained everything, in fact he had explained nothing at all. But we cannot, as critics today seem to be urging, castigate his "duplicity" or his determination to "whitewash" his uncle. In fact, those who have written serious biographies of Carroll—Green, Hudson, Lennon—have never made such an accusation. And Phyllis Greenacre, in her psychoanalytical study, is far more concerned with getting at the cause of his attitude than giving it a name. But nevertheless, as one reads the biographies, one gets the feeling that with them all, a certain sense of "propriety," of respect for a character by and large so enormously "sympathetic," makes them stop just at the point when, logically, they should go further and start talking in terms of sexuality. I see nothing

[1] Collingwood, p. 360.

disgraceful in that, but nor do I see why this unspoken rule should remain binding. So let me say at once what I shall try to demonstrate in the next few pages—that there was a tremendous emotive and sexual content in Carroll's relationships with little girls. It was in them, and there alone,[2] that he sought to satisfy his sexual urges. Whether or not that satisfaction led to orgasm is only of academic interest.

Seeking for Contact

Collingwood writes (p. 369):

> These friendships usually began all very much in the same way. A chance meeting on the sea-shore, in the street, at some friend's house, led to conversation; then followed a call on the parents, and after that all sorts of kindnesses on Lewis Carroll's part, presents of books, invitations to stay with him at Oxford, or at Eastbourne, visits to the theatre.

And his diary gives us the same picture. The notes about his seaside holidays, in particular, are filled with the names of children he has met, and the only reason there are not more of them is that Green has omitted a great many, considering them too repetitive. Meetings of this kind were all the more likely to be successful in that Carroll had enormous charm: first of all, he knew how to talk to children and could tell them stories. This is proved by *Alice*, of course, but also there were the evenings he spent with the Salisburys, when his audience of children sometimes amounted to over a hundred! Then, too, he made a point of always having a supply of games and toys which could be used (in the train, for instance) to pass the time, or at least to rouse the curiosity of children. Ethel Arnold[3] recalls his display of treasures:

> And what an Eldorado of delights those rooms were for his innumerable child friends! The large sitting room was lined with well-filled bookshelves, under which ran a row of cupboards all

[2] This statement can only be disproved if evidence can be found of some other attachment on Carroll's part; at present there is *none*.

[3] Ethel M. Arnold, "Reminiscence of Lewis Carroll," *The Atlantic Monthly*, Boston, June 1929, p. 783.

round the four walls. Oh, those cupboards! What wondrous
treasures they contained for the delectation of youth! Mechanical
bears, dancing dolls, toys and puzzles of every description, came
from them in endless profusion!

In his forethought, he did not neglect the mothers either, and
Collingwood mentions (p. 373) that

> he never went down to the beach without providing himself
> with a supply of safety-pins. Then if he saw any little girl who
> wanted to wade in the sea, but was afraid of spoiling her frock,
> he would gravely go up to her and present her with a safety-pin,
> so that she might fasten up her skirts out of harm's way.

Then there would be the noblest gift he could give, an
inscribed copy of one of his books. This must have been frequent, for his diary contains several notes like the following
(p. 355):

> I made friends with my fellow-travellers from Oxford, a Mrs.
> Dixon, and her daughter, Emily Phyllis (aged 12). The adven-
> ture had the usual ending—of my promising to send the child a
> copy of *Alice*.

This was the trump card he played whenever possible.
  In the following extract there is a phrase that reveals
something of his excitement:

> Called on Dr. Wallich, and sat for a photograph, then at Mr. Du
> Maurier's: only Mrs. Du Maurier and Beatrix at home. I had a
> chat with the former, and partially tamed the latter. (*Diaries*, p.
> 267)

Then there were ". . . two charming little nieces of his, Kath-
leen and Alice Holdsworth (8 and 6) with whom I became
great friends by the time I left next day" (p. 287). It is clear
that Carroll put himself out to win the favour of the little
girls he noticed and found attractive. Here is another
instance of a description of a similar sort of day (p. 383):

> I went, and met her, and Florence (to whom I gave a copy of
> *Doublets*, and promised *Alice*), and a little sister, a veritable
> 'Alice'. But the meeting them was to lead to more pleasure. Flor-
> ence's great friend, Mabel Woodhouse, was with them when we

parted, and I at once made friends with Mabel, who proved to be a quite charming child, and whose elder sister, Nora, and her brother Rowley, joined us. Then again Nora's great friend, 'Toppy' Robertson, joined us, and I made friends with her also.

After luncheon I made acquaintance with my fellow-lodger, Dr. Philps, and brought him and his child Beatrice, up to my room to see photos, etc.

I went down on the beach again, saw three nice-looking children, and addressed a random remark to one, and got a ready and courteous reply. I soon made friends with the three, and found them to be the Coles'. . . . I am suddenly growing rich in child-friends here.

While I was at dinner Evie and Jessie [Hull] arrived to beg me to take them on the pier: it was a lovely evening, and I think we all enjoyed it thoroughly—a very pleasant end to a wholly exceptional day, so full of pleasant surprises.

It does not, in fact, seem as though that particular day was as exceptional as all that. Two years earlier—his first summer at Eastbourne—Carroll had made this magnificent statement in his diary: "It seems that I could, if I liked, make friends with a new set of nice children every day!" (p. 365).

Once the initial contact had been made, the pattern described by Collingwood would then be followed: an outing or a trip to the theatre; sometimes an invitation to Oxford; sometimes—though only in the later part of Carroll's life—a few days' visit to Eastbourne when he was spending his holidays there. The dinners—more like dolls' dinner parties—in his rooms at Oxford have been described by several of his child-friends, especially Alice.[4] When inviting one child, Carroll asked her:

What do you usually drink at dinner? You·can have any of the following beverages: (1) bottled lemonade; (2) ginger-beer; (3) beer; (4) water; (5) milk; (6) vinegar; (7) ink. Nobody has yet chosen either No. 6 or No. 7. (*Diaries*, p. 529)

The meal itself was sober enough: meat and vegetables, and a dessert. So it may well be that the drink, combined with

[4] Captain Caryl Hargreaves, "Alice's Recollections of Carrollian Days."

the entertainment provided by Carroll, formed the major attraction of the meal.

The Fruits of Victory

But what did he gain out of all those manoeuvres, all those not wholly accidental strolls in places where he was very likely to meet children? To that question there are several layers, as it were, of reply. Up until 1880, one of his main aims was to take photographs of all these little girls. But in collecting their portraits, he was in fact collecting their faces and bodies; so this answer simply leads us to the further question: what did those faces and bodies mean to him?

Little girls seem always to have appeared to Carroll in sheerly physical terms: they were "lovely," "pretty": it was their looks that attracted him so much—almost never their liveliness or intelligence. Certainly there is no mention in his diary of any little girl's attracting him in any other way. And the attraction included the whole body as much as the face. The often-quoted example of little Connie Gilchrist is quite unambiguous: "the most gloriously beautiful child (both face and figure) that I ever saw" (p. 362). With a photograph, he could record the glory of that figure immediately and forever.

Bearing this in mind, we can see that Collingwood was not lying, but neither was he explaining very much, when he wrote (p. 362): "Children appealed to his aesthetic faculties, for he was a keen admirer of the beautiful in every form." But what Collingwood does not seem to have noticed, in his biography, is that that beauty was natural beauty, the beauty of the naked body. This became abundantly clear in Carroll's photography, for he would very soon want to record those figures on paper "sans habilement. [sic]" Hence his delight at finding a model who understood this (p. 356): "It is quite a new privilege to have a subject for photography so entirely indifferent as to dress: I have had none such since Beatrice Hatch." It must be added, however, that photography was only one of the means by which he indulged this taste. When he gave that up in 1880, he was to find quite as much satis-

faction in drawing, and we later find him expressing his gratitude to Gertrude Thomson, in whose studio he could contemplate her studies of nudes at leisure. On this subject,
Harry Furniss reports statements by Carroll that leave no
room for doubt:[5]

> I *wish* I dared dispense with all costume; naked children are so
> perfectly pure and lovely, but Mrs. Grundy would be furious,
> and it would never do.

And of Sylvie:

> I *think* we might venture on making her *fairy* dress transparent.
> Don't you think we might face Mrs. Grundy to *that* extent? In
> fact I think Mrs. Grundy would be fairly content at finding her
> *dressed,* and would not mind whether the material was silk or
> muslin or even gauze.

Another artist, Mrs. Shute, gave him the occasion to write
this in his diary (p. 457):

> Went to Mrs. Shute's studio in Chelsea, as she had arranged
> with Ada Frost (a model aged 14 . . .) that I might come and
> draw her too. It was quite a new experience—the only [two]
> studies of naked children I have ever had opportunities for
> having been each at about 5 years old. Ada has sat as a model
> ever since she was 5, and it was very comfortable to see how
> entirely a matter of business it was to her, and also what a quiet
> dignified manner she had. I think a spectator would have to be
> really in *search* of evil thought to have any other feeling about
> her than simply a sense of beauty, as in looking at a statue. . . .
> She seemed to me a good and modest girl, with every prospect
> of growing up a pure and good woman, in spite of the peculiar
> surroundings of her profession.

Few passages in Carroll give such a sense, not precisely of
duplicity, but of such determination *not to see* what must have
been crystal clear to him. But though it may have been a
rejection rather than hypocrisy, surely the end result is the
same? Furthermore, Mrs. Shute tells us more about his attitudes toward the bodies of children (*Diaries,* p. 457):

[5] H. Furniss, *Confessions of a Caricaturist,* vol. I, pp. 106–7.

He confessed to having no interest in boy or grown-up female models, having the 'bad taste' to find more beauty in the unde-veloped than the mature form. 'I think', he adds [in a letter] 'twelve would be my ideal age: children are so thin from seven to ten'.

Was this aesthetic delight the only delight Carroll felt? I feel by no means sure. A contemporary of Carroll's, also a clergyman, Francis Kilvert, actually put into words all that Carroll did not say:[6]

> As I walked from Shanklin to Sandown [a part of the country especially dear to Carroll] along the cliff edge, I stopped to watch some children bathing from the beach directly below me. One beautiful girl stood entirely naked on the sand, and there, as she half sat, half reclined sideways, leaning upon her elbow, with her knees bent and her legs and feet partly drawn back and up, she was a model for a sculptor, there was the supple slender waist, the gentle dawn and tender swell of the bosom and the budding breasts, the graceful rounding of the delicately beauti-ful limbs and above all the soft curves of the rosy dimpled bottom and broad white thigh.

And even allowing for the demonstrations of affection common in Victorian society, it is slightly surprising to find how much stress Carroll laid on the importance of kissing all his little-girl friends. Hudson (p. 265) recounts a story, told to the biographer by the child herself in later life, of how Carroll suddenly kissed her in the middle of a play they were both watching. But on this point his diary is quite explicit— at least from his own point of view. Thus (p. 390), on meet-ing a little American girl, aged eight, he meets with a some-what unexpected reaction:

> [She] declined to be kissed on wishing goodbye, on the ground that she 'never kissed gentlemen'. It is rather painful to see the lovely simplicity óf childhood so soon rubbed off: but I fear it is true that there are no children in America.

Sometimes the opposite happened, as for instance with little Atty Owen (p. 385):

[6] Francis Kilvert, *Diary (selection)*, London, 1944, p. 290.

She does not look fourteen yet, and when, having kissed her at parting I learned . . . that she is seventeen, I was astonished, but I don't think either of us was much displeased at the mistake having been made!

More significant still is this letter[7] written to a mother—who was not, it seems, amenable to Carroll's persuasion:

Also, are they [your daughters] kissable? I hope you won't be shocked at the question, but nearly all my girl-friends (of all ages, and even married ones!) are now on those terms with me (who am now sixty-four). With girls under fourteen, I don't think it necessary to ask the question: but I guess Margery to be *over* fourteen, and, in such cases, with new friends, I usually ask the mother's leave. When my girl-friends get *engaged* (as they are always doing) I always decline to go on with the practice, unless the 'fiancé' gives his permission: and sometimes he gives it—which is rather a wonder to me, as I feel sure that, if I were in his case, I should *not* give it!

There seems little doubt that this "practice" caused him a certain amount of trouble. Especially when he did not stop there, but braved "Mrs. Grundy" still further by bringing little girls, or even quite big girls, home with him without any chaperon. It seems indeed, that, undaunted by the unpleasantness there had been with Mrs. Liddell, he felt it imperative to avoid the constraint of having any third party present at all. In the letter I have just quoted, there is a passage that makes this perfectly clear:

Would you kindly tell me if I may reckon *your* girls as invitable . . . to tea, or dinner, *singly*. I know of cases where they are invitable in *sets* only (like the circulating-library novels), and such friendships I don't think worth going on with. I don't think anyone knows what girl-nature is, who has only seen them in the presence of their mothers or sisters.

If the parents objected, the relationship would end there. That is what happened with some little girls whose mother

never lets her children go out without herself or the nurse! I wrote to say I was sorry not to add them to the list of my little

[7] *Diaries*, p. 527.

friends, who are all available as companions. This ends our brief acquaintance, as I do not care to have child-friends on such distant terms; I shall not call there again. (p. 416)

As he grew older, however, Carroll seems to have taken greater liberties with regard to the social censoriousness of Victorian prudery—or it may be that he enjoyed outraging it more than in the past. But it is true that, as he grew older, so did the age of his girl friends; the fear of "scandal" thus becomes more comprehensible, which may well have made him react by an increasing determination to get people to accept him as he was—or rather as he thought he was. I have quoted elsewhere the letter he wrote to his sister Mary,[8] in which he makes clear that he is well aware of the interpretations put upon his behaviour, but that "his own conscience" is satisfied. Of this latter there can be absolutely no doubt. But the problem remains whether that "conscience" may not have been wilfully blind.

Some elements in his behaviour are matters of fact: his fondness for kissing, and his predilection for nudity in little girls—in other words, he got, and sought to get, *physical* pleasure from them. Furthermore, the emotional intensity displayed in some of his letters would lead one to suspect that the friendship and "purity" for which his nephew gives him credit (and which he indeed gloried in) may not have been unmixed. Here is a letter he sent to one little girl:[9]

> Oh child, child! I kept my promise yesterday afternoon, and came down to the sea, to go with you along the rocks; but I saw you going with another gentleman, so I thought I wasn't wanted just yet: so I walked a bit, and when I got back, I couldn't see you anywhere, though I went a good way on the rocks to look. There *was* a child in pink that looked you: but when I got up to her, it was the wrong child: however, that wasn't her fault, poor thing. . . . So I helped her with her sandcastles and then I went home. I didn't cry *all* the way.
>
> Your loving friend,
> C. L. Dodgson

[8] See "Family."
[9] E. M. Hatch, *Letters*, p. 110.

And another, to Gertrude Chataway:[10]

> Explain to me how I am to enjoy Sandown without *you*. How
> can I walk on the beach alone? How can I sit alone on those
> wooden steps? So, you see, as I shan't be able to do without you,
> you will have to come. . . .

And this, addressed to Agnes Hull:[11]

> My darling Aggie,
>   Oh yes, I know quite well what you're saying—'Why can't
> the man take a hint? He might have *seen* that the beginning of
> my last letter was meant to show that my affection was cooling
> down!' Why, of course I saw it! But is that any reason why *mine*
> should cool down, to match? . . . Haven't I a right to be affec-
> tionate if I like?

And this letter must surely suggest a great deal more than it
says explicitly, even to non-Freudians:[12]

> Oh! you naughty, naughty little culprit! If only I could fly to
> Fulham, with a handy little stick (ten feet long by four inches
> thick is my favourite size), how I would rap your naughty little
> knuckles! However, there isn't much harm done, so I will sen-
> tence you to a very mild punishment—only one year's imprison-
> ment. If you'll just tell the Fulham policeman about it, he'll
> manage all the rest for you, and he'll fit you with a nice comfort-
> able pair of handcuffs, and lock you up in a nice cosy dark cell,
> and feed you on nice dry bread and delicious cold water.

And Phyllis Greenacre, who quotes the following
letter,[13] with its play on the idea of drinking someone's
health, may well be right in seeing in it traces of a passion too
powerful to be totally eclipsed by the humour:

> Tomorrow I will drink your health, if I remember to, and you
> would like it—but perhaps you will object. . . . If I were to sit
> by you and to drink your tea, you wouldn't like that! You would

---

[10] A. G. Atkinson, "Memories of Lewis Carroll." Reprinted from
The Hampshire Chronicle, 13 March 1948, p. 5.
[11] Hudson, p. 263.
[12] E. M. Hatch, *Letters*, p. 216.
[13] Collingwood, p. 381. P. Greenacre, *Swift and Carroll: A psychoanalytic study of two lives*, p. 176.

say 'Boo-hoo! here's Mr. Dodgson's drunk all my tea and I haven't got any left!' I am very much afraid Sybil will find you sitting by the sad sea-wave and crying, 'Boo! Hoo! Mr. Dodgson's drunk my health and I haven't got any left!' Your mother will say [to the doctor] 'You see, she would go and make friends with a strange gentleman, and yesterday he drank her health!' . . . 'The only way to cure her is to wait until next birthday, and then for her to drink his health'. And then we shall have changed healths. I wonder how you'll like mine!

One cannot simply lump together as *nonsense* all the letters and the kisses—there are just too many of both: they play a most significant part. Here is another letter, also to Gertrude Chataway,[14] then seven or eight years old; Carroll has explained to his doctor that he is "tired in the face":

'Well', he said, 'it puzzles me very much. Do you think that it's in the lips?' 'Of course!' I said. 'That's exactly what it is!' Then he looked very grave indeed, and said, 'I think you must have been giving too many kisses'. 'Well', I said, 'I did give *one* kiss to a baby child, a little friend of mine'. 'Think again', he said, 'are you sure it was only *one?*' I thought again, and said, 'Perhaps it was eleven times'. Then the doctor said, 'You must not give her *any* more till your lips are quite rested again'. 'But what am I to do?' I said, 'because, you see, I owe her a hundred and eighty-two more'.

In short, all the evidence—of which the foregoing represents only a tiny sample—seems to show that, in a great many cases, and even when there was no deep or lasting attachment, what Carroll felt for his little-girl friends was, from his own description, an emotion marked by all the normal characteristics of physical love between adults, and of sexual desire. As one final piece of evidence, we may note (following Hudson)[15] that the occasions when Carroll was not the conquered but the conqueror—when he had succeeded in "making friends," or taking really satisfactory photographs, or spending an evening with one of the little girls

---

[14] Collingwood, p. 384.
[15] Hudson, p. 98: he does not expand the point, but considers it of sufficient importance to merit an entry in the index of the book.

—he would write in his diary, "I mark this day with a white stone," or *Die notandus*, or *Die creta notandus*, a phrase that would make it instantly recognizable. It would be hard to make it any clearer.

The Passage of Time

In her old age, Gertrude Chataway, who was one of the most faithful of Carroll's child-friends over the years, published some recollections about him.[16] About the passage of time she has this to say:

> Many people have said that he liked children only as long as they were really children, and did not care about them when they grew up. That was not my experience; we were warm friends always. I think sometimes misunderstandings came from the fact that many girls when grown up do not like to be treated as if they were still ten years old. Personally I found that habit of his very refreshing.

And it is quite true that there were a number of little girls who, as big girls, and later young women, still received the same sort of long, cheerful, and humorous letters from him as when they were eight or ten. Very often the engagement of one of his former child-friends would call forth a response. Mary, daughter of George MacDonald (who had been so influential in persuading him to publish *Alice in Wonderland*), received a letter of this kind in 1874:

> I haven't had such a pleasant piece of news for a long time. . . . I congratulate you on it with all my heart.
>
> They say that, when people marry, they generally find it best to drop all their *former* friends, and begin again with a new set. Is it a *universal* rule, I wonder? And does it include *very* old friends, as well as new ones? If so, I mustn't grumble at my fate, but quietly retire into your list of "bowing acquaintances". If not, then I hope our friendship will continue for a dozen (or more) years to come what it has been for a dozen years past. . . .[17]

16 Atkinson, "Memories of Lewis Carroll."
17 E. M. Hatch, *Letters*, pp. 32–33.

Yet there is a pathos in his situation, which he deliberately accentuates, and we sometimes find in his diary wistful mention of events of this kind, which made him keenly aware of the passage of time. Gertrude Chataway, Isa Bowman, Enid Stevens, to name only the best known, all remained his friends well after childhood. But such was not always the case. Ethel M. Arnold writes:[18]

> I enjoyed the proud distinction of being one of the very few of his child friends with whom he remained on terms of close friendship after they had attained years of discretion. In fact, I believe I was about the only one of his Oxford child friends who could claim that distinction. He always used to say that when the time came for him to take off his hat when he met one of his quondam child friends in the Oxford streets, it was time for the friendship to cease.

Though the fact that some of his friendships persisted undeniably proves that some of these attachments were quite profound, it cannot erase another fact: that their *nature* changed completely. Knowing children as he did, Carroll was well aware how much the personality changes at puberty. Consider only the comment on Alice Liddell in his diary (p. 231): "Alice seems changed a good deal, and hardly for the better—probably going through the usual awkward stage of transition." Some of his comments are harsher; thus, of little Connie Gilchrist, over whom he had rhapsodized a year earlier (when she was eleven), he writes in 1877: "She is losing her beauty, and can't act" (p. 374). It is certainly hard to believe, as some of his biographers and former child-friends would have us believe, that it was merely that the little girls grew away from him as they grew up, when we read phrases like those I have quoted from his own pen, or this one, recorded by Collingwood:[19]

> About nine out of ten, I think, of my child-friendships get shipwrecked at the critical point, 'where the stream and river meet', and the child-friends, once so affectionate, become uninteresting acquaintances whom I have no wish to set eyes on again.

[18] E. M. Arnold, "Reminiscence of Lewis Carroll."
[19] Collingwood, pp. 368–69.

Certainly the change itself was not his doing, since it took place in the heart and in the body of the little girl. But when he says, as he does in one letter: "Usually the child becomes so entirely a different being as she grows into a woman, that our friendship has to change too,"[20] do we feel bound to conclude that, on his side, he was prepared to continue as before? Surely not. Some critics have, in my view, attached too much importance to one interesting development: as Carroll grew older, he became very much more relaxed with older girls; so much so that from 1887, he gave lectures at a girls' high school in Oxford, and in the very last years of his life he even taught logic to the undergraduates at Lady Margaret Hall. The most one can possibly deduce from this is that his efforts to grow up along with his little friends had enabled him to extend his capacity for emotional satisfaction somewhat. But he never ceased to care for little girls.

Everything seems to indicate that the growing apart, the cooling of affection, was due to the ambivalence within the relationship itself. Being a prisoner of his nature, his age, and the language of his age, Carroll could not have maintained beyond the age of childhood strictly so called the fiction that what he was attracted by was a soul—when what he noticed, described in loving detail, and in fact transformed into an object of enjoyment, was a face and a body. He could say, and try to assure himself, that there was nothing wrong in fondling a little girl of eight; but when she became fourteen or fifteen, it was a different matter. In this respect, social conventions are very revealing, and the passage of time shows up the illusions—or blindnesses—of the past.

The vocabulary of the time was used, in the last resort, in an attempt to harmonize real experience with the demands of conscience. But though the reader of 1880 might have been convinced by such passages as the following,[21] we today can hardly help feeling that they really mean almost the opposite

[20] Hudson, pp. 260–61.

[21] These are all taken from a long article by Morton N. Cohen in *The Times*, of November 20, 1971. Cohen is at present working with Green on an edition of Carroll's letters.

of what they say. This, for instance, to a little girl who has
sent him her photograph:

> Photographs are very pleasant things to have, but *love* is the best
> thing in the world. Don't you think so? Of course I don't mean
> it in the sense meant when people talk about 'falling in love';
> that's only *one* meaning of the word, and only applies to a few
> people. I mean in the sense in which we say that everybody in
> the world ought to 'love everybody else'.

Or this, to a mother:

> *Many* thanks for again lending me Enid. She is one of the
> dearest children. It is *good* for one (I mean, for one's spiritual
> life, and in the same sense in which reading the Bible is good)
> to come into contact with such sweetness.

Or this, to another mother:

> You speak of my having seen into Marion's inner nature, and
> having seen what she is in *herself*. Well, I think I have *not* done
> that, as yet. We are excellent friends, but I don't think she yet
> regards me as so *intimate* a friend as to show any of her real
> inner life to me. I *have*, before now, reached such terms and cer-
> tainly a child's nature appears in a new and wonderful light
> when she knows one well enough to say anything about her
> thoughts about God, and death, and such subjects as underlie all
> other thoughts and words. Such intercourse is rather 'aweful' to
> me: one's own nature comes out so poor and mean in the new
> light thus thrown upon it.

I would say quite frankly that this last letter, in particular, seems to me to touch on the bounds of the tolerable:
though we may not see Carroll as a conscious hypocrite, there
does seem a definite uneasiness in this effort to keep recalling
(to himself and others) that he is a clergyman, and that
therefore the attachment he feels for a little girl must be
pure. It is hard to believe in all honesty that he really wanted
to talk about God and death with Connie Gilchrist or any of
his other photographic models: or—for, after all, he talks
about it at some length in *Sylvie and Bruno*—that physical
beauty and moral beauty really aroused equivalent sensations
in him. Yet he says as much in that same letter:

I have no doubt that Marion will be loved by many for her beauty, but I can honestly say my love for her, such as it is, is for *herself*, and not for her good looks.

And Collingwood warms to this theme, recalling Walter Pater, Francis Thompson, and a whole background of neo-Christian romanticism:[22]

Recognising, as he did, what Mr. Pater aptly terms 'the curious perfection of the human form', in man, as in nature, it was the soul that attracted him more than the body.

One can only conclude unhesitatingly that, behind the conventional vocabulary and all the moral and religious attitudinizing of the age, Carroll's very denials make it clear how fundamentally sexual was the importance of little girls in Carroll's life. They were the only sexual object he allowed himself—a man who in theory rejected sexual objects altogether—and they provide the key to his entire sexuality.

[22] Collingwood, p. 362.

Illustrators

Carroll's earliest writings (things produced for family consumption, like "Useful and Instructive Poetry," "Mischmasch," and "The Rectory Umbrella") were all illustrated by himself. The same was the case with the manuscript of *Alice's Adventures Under Ground,* completed in 1863; for this he sought the help of a natural history book. But on the advice of his friend MacDonald, and perhaps also of Ruskin —and undoubtedly also, as Collingwood notes, from lack of confidence in his own ability—he resolved to employ an artist to illustrate the published version, and settled finally upon John Tenniel.

But after *Through the Looking-Glass,* Tenniel decided that it was impossible to continue collaborating with Carroll (see below), and for his later works, Carroll had to find other illustrators. There were four altogether: Henry Holiday (for *The Hunting of the Snark*), Arthur B. Frost (for *A Tangled Tale* and a collection of poems), Harry Furniss (for *Sylvie and Bruno*), and Gertrude Thomson, who provided pictures for the cover of *The Nursery Alice*—otherwise illustrated by Tenniel pictures, enlarged and coloured—and for *Three Sunsets.*

The Amateur and the Professionals

Carroll's drawings have very little in common with what normally appeared in the children's books of the period, but are very similar to the kind of thing Edward Lear was doing from 1845 onward in his *Books of Nonsense*. They were indubitably "children's drawings," but showed so strong a tendency to distortion as to be really caricatures, and in some cases—as when Alice grows too large in the White Rabbit's house—contain a wealth of meaning.

There is no doubt at all that Carroll's eclipse by his professional illustrators was due to his own modesty: we may consider it excessive, but it was certainly genuine and not contrived. However, it posed two sets of problems, especially with the Alice books.

For Carroll himself, there was the problem of day-to-day collaboration with people who could not, he knew, have the same attitude to his work as he had. With them all he exchanged innumerable letters; he studied carefully every drawing, indeed every line. (And this carefulness extended to the printing, and then the final reproduction.)[1] The result was incessant friction, which strained his relations with all his illustrators, but especially the first of them, Tenniel. It must indeed have been exasperating for a famous caricaturist to be given advice by an obscure young don, and especially one who was so outrageously demanding. Tenniel flatly refused, for instance, to draw "a *wasp* in a *wig*"—and thus caused one episode of the *Looking-Glass* to disappear altogether. In any case, after Alice, neither of them wanted to continue their collaboration, and it was as much by Carroll's wish as by Tenniel's that the attempt was abandoned. However, when Carroll did approach Tenniel once, later on, the latter replied:

It is a curious fact that with *Through the Looking-Glass* the fac-

[1] Harry Furniss was to write to Collingwood: "I have illustrated stories of most of our leading authors, and I can safely say that Lewis Carroll was the only one who cared to understand the illustrations to his own book." (Collingwood, p. 319)

ulty of making drawings for book illustrations departed from me, and, notwithstanding all sorts of tempting inducements, I have done nothing in that direction since. (Collingwood, p. 146)

Harry Furniss, whether because he was less discreet or more touchy, was to make a great many harsh comments about his collaboration with Carroll. In the *Strand* magazine, in 1908, he wrote an article containing the following remarks:

> He would take a square inch of the drawing, count the lines I had made in that space, and compare their number with those on a square inch of an illustration made for *Alice* by Tenniel! And in due course I would receive a long essay on the subject from Dodgson the mathematician. Naturally this led to disagreements, particularly when it came to foreshortening a figure, such as 'Sylvie and the Dead Hare', which is a question for the eye, not for the foot-rule and compass. In fact, over a criticism of one drawing, I pretended that I could stand Dodgson the Don no longer, and wrote to Carroll the author declining to complete the work.[2]

In his memoirs,[3] Furniss gives a fascinating description of his professional relationship with Carroll. For instance, this was in a letter from Carroll about *Sylvie and Bruno*:

> I think I had better explain part of the plot, as to these two—Sylvie and Bruno. They are not fairies right through the book—but *children*. All these conditions make their *dress* rather a puzzle. They mustn't have *wings*: that is clear. . . . Their friends might be able to say 'What oddly-dressed children!' but they oughtn't to say 'They are not human!'

And of Sylvie, Furniss tells us:

> Then for months we corresponded about the face of the Heroine alone. My difficulty was increased by the fact that the fairy child Sylvie and the Society grown-up Lady Muriel were one and the same person! So I received reams of written descriptions and piles of useless photographs intended to inspire me to draw with

[2] *Diaries*, p. 474.
[3] *Confessions of a Caricaturist*, vol. I, pp. 101–12.

Drawing by Holiday for the *Snark*.

a few lines a face embodying his ideal in a space not larger than a threepenny-piece. . . . I received the author's recipe for constructing the ideal heroine. I am not to take *one* model for the lady-child or child-lady. I am to take *several*. . . . I am therefore to go to Eastbourne to see and study the face of Miss Matilda Smith, in a pastry-cook's shop, for the eyes. . . . Then in Glasgow there is a Miss O'Grady, 'with oh, such a perfect nose! Could I run up to Scotland to make a sketch of it?' A letter of introduction is enclosed, and, as a precaution, I am enjoined that 'I must not mind her squint'. . . . For the ears a journey to Brighton to see Miss Robinson, the Vicar's daughter, is recommended. . . . The mouth I shall find in Cardiff—not an English or Welsh mouth, but a sweet Spaniard's, Señora Niccolomino, the daughter of a merchant there. . . . For the hair I must go to Brighton; for the figure to a number of different places. In fact my author had mapped out a complete tour for me.

For the reader, the question is how the illustrations relate to the written text. Here there is no room for doubt: *the illustrations constitute an integral part of Carroll's books.* Personal disagreements notwithstanding, Carroll demonstrated an extraordinary attention to detail in his advice, his criticism, and his approval. Consequently, whatever his illustrators did (or did not do, as in the case of a drawing by Holiday of the Snark which Carroll made him remove, explaining that "it was a beautiful beast but that he had made the Snark strictly unimaginable, and desired him to remain so") [4] was generally what Carroll intended.

This is a vital point, especially with the Alice books. For the characters in them emerge not only from Carroll's written text, but also from the "text" of Tenniel's drawings: the White Knight *is* that old man with the long white moustache; and the father of Sylvie and Bruno, too, is the handsome old man in Furniss's frontispiece. With a less punctilious author, the illustrations might be merely extras: with Carroll they are the necessary complement to the text. Though we can only lament the fact that he lacked the courage to publish his own drawings, there can certainly be no question of

[4] Cf. *The Lewis Carroll Handbook,* p. 86.

saying that he was "betrayed" by Tenniel, Holiday, or Furniss. Despite all their temperamental differences, the text and
pictures always form a harmonious whole.

Inventions and Games

Carroll was a born inventor. Collingwood describes him in his childhood inventing games for his brothers and sisters; but this ability, fairly commonplace in a child, was to develop in the adult into a wealth, and indeed at times a positive fever, of inventions of every description. From the wrapping of parcels to the most complex arithmetical problems; from gadgets and commonsense solutions, to tiresome practical problems, to important mathematical discoveries. Thus, Carroll writes in his diary for January 27, 1865:

> Wrote to the manager at Covent Garden, suggesting an idea that had occurred to me for managing the carriages—to divide the three exit doors among the alphabet, and arrange the carriages outside so that they should drive in, in sets of three, in the proper order. (p. 226)

In 1871, having given a dinner party in his room for eight guests, he writes to Macmillan's, his publishers, to suggest (perhaps for publication?) a table plan to be given to each guest, with parentheses to show who was to give an arm to whom on going in to dinner; he considered this to have many advantages:[1]

> (1) It saves the host the worry of going round and telling every gentleman what lady to take in.

---

[1] Hudson, p. 170.

(2) It prevents confusion when they reach the dining-room (the system of putting names round on the plates simply increases the confusion, though it would work well *with* this plan).

(3) It enables everybody at table to know who the other guests are—often a very desirable thing.

(4) By keeping the cards one gets materials for making-up other dinner-parties, by observing what people harmonise well together.

In 1880, he writes in his diary (p. 391):

Thought of a plan for simplifying money-orders, by making the sender fill up two duplicate papers, one of which he hands in to be transmitted by the postmaster—it contains a key-number, which the receiver has to supply in order to get the money. I think of suggesting this, and my plan for double postage on Sunday, to the Government.

In 1891, we find this enthusiastic entry (p. 486):

An inventive day. It has long been a 'desideratum' with me to be able to make short memoranda in the dark, without the unpleasant necessity of having to get up and strike a light. I have tried writing within oblongs cut out of cardboard: but the result is apt to be illegible. Today I conceived the idea of having a series of *squares*, cut out in card, and devising an alphabet, of which each letter could be made of lines along the edges of the squares, and dots at the corners. I invented the alphabet, and made the grating of sixteen squares. I shall call it 'The Typhlograph'. ([A month later]: Instead of 'typhlograph' I have adopted 'Nyctograph' at the suggestion of Warner.)

Nothing seems to have been outside the scope of his inventive talent. It was at his suggestion that his publisher replaced plain book-jackets with covers with titles on the spine, so that they could be read when standing on the shelf. In 1896, he invented "a substitute for gum, for fastening envelopes (as used to be done with wafers), mounting small things in books, etc.—viz: paper with gum on *both* sides. It should be supplied in sheets, and also in discs." (p. 526). In 1879, he invented a folding map:

Planned a mode of cutting up and mounting two Post Office Directory maps of London, so as to make a handy book for referring to when walking about. I think of suggesting to the publishers to bring out a map so arranged. (p. 378)

But in this area, the publishers only took his advice once. His one and only success was a holder for stamps, "The Wonderland Postage-Stamp Case," invented in 1888 and produced in Oxford in 1890 (copies could still be seen at the publishers in 1958).

All these schemes and inventions are clearly reminiscent of Chapter VIII of *Through the Looking-Glass*, aptly entitled, "It's My Own Invention," in which the White Knight describes some of his inventions to the polite but sceptical Alice, and sings her a song whose hero is an inventor, too. They also link up with the Professor/Mein Herr in *Sylvie and Bruno* and its sequel, who invents special boots for horizontal rain, and describes the "artificial selection" of people who are "lighter than water." If we compare the inventions in his fictional writing with those he tried, sometimes successfully, to make himself, we find ourselves having to treat both relatively seriously. And taking them seriously means, first and foremost, recalling to what extent the nineteenth century was an age of technical discoveries, perhaps more in England than anywhere else;[2] and to what extent a belief in the possibility of indefinite progress was sustained by inventions that, in fact, continued to make daily life ever easier and more comfortable. "The age of the machine" really began in the reign of Queen Victoria, and Carroll lived to see the appearance of the phonograph, the bicycle, the fountain pen, and the first copying machine. And, a fact that also indicates the way in which Carroll "adjusted" to his time, all these inventions interested him. We find him in his diary closely following, and at times actually forestalling, advances in all sorts of spheres: the cyclostyle in 1877 ("spent the evening in trying an 'electric pen' sent from Parker's with moderate success"); the fountain pen in 1879 ("Received the new American pen

---

[2] Cf. the splendid book by L. de Vries, *Victorian Inventions* (*1865–1900*), London, 1971.

—the 'Stylograph'—with which I am writing this entry");
and the phonograph in 1890:

> Went to the exhibition of 'Edison's Phonograph'. It is indeed a
> marvellous invention. As heard through the funnel, the *music*
> (particularly trumpet-music) was flat: the singing and speaking
> were better, though a little inarticulate. (p. 479)

And with this particular invention, we see how much he was
a man of his time:

> Went to the 'Phonograph' again, at the end of the lecture. . . .
> Listening through tubes, with the nozzle to one's ear, is far
> better and more articulate than with the funnel: also the music is
> much sweeter. It is a pity that we are not fifty years further on in
> the world's history, so as to get this wonderful invention in its
> *perfect* form. It is now in its infancy—the new wonder of the
> day, just as I remember Photography was about 1850. (*Ibid.*)

With regard to the bicycle, in his passion for exercise,
Carroll had various suggestions to make; he had tried a
"Velociman" (a treadle-tricycle, worked by hand), and a few
days afterward sent its inventor some proposals for technical
improvements, one of which was typical of his concern for
making life easier; he considered that the steering would be
improved by a system of horizontal wheels with a chain so
that "you lean the way you want to turn, which is instinctive
and safer as to upsetting" (pp. 406–07).

So deep-rooted was his love of innovation that, during
his period as Curator of the Common Room at Christ
Church, Carroll was always ready to suggest technical
improvements to his colleagues, especially in the matter of
heating and lighting. Was he, in fact, an inventor who never
got a lucky break? Yes and no. Yes, because he really thought
that absolutely everything could be improved upon, and was
prepared to consider any solution that was not a physical
impossibility: thus the fantasies devised in the *Sylvie and
Bruno* books are not to be dismissed as sheer nonsense—nor
have they always been, as witness the "black light" described
in the Professor's lecture. But no, also, for he was perfectly

satisfied with the *intellectual* pleasure he got from each discovery, and his delight at having *found* something new. We can see this even more clearly in relation to mathematical problems. Above all, we must not foist upon him the image of the delightful lunatic that might be suggested by the White Knight and the Professor, nor that of the dreamer in an ivory tower who can never descend from his logico-mathematical cloud-world. Practical technology was very much a part of his total makeup.

Puzzles, Games, and Problems

One of his little-girl friends, when an adult, recalled how, when travelling, Carroll always provided himself with various games so that he could entertain any travelling companions he might have.[3] A great many of these games were also invented by himself. From the end of his youth, his diaries are liberally scattered with notes like this, in 1858: "Completed the rules of the game at cards I have been inventing during the last few days, *Court Circular*" (p. 139). A number of them he found so satisfactory as to have their rules actually published, with a view to offering increased sources of amusement to other card players. He did this with Court Circular (1860, revised in 1862); with Croquet Castles, a variant of croquet (1863, revised in 1866); and with his new rules for lawn tennis tournaments (1883). On other occasions, he noted a new game in his diary, saying how he had tried it out with one or other of his child-friends, and then never refers to it again. This was the case with several variants of backgammon, in which he became very interested during 1868; and "a new Arithmetical game for two, which I think of calling *Numerical Dominoes*" (1875). Nor do we hear any sequel to this entry: "The idea occurred to me that a game might be made of letters, to be moved about on a chess-board till they form words" (1880—perhaps a precur-

[3] Even in Russia he made sure of always having a portable chess set with him, and was very glad of it on the journey from Moscow to Warsaw.

sor of Scrabble?). One of his little friends later spoke of his
showing her "how to make a paper pistol go off with a bang,"[4]
but we hear no more of that either.

Among all his games, those in which letters and words
were the materials used—the chessmen, if you like—were the
ones in which his genius had freest rein.[5] He has left us at least
three games of this nature: Doublets, (1878–79, known first
as Word-Links), Mischmasch (1881–82), and Syzygies (1891).
All are based on the idea that by changing a letter in a word
you can produce a different word, and the object in all the
games is to cover the maximum range of possibilities. In
Doublets, you have to move from one word to another in as
few moves as you can; in Mischmasch, you build words from
a kernel of two or three letters given you by your opponent.
In Syzygies (to which, when he published it, he added the
words "Phoebus, what a name!"), the player has to find a
series of links (one letter or several consecutive letters) that
yoke two words together; for instance, from *walrus* to *carpenter,* the chain might be like this:

WALRUS

(rus)

peruse

(per)

harper

(arpe)

CARPENTER

His games got more difficult as he went on, and though
Doublets became quite popular, the other two (and Lanrick,
played on a chessboard) never really gained a following
among the public for whom they were intended. For they
were all published in magazines, for women or children—and
even, in the case of his variant on backgammon, in *The Times*!
As the good teacher he was, Carroll in each case provided
some sample problems, gave the answers, and was prepared to
go on endlessly providing more.

[4] *Diaries*, p. 487.
[5] On this point, see my *Lewis Carroll*, pp. 361–68.

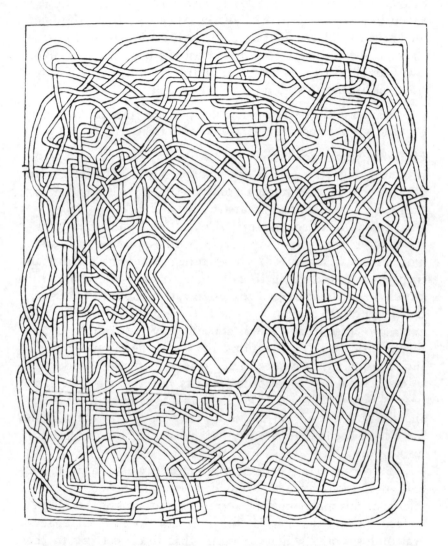

Drawing by Lewis Carroll for Mischmasch.

The same thing was true of his riddles. The best known, of course, is the riddle the Mad Hatter asks Alice: "Why is a raven like a writing-desk?" When Alice could not think of an answer, and the Hatter said flatly that he "hadn't the slightest idea," that would seem to have been the end of it. But Carroll, for the last edition of *Alice* published in his lifetime, Christmas 1896, did try to give a reply:

> Because it can produce a few notes, though they are *very* flat; and it is never put with the wrong end in front.

Hudson, who quotes this (p. 300), suggests that Carroll probably felt it needed some excuse, since he went on to explain that it was "merely an after-thought: the Riddle, as originally invented, had no answer at all."

But quite independent of *Alice*, Carroll took great trouble to offer his readers innumerable riddles, puzzles, charades, and acrostics; and in 1875 he planned to assemble them all into what he was going to call *Alice's Puzzle Book*, and for which Tenniel had agreed to design a frontispiece. The work never appeared, though. Towards the end of his life Carroll again projected it, and it was actually advertised under a different title, with illustrations by Gertrude Thomson.[6] To judge from the few specimens available to us,[7] we do not seem to have lost a great deal by its never having, in fact, been achieved. We learn more, from the entries in his diary and the recollections of his young friends, of how marvellous must have been his apparently inexhaustible fund of ideas for passing the time.

However, things became more serious when, in the latter half of Carroll's life, he decided to employ his considerable talents in this sphere in the teaching of mathematics and logic. Indeed, I think that it is in this light that we have to see several of his works which are somewhat disconcerting to the reader of *Alice*: *Curiosa Mathematica, A Tangled Tale, The Game of Logic*, and *Symbolic Logic*. All four occurred in the later part of his life, appearing between 1885 (*A Tangled Tale*) and 1896 (*Symbolic Logic*). All four represent a delib-

---

[6] *Diaries*, pp. 337–38; *LCPB*, p. 270.
[7] *Works*, pp. 819–822.

erate effort on Carroll's part—in the words of the preface to
A Tangled Tale—to

> embody in each Knot[8] (like the medicine so dexterously, but
> ineffectually, concealed in the jam of our early childhood) one
> or more mathematical questions—in Arithmetic, Algebra, or
> Geometry, as the case might be—for the amusement, and possi-
> ble edification, of the fair readers of that magazine.

Curiosa Mathematica, of which two successive parts were
published, in 1888 and 1893, was presented in a slightly different way, perhaps because, unlike the other three, this work
was signed by C. L. Dodgson, rather than by Lewis Carroll.
The second volume was subtitled *Pillow Problems,* which
Carroll explained in this way:[9]

> It is not in the hope of remedying insomnia that I have proposed
> mathematical calculations, but rather in order to remedy the
> worrying thoughts which are liable to invade a mind that is
> wholly unoccupied. . . . Once my brain is so wide awake that, do
> what I may, I can be *sure* not to sleep for at least an hour, I have
> to choose between two solutions: either submitting to fruitless
> torture, self-inflicted, by turning within myself to a problem that
> disturbs me; or filling my mind with a subject sufficiently
> absorbing to keep worry at bay. For me, any mathematical prob-
> lem will do this. . . .

But, in addition to this information, which more or less
explains the *genesis* of the work, we discover one fascinating
point: these problems and their solution were indeed the fruit
of sleepless nights, but what is extraordinary about them is
the fact that they were all done *in his head*—he wrote nothing down until he got up the following morning. So the
training Carroll was proposing to his readers was as much a
personal as a mathematical discipline. This time, the jam was
there to disguise a different medicine—intellectual effort.

The two works of logic are more in line with the

---

[8] Calling the chapters *knots* is a literal return to the pun that figures
in Alice's conversation with the Mouse, in Chapter III of *Alice in Wonderland*.

[9] *Pillow Problems*, New York, Dover, 1958, introduction, p. x.

declared aim of *A Tangled Tale*. Of *The Game of Logic*, Carroll says:[10]

> A second advantage, possessed by this game, is that, besides being an endless source of amusement (the number of arguments, that may be worked by it, being infinite) it will give the players a little instruction as well. But is there any great harm in *that*, so long as you get plenty of amusement?

And, in the preface and introduction to *Symbolic Logic*, he defines his intention more forcefully, and in a more logical tone:[11]

> This is, I believe, the very first attempt that has been made to popularize this fascinating subject. It has cost me *years* of hard work, but if it should prove, as I hope it may, to be of service to the young, and to be taken up . . . as a valuable addition to their stock of healthful mental recreations . . . such a result would more than repay ten times the labour I have expended on it. . . . Once master the machinery of Symbolic Logic, and you have a mental occupation always at hand, of absorbing interest, and one that will be of real *use* to you in *any* subject you may take up. . . . *Try it.* That is all I ask of you!

This enthusiasm breaking through in the published preface becomes more and more evident in the increasingly frequent notes Carroll makes in his diary over the years of a "discovery" he has just made in some scientific domain or other, usually that of mental arithmetic.

March 8, 1887:

> Discovered a Rule for finding the day of the week for any given day of the month. There is less to remember than in any other Rule I have met with. (p. 449)

November 27, 1888:

> Devised a Logic Board, with which *five* attributes can be worked. (p. 466)

September 27, 1897:

> *Die notandus !* Discovered a rule for dividing a number by 9, by

---

[10] *The Game of Logic*, New York, Dover, 1958, preface.
[11] *Symbolic Logic*, New York, Dover, 1958.

mere addition and subtraction. I felt sure there must be an analo-
gous one for 11, and found it, and proved the first rule by Algebra, after working about nine hours! (p. 539)

September 28, 1897:

Die creta notandus! I have actually superseded the rules discovered yesterday! . . .

October 12, 1897:

Completed my discovery of a rule for dividing by 13. (p. 540)

November 4, 1897:

Completed a rule, much better than the one done on Oct. 12. . . .
(p. 541)

November 12:

An inventive morning! After waking, and before I had finished
dressing, I had devised a new, and much neater, form in which
to work my Rules for Long Division. (p. 542)

In these few weeks of the last year of his life, we find him
delighting, indeed exulting, in the discoveries that come
crowding into his mind. Whatever the reservations of those
who value him only for his nonsense writings, it is impossible
not to recognize in them a jubilation that surely indicates an
essential dimension of Carroll's personality. Not only is he a
pedagogue, anxious to convey knowledge in the most attractive manner possible; not only is he a mathematician, a man
of reasoned thought, of logical steps and demonstration; he is,
first and foremost, a real *inventor*, for whom the joy of discovery is one of the greatest delights life has to offer. It is significant indeed that the triumphant Latin phrase with which
he opens the last entries I have quoted is the same that he uses
for his days of richest emotional fulfilment. On those few
occasions when he reached certain intellectual high points (or
what seemed to him high points), the satisfaction he felt was
as profound as, and similar in kind to, what he felt after
spending the afternoon with an enchanting little girl. A joy
of discovery, of invention: this is an element we must be very
careful never to forget in any effort to capture the personality of Lewis Carroll.

Juvenilia

———◆———

Carroll began writing before the end of his childhood. Collingwood quotes six lines of Latin verse written when Carroll
was twelve, and refers also to his having written a story, "The
Unknown One," published in the Richmond School magazine
in 1845; though no trace can be found of it, Collingwood
remarks (p. 24) that it "was probably of the sensational type
in which small boys usually revel." At about the same time,
there began the series of family magazines: first *Useful and
Instructive Poetry*, in 1845; then *The Rectory Magazine*,
bound into a volume in about 1850; *The Rectory Umbrella*,
1850–53; and *Mischmasch*, 1853–62. In 1850 he wrote *La
Guida di Bragia*. And, between 1851 and 1855, the date of his
first contribution to *The Comic Times*, he wrote a short
humorous story, and a number of poems, two of which seem
to have been published in an Oxford local magazine.

It is worth noting here certain features common to all
these youthful works:[1] first, his fondness for parody, naturally tending to choose as its target the great writers studied
at school. He parodied Macaulay, for instance (in *The Rectory Umbrella*, "Lays of Sorrow").[2] Also Shakespeare; indeed,

---

[1] For a more detailed discussion, I would like to refer readers to my
Lewis Carroll, Part I.

[2] *LCPB*, pp. 12–14. *Works*, p. 791. *The Rectory Umbrella and
Mischmasch*, New York, Dover, 1971.

his parody of *Henry IV*, Part II, merits special mention for the way it combines a sense of parody with an early taste for logic.[3]

La Guida di Bragia is a splendid example of how Carroll's early writings displayed some of the features that were to be so characteristic of his mature work. It was a ballad opera written for the marionette theatre. The title itself introduces a note of parody, indeed of lunacy: it is an Italianization of *Bradshaw's Guide*—the voluminous timetable of all the railway lines in England. The plot is complex and Shakespearean: it juxtaposes the vicissitudes of two aristocratic characters, Orlando and Sophonisba, in connection with a train journey Orlando has to make, with those of two comic characters, Mooney and Spooney, who become involved with a rather odd fellow traveller. The element of parody runs strongly in a passage in which Mooney recounts a strange adventure he has just had:[4]

> Mooney: Do you know, Spicer, what an awful thing I saw just now?
> Spooney: No, what?
> Mooney: A Bradshaw's Railway Guide on legs stood visibly before me, and at the same moment I heard a hollow voice.
> Spooney: Oh, I say, how you terrify me!
> Mooney: Yes, sir, a hollow voice which said: 'Mooney, why singst thou not? Spooney, why singst thou not? Spooney hath murdered singing. And therefore, Mooney shall sing no more, Spooney shall sing no more'.
> Spooney: Did it say any more?
> Mooney: Oh, ever such a lot more! It said:
> 'Oh, I have passed a miserable day
> Spooney sings worse than any man can say'.
> Spooney: Any more?
> Mooney: Rather. It said:
> 'Tunes, music, thorough-bass lend me your ear,
> I came to see if Spooney sang: he didn't! ...

[3] *Useful and Instructive Poetry*, first published with an introduction by Derek Hudson, London, Geoffrey Bles; Macmillan, New York, 1954, pp. 25–27.
[4] *La Guida di Bragia* was published for the first time in *The Queen*, London, 18 November 1931.

> Did this in Spooney look like knowing music?
> Yet Spooney thinks he knoweth how to sing,
> But Spooney he is very much mistaken!
> Each time he tried he always missed a note,
> Now sharp, now flat, but never natural,
> Yet Spooney thinks he knoweth how to sing,
> But Spooney he is very much mistaken!'

The obvious likeness to Macbeth and to Antony's speech from *Julius Caesar* make Spooney exclaim: "Such an odd thing! To think of a book coming and talking Shakespeare like a human being. . . ."

The other element is the vein of nonsense, and here we find some rather more modern overtones:

> Mooney: Who's you?
> Spooney: Why, me.
> Mooney: Nonsense, it can't be, what's your name?
> Spooney: Oh, that's quite another question: I shan't tell.
> Mooney: Yet there is something familiar in those tones; something which recalls to my memory visions of earlier and happier days. Speak, speak! *Have* you the mark of a gridiron on the back of your left wrist?
> Spooney: No, certainly not; nothing of the sort!
> Mooney: Then you are my long-lost friend, my Spooney.
> Spooney: My Mooney!   (They embrace.)

There is also his love of illustration, including caricature —the pictorial equivalent of parody. *The Rectory Umbrella*, for instance, contains caricatures of some pictures by Reynolds, with commentaries. Carroll drew freely, and there is no hint of the modesty that was to overtake him when it came to the publication of *Alice*.

The vein of nonsense, which runs through *Useful and Instructive*, appears in the limericks, the word games like "Rules and Regulations," and in poems like this one:[5]

> Were I to take an iron gun,
> And fire it off towards the sun;
> I grant 'twould reach its mark at last,
> But not till many years had passed.

[5] *Works*, p. 783.

> But should that bullet change its force,
> And to the planets take its course,
> 'Twould *never* reach the *nearest* star,
> Because it is so *very* far.

Another form his nonsense took was the logico-mathematical problems, like "The Two Clocks,"[6] in which a paradox is disguised under a mask of apparent absurdity:

Which is better, a clock that is right only once a year, or a clock that is right twice every day? 'The latter', you reply, 'unquestionably'. Very good, now attend.

I have two clocks: one doesn't go *at all*, and the other loses a minute a day: which would you prefer? 'The losing one', you answer, 'without a doubt'. Now observe: the one which loses a minute a day has to lose twelve hours, or seven hundred and twenty minutes before it is right again, consequently it is only right once in two years, whereas the other is evidently right as often as the time it points to comes round, which happens twice a day.

So you've contradicted yourself *once*.

'Ah, but', you say, 'what's the use of its being right twice a day, if I can't tell when the time comes?'

Why, suppose the clock points to eight o'clock, don't you see that the clock is right *at* eight o'clock? Consequently, when eight o'clock comes round your clock is right.

'Yes, I see *that*', you reply.

Very good, then you've contradicted yourself *twice*: now get out of the difficulty as best you can, and don't contradict yourself again if you can help it.

You *might* go on to ask, 'How am I to know when eight o'clock *does* come? My clock will not tell me'. Be patient: you know that when eight o'clock comes your clock is right, very good; then your rule is this: keep your eyes fixed on your clock, and *the very moment it is right* it will be eight o'clock. 'But—', you say. There, that'll do; the more you argue the farther you get from the point, so it will be as well as stop.

The Published Works

The first piece of writing by the young Dodgson was published in 1854. Carroll mentions (in *Mischmasch*) that

[6] *LCPB*, p. 6. *The Rectory Umbrella and Mischmasch*, p. 78.

two of his poems were published in 1854 in *The Oxonian
Advertiser* (he being a Student in Oxford by then); but he
gives no title, and as nothing in that long-since defunct magazine was signed by him, and he gives us no information as to
any pseudonym, we are none the wiser. On the other hand, in
that same year he published two pieces in *The Whitby
Gazette*: "Wilhelm von Schmitz" in prose, and "The Lady
of the Ladle" in verse; both were to be reproduced in the
family magazine, *Mischmasch*, the preface[7] of which is
worth quoting at some length, since in it Carroll is already
adopting the stance of the writer looking back upon his past:

> 'Yet once more' (to use the time-honoured words of our poet
> Milton) we present ourselves before an eager and expectant
> public [i.e. his family], let us hope under even better auspices
> than hitherto.
>
> In making our bow for the—may we venture to say so?—
> fourth time, it will be worth while to review the past, and to
> consider the probable future. We are encouraged to do so by
> Mrs. Malaprop's advice: 'Let us not anticipate the past; let all
> our retrospections be to the future', and by the fact that our
> family motto is '*Respiciendo prudens*'.
>
> We purpose then to give a brief history of our former
> domestic magazines in this family, their origin, aim, progress,
> and ultimate fate, and we shall notice, as we go on, the other
> magazines which have appeared, but not under our own editor-
> ship.

There follows a list of the magazines: *Useful and Instructive
Poetry, The Rectory Magazine, The Comet, The Rosebud,
The Star, The Will-o-the-Wisp*, and finally

The Rectory Umbrella

This we started, we believe, in 1849 or 1850. . . . It was
admired at the time, but wholly unsupported, and it took us a
year or more to fill the volume by our own unaided efforts. . . .

We will here notice one or two of our own writings, which
have seen more extended publicity than the above mentioned. In
the summer of 1854 we contributed two poems to the 'Oxonian
Advertiser', neither at all worth preservation; and in the Long

7 LCPB, p. 15. *The Rectory Umbrella and Mischmasch*, p. 89.

The Rectory Umbrella; drawing by Lewis Carroll.

Vacation of the same year, when staying with a reading party at
Whitby, we contributed 'The Lady of the Ladle' and 'Wilhelm
von Schmitz' to the weekly Gazette of that place. . . .

Of *Mischmasch* itself, Carroll declares:

The best of its contents will be offered at intervals to a contemporary magazine of a less exclusively domestic nature: we allude
to the Comic Times; thus affording to the contributors to this
magazine an opportunity of presenting their productions to the
admiring gaze of the English Nation.

Thus, it was in collaboration with the *Comic Times* that
Carroll was launched on his public career as a writer. He had
just completed the first part of his university studies, having
received his B.A. in December 1854. On July 10, 1855, he
noted in his diary (p. 55):

Yesterday I heard from Menella Smedley [a cousin], returning
'The Three Voices' which she borrowed to show Frank Smedley:
she says that he wishes to be instrumental in publishing it and
others.

And things moved so fast that we find him writing on July 27
(p. 56):

Heard from Frank Smedley, who wants me to become a contri-
butor to the *Comic Times*, which Ingram, the publisher of *The
Illustrated London News*, is going to begin. A friend of his,
Edmund Yates, is the Editor.

Carroll's first piece appeared in the number dated August
18; it was (predictably) a parody on a poem popular at the
time. His second, which appeared on September 8, was the
first version of the text read by the White Rabbit at the
Knave of Hearts's trial. His third was a prose piece, which
gives us a foretaste of the style of the Oxonian pamphlets,
and is worth quoting in full:[8]

Hints for Etiquette;
or, Dining Out Made Easy

As caterers for the public taste, we can conscientiously recom-

8 *LCPB*, p. 33. *The Rectory Umbrella and Mischmasch*, p. 115. *Works*,
p. 1235.

mend this book to all diners-out who are perfectly unacquainted with the usages of society. However we may regret that our author has confined himself to warning rather than advice, we are bound in justice to say that nothing here stated will be found to contradict the habits of the best circles. The following examples exhibit a depth of penetration and a fulness of experience rarely met with:

I

In proceeding to the dining-room, the gentleman gives one arm to the lady he escorts—it is unusual to offer both.

II

The practice of taking soup with the next gentleman but one is now wisely discontinued; but the custom of asking your host his opinion of the weather immediately on the removal of the first course still prevails.

III

To use a fork with your soup, intimating at the same time to your hostess that you are reserving the spoon for the beef-steaks, is a practice wholly exploded.

IV

On meat being placed before you, there is no possible objection to your eating it, if so disposed; still, in all such delicate cases, be guided entirely by the conduct of those around you.

V

It is always allowable to ask for artichoke jelly with your boiled venison; however, there are houses where this is not supplied.

VI

The method of helping roast turkey with two carving-forks is practicable, but deficient in grace.

VII

We do not recommend the practice of eating cheese with a knife and fork in one hand, and a spoon and wineglass in the other; there is a kind of awkwardness in the action which no amount of practice can entirely dispel.

VIII

As a general rule, do not kick the shins of the opposite gentleman under the table, if personally unacquainted with him; your pleasantry is liable to be misunderstood—a circumstance at all times unpleasant.

IX

Proposing the health of the boy in buttons immediately on the removal of the cloth is a custom springing from regard to his tender years, rather than from a strict adherence to the rules of etiquette.

His fourth contribution, published in November, was the first piece Carroll ever wrote about photography.

According to his diary, all the pieces he ever sent to the *Comic Times* were published, but the paper itself soon failed, and Smedley and Yates founded another, *The Train*. Carroll published a poem in this in March 1856—the first piece to be signed "Lewis Carroll." Between March 1856 and December 1857, eight pieces of his were published in *The Train*, including the first version of the White Knight's song, a parody of one of Wordsworth's best-known poems, a parody of Tennyson, and one of Longfellow (this last being also about photography).

The Train soon went the way of the *Comic Times*, with the result that Carroll published very few literary pieces before *Alice*. A paradox, in the form of a letter, entitled "Where does the day begin?" was published in *The Illustrated London News* in 1857; a poem appeared that same year in *The Oxford Critic*; in 1860 he wrote another piece on photography, and a poem, "Faces in the Fire"; and between 1860 and 1863 he contributed a number of poems to the interuniversity magazine, *College Rhymes*. But in 1860, his mathematical works began to appear.

There are two comments that spring to mind in relation to all these pieces: Carroll would "publish"—in the sense described in the preface to *Mischmasch*—simultaneously at

home (at Croft) and outside it, without making any alterations in the text to suit his two publics; and consequently,
not only did he never disown any of his youthful works
(except the two "neither at all worth preservation"), but
actually managed over the course of the years to get all of
them into print. Either he reworked them and incorporated
them into one of the *Alice* books, as with the two aforemen-
tioned poems, and also "A Stanza of Anglo-Saxon Poetry,"
originally included in *Mischmasch*, which was to become the
first verse of "Jabberwocky." Or he included them in later
collections, such as *Phantasmagoria*, published in 1883, or
Rhyme? and Reason? (1869). In this sense, then, though obviously *Alice* represented a totally new departure, we must resist
the temptation of making a division between his youthful and
his later works. Carroll's literary career extended over fifty-
four years, and though it certainly had its high points, it is
quite wrong to think that nothing before *Alice* was of any
value. His early writings contain the seeds of all his later stylis-
tic idiosyncrasies, and they draw on the same inspirations:
parody, nonsense, and logic.

The Liddells

Carroll's university career reached its culmination in 1855: at the end of the academic year 1854-55, he was given a permanent appointment as "master and tutor," after which he never sought further advancement. That same year also saw the death of the Dean of Christ Church, Thomas Gaisford, under whom Carroll studied as an undergraduate and also went rapidly up the few rungs of the academic ladder he was to climb. The election of the new Dean should have made no difference at all in Carroll's circumstances.

The new Dean was Henry George Liddell, formerly Headmaster of Westminster, one of the major English public schools, but best known for having collaborated in *Liddell and Scott*—not just a Greek dictionary, but *the* Greek dictionary. In fact, Liddell's coming to Christ Church turned out to be of cardinal importance in Carroll's life, and his Deanship was practically coterminous with that life, ending in 1891. It began badly, however. We read in the diary, June 7, 1855:

> *The Times* announces that Liddell of Westminster is to be the new Dean; the selection does not seem to have given much satisfaction in the college. (p. 51)

A contemporary, W. B. Richmond, quoted by Green describes the man thus:

> The Dean inspired awe. . . . He disliked shyness in others,

124

although he was the shyest of men himself. A certain aloofness of manner was the result, which could easily be broken down by meeting him with perfect straightforwardness.

And Richmond adds:

His relationship with his family was beautiful. They feared him not one whit, although he would at times reprimand them with asperity, if they were inaccurate or made what he considered silly statements. It was a household of quite exceptional physical beauty. The Dean was as handsome a specimen of aristocratic manhood as could be seen in a lifetime. (*Diaries*, pp. 51–52)

These comments cast considerable light on the elements that might have caused friction—and attraction, too—between Carroll and Liddell: the masculine handsomeness of which Carroll had so little; the authoritarianism, combined with shyness, which would make it very difficult for the two shy men to communicate. And yet, though not exactly contemporaries (Liddell was twenty-one years older than Carroll, though he died five days after him), the two had quite a lot in common. For instance, there was a similarity in their schoolboy experiences. Liddell had this to say of his:

In July or August 1829 I left Charterhouse [a public school]. Never did pilgrim departing from an inhospitable mansion shake the dust from off his feet with more hearty satisfaction than I did. . . .[1]

But it would appear that they must have confided in each other little or not at all, for relations between the two men were never good and soon became undisguisedly bad.

Carroll and Mrs. Liddell

Dean Liddell arrived in the company of his wife and four children: Harry, the eldest, and three little girls: Lorina, Alice, and Edith. Alice was then just three. Oddly enough, it was through the boy (aged eight) that Carroll first made contact with the family. He writes on March 6, 1856: "Made

[1] *Henry George Liddell, D.D.: A Memoir*, by Henry L. Thompson, London, 1899.

friends with little Harry Liddell (whom I first spoke to
down at the boats last week): he is certainly the handsomest
boy I ever saw" (*Diaries*, p. 79). Two days later, he made
friends with Lorina (aged six). And the following month, he
met the three little girls together:

> Went over with Southey in the afternoon to the Deanery, to try
> and take a photograph of the Cathedral: both attempts proved
> failures. The three little girls were in the garden most of the
> time, and we became excellent friends: we tried to group them
> in the foreground of the picture, but they were not patient sit-
> ters. I mark this day with a white stone. (p. 83)

The last sentence is enough to indicate the "emotional
charge" involved in the meeting. This marked the beginning
of frequent visits to the Liddell household. And the object was
always to visit the children, for their father is never mentioned except in connection with some administrative matter
or other. But their mother appears very early on, for by November—after he had visited the children a great many times
and taken photographs of them—Carroll writes:

> Was at the Deanery in the morning taking pictures, and went
> again in the afternoon by Harry's request to take him and Ina
> [Lorina]. However I found Mrs. Liddell had said they were not
> to be taken till all can be taken in a group. This may be meant as
> a hint that I have intruded myself on the premises long enough:
> I am quite of the same opinion myself, and, partly for this
> reason, partly because I cannot afford to waste any more time on
> portraits at such a bad season of the year, I have resolved not to
> go again for the present, nor at all without invitation, except just
> to pack up the things and bring them back. (p. 95)

Thenceforth, it was always she, as the children's guardian, with whom Carroll was involved. With her he talked
over Harry's education, offering to "teach him sums, etc."
(p. 97), and he presented her with two portraits. (On her
departure to Madeira with the Dean just before Christmas
1856, he went to lunch with the children!) With her agree-
ment, shortly after an initial refusal, he did teach Harry,
writing after the first lesson: "He is quick, but knows very
little" (p. 102). During this period, it was Ina, the eldest of

the girls, whom he saw regularly, though always under the watchful eye of her governess. But this led to trouble, as gossip began to spread:

> I find to my great surprise that my notice of [the Liddell children] is construed by some men into attentions to the governess, Miss Prickett. I had a long talk with Joyce about it in the evening, and though for my own part I should give little importance to the existence of so groundless a rumour, it would be inconsiderate to the governess to give any further occasion for remarks of that sort. For this reason I shall avoid taking any public notice of the children in future, unless any occasion should arise when such an interpretation is impossible. (pp. 110–11)

Shortly afterward, things improved somewhat and in June 1857 (just before the summer vacation), Carroll was again indulging in the joys of photography at the Deanery, and Mrs. Liddell even went so far as to bring her children to his rooms. Of the next four years, unfortunately, we know next to nothing about their relationship—or anything else—because the diaries for those years are missing, and Collingwood tells us nothing on the subject.[2] But in that time, Harry went to school, and Alice became older—in 1862 she was ten. It seems quite natural that Carroll should have taken the three little girls out on the river during the spring and summer of 1862 and told them the story of Alice in Wonderland. But it was during that year that something—and we do not know what it was—happened to cause a breach between him and Mrs. Liddell; he writes on October 28, 1862: "I have been out of her good graces ever since Lord Newry's business" (p. 188); and two weeks later: "On returning to Christ Church I found Ina, Alice and Edith in the quadrangle, and had a little talk with them—a rare event of late." All his comments on this theme tend to a certain acidity. On November 21, for instance:

[2] Alice herself was to say, when an old lady of eighty, that Carroll had visited her family in Wales during summer vacations; but Green, who quotes her statement (*Diaries*, pp. 170–71), thinks it probable that this was a confusion of memory.

Was surprised by a message from Mrs. Liddell asking whether the children should come over to me, or if I would go to them. No other alternative being offered, I chose the latter, and found that Alice and Edith had originated the idea, that I must put their crests into their books for them. With that and a game of parlour croquet, I had a very pleasant two hours with them (Ina being in bed with a cold) and Mrs. Liddell did not appear. (pp. 189–90)

And in December 1863, after referring to a theatrical evening at Christ Church, he comments: "Mrs. Liddell and the children were there—but I held aloof from them as I have done all this term" (p. 208). And, on May 12, 1864: "During these last few days I have applied in vain for leave to take the children on the river, i.e. Alice, Edith and Rhoda; but Mrs. Liddell will not let *any* come in future. . . ." (p. 215). Three years later, he writes: "Paid a visit to Mrs. Liddell, and had a long chat with her, walking about the Deanery garden—a thing I have not done for years" (p. 260).

From then on, he and Mrs. Liddell seem to have met only very occasionally; not until 1870 does he mention her again in his diary, and then it is again with a touch of acidity: "This morning an almost equally wonderful thing occurred, Mrs. Liddell brought Ina and Alice to be photographed, first visiting my rooms, and then the studio" (p. 288). At three-year intervals (in 1870, 1873, and 1876) they exchanged visits and photographs. The last such occasion seems to have been in 1892 (after the announcement of the Dean's resignation): "A yet more wonderful experience: Mrs. Liddell and Mrs. Skene [Lorina] came to tea, and proved very pleasant guests" (p. 488).

This steady hostility between Carroll and Alice's mother was surely significant—in at least two ways: first, Carroll demonstrated a degree of attachment to the Liddell children that must have surprised and shocked (perhaps upset?) a Victorian mother; and second, Carroll was well aware that Mrs. Liddell, beneath all the polite good manners the situation demanded, was his enemy. It seems highly probable that he knew very well why. But here we must go cautiously. Mrs.

Portrait of Alice's father, Dean Liddell, in 1858, near the
time of his arrival at Christ Church.

Liddell was certainly convinced that there was something peculiar in Carroll's attentions to Alice, or she would not have insisted on destroying all his letters to her.[3] And it may well be that, aside from the moral risks the child might be running, she saw him as an obstacle in the way to her daughter's making a good match. This would explain the constant need for chaperoning, and so on. On the other hand, it is arguable that, on Carroll's side, given his own well-founded conviction that his affectionate behaviour to children (for after all, the Liddell children were very far from being the only ones) was a response to what they themselves wanted, his hostility—and *also* his persistence—was as much an indication of his clear conscience as a true "friend to children" as of any more profound attachment to his little-girl friends. In any case, he was confronted by a Victorian wife and mother, the vigilant guardian of hearth and home, the defender of family morality. Everything about Carroll's situation and behaviour must have seemed to her dubious in the extreme: a semi-priest, a bachelor enormously attracted to children, and a writer of nonsense stories—none of this fitted in with the conventions it was her duty to preserve. They could not but be enemies. And that was certainly how they saw one another.

Dean Liddell

Relations with Dean Liddell were less complex. He was a symbol of authority—and we must remember that Carroll's position in the college was too junior for him to have had any part in the deliberations that preceded the Dean's appointment. To make matters worse, Liddell arrived at Christ Church with the reputation of being a reformer; and to Carroll, a reformer might well be equivalent to a dangerous revolutionary. The campaign Carroll was to conduct against him, most of it anonymous but not all, both expressed and served to intensify the almost instantaneous dislike that Liddell's personality seems to have aroused in him.

[3] Hudson, p. 200.

Their first disagreement centred on the fact that Carroll did not take full Holy Orders. A second followed in 1864 over the giving of Junior Studentships in Christ Church; Carroll refers in his diary (p. 209) to their "rather disagreeable correspondence." In 1865, when Liddell wanted to simplify the complex structure of the teaching staff, Carroll speaks of possibly writing a pamphlet to ridicule the debate. In 1870, when Carroll suggested to Liddell a reduction in his own work, with a corresponding reduction in salary, he says, "He quite approved of the plan" (p. 290). But from 1872 onward, there was open war: Liddell had plans for Christ Church itself, and Carroll published his first pamphlet: *The New Belfry*.[4] It was a violent attack, and the Dean, referred to directly, and also indirectly in the guise of "Scott, the great architect" (who is linked with the Scott of the Greek dictionary), must have felt no love for the author whose anonymity was anything but complete in the initials D.C.L. The following year, Carroll returned to the charge, upon seeing more of the Dean's alterations: "The new West entrance to the Cathedral was revealed today (Wed.): and almost rivals the 'Belfry' in ugliness" (p. 320). He thereupon wrote an even longer pamphlet, *The Three T's*.[5] To make himself abundantly clear, he also wrote under his own name "Objections submitted to the Governing Body of Christ Church, Oxford, against certain proposed alterations in the Great Quadrangle," a straightforward statement of his views on the subject, and especially his opposition to the rebuilding of cloisters in the Great Quadrangle. The year after that, he published *The Blank Cheque*, signed by "The author of 'The New Belfry' and 'The Vision of the Three T's.'"[6] Though this last was not actually directed against Liddell, the reference to the author of the earlier pamphlets could only reopen the wound; and to make sure it did, Car-

[4] *The New Belfry of Christ Church, Oxford*: a Monograph by D. C. L.; *Works*, p. 1139. *LCPB*, pp. 96–117.
[5] *The Vision of the Three T's: a Threnody*; by the author of *The New Belfry*, *LCPB*, pp. 118–46. *Works*, p. 1150.
[6] *Works*, p. 1170. *LCPB*, pp. 149–59.

roll added on the title page a quotation from *Pickwick Papers* which could hardly miss its target:

> 'Vell, perhaps', said Sam, 'you bought houses, vich is delicate English for goin' mad; or took to buildin', vich is a medical term for bein' incurable'.

Carroll mentions Liddell's name again only three times in his diary: in 1881 (when he resigned the Mathematical Lectureship), in 1884 (in reference to the position of the cathedral organ), and in 1891 (when he heard of the Dean's resignation). When Collingwood writes (p. 297) that this was "a great blow to Mr. Dodgson," one can only hope that he was speaking ironically. Everything goes to indicate that no sympathy of any kind ever existed between the two men, and it is obvious that, to a dedicated university man like Liddell, Carroll's scientific—and still more, his literary—work could do nothing to redeem the insolence of his behaviour. And it is surely significant that, in the short biography of Liddell written in 1899 at the request of his widow, there is not even a mention of Carroll-Dodgson.

Cakeless

Cakeless was a short play in verse written anonymously in 1874, which Derek Hudson quotes; it was an attack on both the Liddell family and Carroll. Mrs. Liddell is ridiculed for all her efforts at matchmaking for her daughters. Enter Kraftsohn (clearly Dodgson), furiously biting his nails and protesting against the triple wedding; Hudson tells us that at this point, in the copy at the British Museum, a reader has pencilled in the note "—dgs-n had been rejected" (p. 205)—an intriguing bit of information. Whereupon the scouts (college servants) advance upon him and subject him to various outrages, all of which are explicitly related to Carroll's pamphlets attacking the Dean. And, with oddly unerring aim, the text refers to those parts of Carroll's pamphlets which had most irritated the Liddells, especially his unkind allusions to Mrs. Liddell's matrimonial hopes.

The Deanery at Christ Church in Dean Liddell's day.

Macmillan's

___◆___

When, upon the advice of his friends Duckworth and Mac-
Donald, Carroll decided in 1863 to publish the manuscript
of *Alice*, he did not think in terms of dealing with a publisher. He intended to have the story printed at his own
expense by the university press. It was probably the problems
of binding and distribution that caused him to change his
mind. Macmillan's was the obvious choice, since they already
published for the university, and had just brought out Kingsley's *The Water Babies*.[1] (According to Charles Morgan,[2]
the firm's official historian, however, it was Carroll who
actually inaugurated their list of children's books.) Since
there was no financial risk, and since the illustrator, John
Tenniel, had a tremendous reputation, Macmillan's made no
objections—and have surely never had cause to wish they
had! Yet Carroll turned out to be a demanding, indeed an
exhausting, author.

From the beginning he wanted to be original, and he
wrote to his publishers on November 11, 1864:

> I have been considering the question of the *colour* of *Alice's
> Adventures*, and have come to the conclusion that *bright red* will
> be the best—not the best, perhaps, artistically, but the most

[1] See Hudson, p. 135.
[2] Charles Morgan, *The House of Macmillan*, London, 1943.

attractive to childish eyes. Can this colour be managed with the same smooth, bright cloth that you have in green?[3]

He had at first tried to get them to agree to a special quarto format, with double columns, and had gone so far as to print a specimen page; but in the end, Macmillan's convinced him that it was better to keep to the normal octavo size.[4] He then suggested that the book should appear on April 1 (1865), which Macmillan's approved but could not in the end manage. He also suggested that "it would look better with the edges merely cut smoothe, and no gilding."[5] When the book finally came out in June 1865, Carroll asked for fifty copies immediately because his "young friends ... are all grown out of childhood so alarmingly fast."[6] Then came the bombshell: in his diary on July 20 we read:

> Called on Macmillan, and showed him Tenniel's letter about the fairy-tale—he is entirely dissatisfied with the printing of the pictures, and I suppose we shall have to do it all again. (p. 234)

(It is noteworthy that, though of the criticisms most frequently made of Carroll by his commentators was that of carrying perfectionism to the point of mania, it was, in fact, not he but Tenniel who was responsible for the suppression of this first edition.) Thereupon, Carroll decided that the first two thousand copies should be sold "as waste paper"! (p. 234). He later had second thoughts, presenting to a number of hospitals the copies returned by their first recipients; the impression had never been on sale, and the rest of it was sold to a New York publisher who seems not to have been troubled by Tenniel's scruples.[7]

Macmillan's, who were thenceforth to publish all Car-

[3] Hudson, p. 136.
[4] *Diaries*, pp. 217, 229.
[5] *Handbook*, p. 28.
[6] Hudson, p. 137.
[7] In 1886, Carroll wrote a letter to Macmillan's, making his views quite clear: substandard copies of his books "will do very well for the Americans, who ought not to be very particular as to *quality*, as they insist on having books for very cheap" (*Handbook*, p. 132).

roll's writings—starting with a mathematical work published
under his real name in 1867—were to experience problems of
this nature in an incredible variety of circumstances. In 1889,
for instance, the appearance of the first edition of *The Nursery
Alice* was a disaster. The colours, thought Carroll, were too
gaudy, and the first impression was withdrawn to be sold only
in America (where, Charles Morgan tells us, they were
"declined as not being gaudy enough").

> Then the covers were wrong: the thickness of the book had not
> been allowed for and the March Hare was out of centre. When
> all this had been put right, still the early copies were returned.
> They cracked when he opened them; their leaves curled
> obstinately.[8]

It was all done, as Morgan freely admits, at Carroll's
own expense; he was quite prepared to sacrifice his own roy-
alties in order to achieve what he considered excellence in the
production of a book. He had a slip inserted in *Sylvie and
Bruno Concluded*, which is worth quoting in full for the way
in which it demonstrates his passion for perfection, his wish
to be efficient, and, indeed, his generosity:

Advertisement

> For over twenty-five years I have made it my chief object with
> regard to my books, that they should be of the best workmanship
> attainable for the price. And I am deeply annoyed to find that
> the last issue of *Through the Looking-Glass*, consisting of the
> sixtieth thousand, has been put on sale without its being noticed
> that most of the pictures have failed so much, in the printing, as
> to make the book not worth buying. I request all holders of
> copies to send them to Messrs. Macmillan & Co., 29 Bedford
> St., Covent Garden, with their names and addresses; and copies
> of the next issue shall be sent them in exchange.
>   Instead, however, of destroying the unsold copies, I pro-
> pose to utilise them by giving them away, to Mechanics' Insti-
> tutes, Village Reading Rooms, and similar institutions, where

---

[8] Morgan, *The House of Macmillan*, p. 112. See also *The Nursery
Alice*, New York, Dover, 1966, p. vi.

the means for purchasing such books are scanty. Accordingly I invite applications for such gifts, addressed to me, 'care of Messrs. Macmillan'. Every such application should be signed by some responsible person, and should state how far they are able to buy books for themselves, and what is the average number of readers.

I take this opportunity of announcing that, if at any future time I should wish to communicate anything to my Readers, I will do so by advertising, in the 'Agony' column of some Daily paper, on the *first Tuesday in the Month*.

Lewis Carroll

Christmas 1893

Charles Morgan recalls quite a number of things of this kind that Carroll made his publishers do. Thus, when *Euclid and His Modern Rivals* appeared, Carroll suggested adding a few lines to the title page to make it clear that it was not a comic work; and with *The Game of Logic* (the earlier, not yet developed version of *Symbolic Logic,* the first edition of which was also deemed unworthy to sell to English readers), Macmillan's had to sell along with the book an envelope containing a card diagram and nine counters, four red and five grey, three-quarters of an inch wide. And his author's copies of *Through the Looking-Glass* he wanted bound as follows:

> Fifty copies in red, twenty in blue, twenty in green, two in vellum, one with edges uncut, one with primrose edges, and one with a piece of mirror in the cover.[9]

There were times when his interest in publishing problems exceeded the purely technical, as for instance when he realized (Collingwood says he "was advised" to take action) that overlarge discounts were given to booksellers, by which the public were the sufferers. In 1883, his books appeared with the following notice:

> In selling Mr. Lewis Carroll's books to the Trade, Messrs. Macmillan and Co. will abate 2d. in the shilling (no odd copies),

[9] Morgan, *The House of Macmillan*, p. 81.

and allow 5 per cent. discount within six months, and 10 per cent for cash. In selling them to the Public (for cash only) they will allow 10 per cent discount.[10]

Some booksellers reacted with vocal hostility, and Carroll decided to explain himself in a short pamphlet, *The Profits of Authorship*, showing that the bookseller makes as much profit as that of the publisher and author combined, for considerably less work. The piece itself is lost to us, but Collingwood gives an excerpt. It provided Carroll with an opportunity to pay an unexpected tribute to his own publisher:

> The publisher contributes about as much as the bookseller in time and bodily labour, but in mental toil and trouble a great deal more. I speak with some personal knowledge of the matter, having myself, for some twenty years, inflicted on that most patient and painstaking firm, Messrs. Macmillan and Co., about as much wear and worry as ever publishers lived through. The day when they undertake a book for me is a *dies nefastus* for them. From that day till the book is out—an interval of some two or three years on an average—there is no pause in 'the pelting of the pitiless storm' of directions and questions on every conceivable detail. To say that every question gets a courteous and thoughtful reply—that they are still outside a lunatic asylum —and that they still regard me with some degree of charity—is to speak volumes in praise of their good temper and of their health, bodily and mental. I think the publisher's claim on the profits is on the whole stronger than the bookseller's.[11]

However, this must not lead anyone to suppose that Carroll failed to stand up for his rights as an author. He attempted to defend himself in advance against the voraciousness, not of imitators (at whom he launches a barb or two in the preface to *Sylvie and Bruno*) but of pirates. He wrote this letter to Macmillan's on November 26, 1872:

> Dear Mr. Macmillan,
>   Will you kindly, with all reasonable expedition on receipt of this, engage a couple of copying-clerks, and have *all* the speeches in 'Alice' and the 'Looking-Glass' written out, with the

[10] Collingwood, p. 226.
[11] Collingwood, pp. 226–28.

names of the speakers, and such directions as 'Enter the White Rabbit', 'Exit the Red Queen', in the ordinary dramatic form, *and get them registered as two dramas,* with the same names as the books—I am told that is the only way to retain a right to forbid their being represented by any one who may choose to dramatise them. I trust to you to get it all done in such a way as will satisfy the requirements of the law. Please put in *all* the speeches.[12]

Indeed, he even entered (politely) into dispute with his publisher: another firm had proposed including some of his poems in an anthology, and on Macmillan's showing very little enthusiasm for this, Carroll wrote:

I don't think our views quite harmonise. You take the publisher's view, doubtless, that it might injure the sale of the book [published by you]. But really I don't feel much fear of that.[13]

But such brushes were rare. And the encounters he had with Macmillan's could arise out of all manner of things that had little to do with publishing. We read in Carroll's diary (p. 460): "Got tickets (by telegraphing to Macmillan) for Monday afternoon and evening." And Charles Morgan comments (p. 110):

When he wished to go to a theatre, Macmillan's were asked to buy the tickets—on the extreme right, if possible, because he was deaf in the right ear, and at all costs not in the centre of the first rows because, from there, his line of sight was interrupted by waving conductors. When he sent his watches to be mended, his publishers were asked to retrieve, and did retrieve them, by what he called 'a trusty and resolute messenger'.

But his wish to be personally involved at every stage produced splendid results when based upon his inventive talent. Thus, he worked out the best way of wrapping up a parcel, and sent it to Macmillan's where it was hung in the dispatch department, so that all the staff could benefit from studying the Carrollian method. Most important, it would seem that we owe to him the modern book jacket: he suggested, for *The*

[12] Hudson, p. 209.
[13] Hudson, p. 210.

Hunting of the Snark, that the plain paper covers used to protect books on the shelves of booksellers should have the title printed lengthways on the back.

By and large, two major features stand out in this not always easy relationship—features that appear again and again in Carroll's relations with other people, and indeed with himself. First the concern, indeed the mania, for *quality*: he could not bear the slightest imperfection. (Of his attitude to the format and makeup of his books, Charles Morgan says charmingly that "he felt them as an old lady feels draughts.") Second, his concern, also almost amounting to mania, for dealing with every detail personally, fearing neither ridicule for himself, nor to offend the susceptibilities of his collaborators. Consequently, each of his works is representative and revealing of the man to an extraordinary degree; every habit, every editorial idiosyncrasy—like the plethora of italicizations—is not just part of the text, but a portrayal of the author. From this point of view, it is worth noting what he says about the "genesis" of his books in the preface to *Sylvie and Bruno*,[14] and if one links that with what I have said here, it becomes evident that Carroll was, very early on, a practitioner of *writing as an art*.

[14] *Works*, pp. 277–80.

Mathematics

———◆———

When he wrote letters to the newspapers, one of the styles Carroll used was that of "Charles L. Dodgson, Mathematical Lecturer at Christ Church." In fact, though his university career had brought success in two subjects, classics and mathematics, it was in the latter that he succeeded most brilliantly, getting a first-class degree in December 1854. The first entry in his diary for January 1, 1855—in fact, the first surviving entry—shows him pursuing his mathematical bent, and hoping to get the Mathematical Lectureship. In March 1855 he tried for the Senior Mathematical scholarship, but failed to win it; then, upon learning in the summer that the Dean was going to make him Mathematical Lecturer, he decided not to try for it again. So, in university terms, the high point of his mathematical career came with the Lectureship in 1855, a post he occupied until 1881.

Upon starting to teach, that same year, he was led to study the actual *teaching* of mathematics. In May 1855, he writes in his diary (p. 50):

> I began arranging a scheme for teaching systematically the first part of Algebraic Geometry: a thing which no one hitherto seems to have attempted—I find it exceedingly difficult to do it in anything like a satisfactory way.

And he notes at the end of the month that he has completed work on *The Fifth Book of Euclid proved Algebraically,* which was to be published in 1858—his first mathematical book. It was published anonymously, however, and not until 1860 did something actually appear under the name of C. L. Dodgson—*A Syllabus of Plane Algebraical Geometry*—the fulfilment of a project begun in May 1855.

In the years following, the diaries contain few mentions of mathematics, whether because Green has excluded them; or because Carroll followed the decision he made on January 29, 1856 (p. 75): "In future I shall record all matters connected with the Mathematical Lecture in a separate book" (Green tells us that no such book has been found); or perhaps because other interests predominated—photography above all, the theatre, museums, and his friendship with the Liddell children. In any case, the public career of Dodgson the mathematician only really began in 1860: in that year, as well as the work already mentioned, he also produced *Notes on the First Two Books of Euclid* for examination candidates; in 1861, *The Formulae of Plane Trigonometry*, notable for the symbols he invented for sine, cosine, etc., and some further algebraical notes; in 1863, a compilation of the propositions in the first two books of Euclid; in 1864, *A Guide to the Mathematical Student*; in 1866, a further Euclidian text, and the *Condensation of Determinants*.[1] Determinants also provided the subject matter for an *Elementary Treatise* in 1867. In 1868 came *The Fifth Book of Euclid Treated Algebraically*; in 1868, 1870, and 1873, collections of algebraic and arithmetical formulas to assist examination candidates; more works on Euclid in 1872, 1873, 1874, and 1875, and most important, in 1879, *Euclid and His Modern Rivals*; in 1882, a new edition of the first two books of Euclid. In 1885, he published a *Supplement to "Euclid and His Modern Rivals,"* and a second edition of the original work. From then on, logic was to replace mathematics as the subject matter for the major part of Carroll's non-literary output, though in 1888 he published *Curiosa Mathematica, Part I*—devoted to a defence of

---

[1] It was this work which figured in the legend that Queen Victoria, having expressed a wish to see further books by the author of *Alice*, was rewarded by being sent a mathematical treatise (see "Victoria").

Euclid's definition of parallel lines against "circle-squarers" —and in 1893, *Curiosa Mathematica, Part II.*

The last-named actually belongs to a totally different category. As long as he was lecturing—in other words, until 1881—Carroll used his mathematical talents in the service of pedagogy, producing manuals, glossaries, books of problems and exercises, etc., for students. His many works on Euclid were also, in a more general way, written with this kind of concern to popularize. He certainly sought, in addition, to defend a geometry that was under attack from all sides, though he never examined the non-Euclidian geometries. Equally certainly, in his linking of algebra and geometry, he was trying to follow the mathematical developments of the day. But the thing above all that he was aiming to do was to translate into a language accessible to everybody (or almost everybody) ideas and problems traditionally the preserve of specialists. His method of popularizing was intelligent and sometimes humorous, especially in his masterpiece in that field, *Euclid and His Modern Rivals.* As the title indicates, the author wanted to ensure Euclid's triumph over his rivals—in respect to his fundamental postulate concerning parallels. But the form he chose is somewhat unusual: a trial in Hades, with Minos and Rhadamanthus sitting in judgement on the "Euclid-wreckers." In this dramatic style, twelve of the latter (with their manuals) are dispatched by Carroll to Mathematical Hades. Aware that his readers might find this approach surprising, especially coming from the pen of "Charles L. Dodgson, M.A., Senior Student and Mathematical Lecturer of Christ Church, Oxford," the author provides an apologia in a prologue, headed with a quotation from Horace:

> *Ridentem dicere verum*
> *Quid vetat?* [2]

It is presented in a dramatic form partly because it seemed a better way of exhibiting in alternation the arguments on the two sides of the question; partly that I might feel myself at liberty to

[2] "What is to prevent a laughing man from saying what is true?" (*Euclid* . . . London, 1882, pp. ix-x).

treat it in a rather lighter style than would have suited an essay, and thus to make it a little less tedious and a little more acceptable to my unscientific readers.

In one respect this book is an experiment and may chance to prove a failure: I mean that I have not thought it necessary to maintain throughout the gravity of style which scientific writers usually affect, and which has somehow come to be regarded as an 'inseparable accident' of scientific teaching. I never could quite see the reasonableness of this immemorial law: subjects there are, no doubt, which are in their essence too serious to admit of any lightness of treatment—but I cannot recognize Geometry as one of them. . . .

Pitying friends have warned me of the fate upon which I am rushing: they have predicted that, in thus abandoning the dignity of a scientific writer, I shall alienate the sympathies of all true scientific readers, who will regard the book as a mere *jeu d'esprit*, and will not trouble themselves to look for any serious argument in it. But it must be borne in mind that, if there is a Scylla before me, there is also a Charybdis—and that, in my fear of being read as a jest, I may incur the darker destiny of not being read at all.

In furtherance of the great cause which I have at heart—the vindication of Euclid's masterpiece—I am content to run some risk; thinking it far better that the purchaser of this little book should *read* it, though it be with a smile, than that, with the deepest conviction of its seriousness of purpose, he should leave it unopened on the shelf.

Aside from the originality of this approach to Euclid, the style is noteworthy, for it prefigures an event then in gestation, which was to occur the following year: the entry into mathematics of "Lewis Carroll." Though, in fact, all the works I have so far mentioned were attributed to C. L. Dodgson, in 1880 there began to appear in a magazine for young people, *The Monthly Packet,* what was to be published in full in 1885 as *A Tangled Tale.*[3] The terms in which Carroll introduces it are strongly reminiscent of the Euclid prologue:

[3] London, 1885. Reproduced in *Pillow Problems and a Tangled Tale,* New York, Dover, 1958.

The writer's intention was to embody in each Knot[4] (like the medicine so dexterously, but ineffectually, concealed in the jam of our early childhood) one or more mathematical questions—in Arithmetic, Algebra, or Geometry, as the case might be—for the amusement, and possible edification, of the fair readers of that Magazine.

It is not only in its title, plainly avowing itself a "tale," and its structure, divided into ten short stories, independent yet interlinked, that Carroll takes over from Dodgson, the Mathematical Tutor. Above all, it is in the reference to *Alice*, explicit in the word "knot," which sends us directly back to one of Alice's unintentional puns in the chapter, "A Caucus-Race and a Long Tale." And lest any doubts remain, Carroll returns to the theme in his conclusion, explaining why he cannot continue the tale *ad infinitum*:

> My puppets were neither distinctly *in* my life (like those I now address), nor yet (like Alice and the Mock Turtle) distinctly *out* of it.[5]

A Tangled Tale, then, with its mixture of fiction-cum-nonsense and mathematics (Carroll always gave the answers to the problems he had set after his readers had sent in their own) represents a marked change. Mathematics, which the literary writer had up to then excluded from his domain, was now invading it, but being altered in the process. *From having been a science, it was becoming a game*.[6] And it was his vocation as a teacher, his desire to communicate, that led to the change. Indeed, the thing was all of a piece: remember that it was in 1881 that Carroll resigned the Lectureship, and in 1877 that he had written the first *Memoria Technica*,[7] a mnemonic game in which his taste for figures and his love of words are

[4] See also p. 111.

[5] *Pillow Problems and A Tangled Tale*, p. 152.

[6] Note, though, that the idea of trying to turn mathematics into a game dated back to 1856 at least. During his brief experience at teaching schoolchildren, he wrote in his diary (p. 75): "Varied the lesson at the school with a story, introducing a number of sums to be worked out."

[7] Quoted in Collingwood, pp. 268–69.

perfectly combined. And, though the first part of *Curiosa Mathematica* (published in 1888) was still very Euclidian, the second (1893) had developed into something quite different— a series of "Pillow Problems," as the subtitle called them. Both were, in fact, signed "Charles L. Dodgson," but the changeover from the demonstration of the first to the problems (with solutions appended) of the second represented precisely that changeover from theory to games that we have been witnessing.

The introduction to *Pillow Problems*[8] leaves us in no doubt, since Carroll makes a point of stressing that it is not with any aim of advancing science, but simply to satisfy the need to occupy the empty hours of the day, or the night, that he presents these games:

> My motive, for publishing these Problems, with their mentally-worked solutions, is most certainly *not* any desire to display powers of mental calculation. Mine, I feel sure, are nothing out-of-the-way; and I have no doubt there are many mathematicians who could produce, mentally, much shorter and better solutions. It is not for such persons that I intend my little book; but rather for the much larger class of *ordinary* mathematicians, who perhaps have never tried this resource, when mental occupation was needed, and who will, I hope, feel encouraged—by seeing what can be done, after a little practice, by one of *average* mathematical powers—to try the experiment for themselves, and find in it as much advantage and comfort as I have done.

The word *comfort* is perhaps a little surprising, as Carroll himself remarks, and it leads him on to a passage which is often quoted in support of hypotheses regarding his "religious doubts" and "sexual obsessions":

> Perhaps I may venture, for a moment, to use a more serious tone, and to point out that there are mental troubles, much worse than mere worry, for which an absorbing subject of thought may serve as a remedy. There are sceptical thoughts, which seem for the moment to uproot the firmest faith; there are blasphemous thoughts, which dart unbidden into the most reverent souls;

[8] *Pillow Problems and A Tangled Tale*, pp. xiii–xiv.

there are unholy thoughts, which torture, with their hateful presence, the fancy that would fain be pure.

A far cry, it seems, from the "games" we were speaking of earlier. But only partly so. For, though it is true that these lines express a gravity we do not associate with entertainment, they also introduce a new factor into mathematics, and use it for a purpose very different from its traditional role. The aim here is not mathematical, or scientific—not even as in applied science—but something quite different: to turn mathematics into a pure *pastime* is a really fundamental change.

It was as a pastime, furthermore, that Carroll returned to mathematics and made it part of his everyday life. To judge from his diaries, the last years of his life were absolutely shot through with his "discoveries"—always worked out mentally, and always following the same pattern: sleeplessness or interrupted sleep, and then a sudden illumination. This note, dated November 12, 1897 (p. 542), is a typical example:

> An inventive morning! After waking, and before I had finished dressing, I had devised a new, and much neater, form in which to work my Rules for Long Division, and also decided to bring out my *Games and Puzzles* and Part III of *Curiosa Mathematica*, in *Numbers*, in paper covers, paged consecutively, to be ultimately issued in boards.

Mathematics, from the science it had been when he was an undergraduate, from the discipline it had represented when he was a Lecturer, had become both a "curiosity" and, literally, an essential pastime.[9]

That it was essential to him is not sufficiently recognized. Several of his biographers, referring to one of the very few mathematicians who have troubled to compare Carroll's work with the mathematics of his day,[10] have assented to his conclusion: "In all of Dodgson's mathematical writings, it is evi-

[9] See "Inventions and Games."
[10] Warren Weaver, "Lewis Carroll Mathematician," *Scientific American*, April 1956.

dent that he was not an important mathematician." And even though Bourbaki[11] is of a somewhat different opinion, I would not go to the stake in defence of Carroll's contribution to the science of mathematics. On the other hand, I think it important to stress the major part played not only by his mathematical training, but, more important, by his profound immersion in mathematics, in both his work[12] and his life. For it is that immersion that accounts for the mass of pamphlets, letters, and lampoons which filled so much of his leisure during the second half of his life—pieces which, whether arguing the finer points of a system of proportional representation or proposing a new method for the rotation of proctors[13] (and in one year he published no fewer than five texts on each of these subjects), were all quite definitely mathematically inspired.

And he was well aware of the fact. This is clear not only from the sheer quantity of writings of which mathematics is obviously the mainspring, of which the perfect model is probably *A Tangled Tale*, but also from statements like the one he puts in the mouth of Arthur Forester in *Sylvie and Bruno Concluded*:[14] "One can't imagine *any* form of Life, or *any* race of intelligent beings, where Mathematical truth would lose its meaning." And in the first part of *Curiosa Mathematica* he presents the argument with great verve:[15]

> It may well be doubted whether, in all the range of science, there is any field so fascinating to the explorer—so rich in hidden treasures—so fruitful in delightful surprises—as that of Pure Mathematics. The charm lies chiefly, I think, in the absolute *cer-*

[11] N. Bourbaki speaks of the "theorems on linear systems with real or complex coefficients thus elucidated, in an obscure textbook, with characteristic attention to detail, by the famous author of *Alice in Wonderland*" (*Eléments d'histoire des mathématiques*, Paris, 1969, p. 87).

[12] I would refer readers to Elizabeth Sewell's excellent book, *The Field of Nonsense*, London, 1952.

[13] "Proctors" were members of the teaching staff appointed in rotation to ensure the maintenance of discipline among the students within the area of the university.

[14] Chapter XVI.

[15] London, 1888; preface, pp. ix–x.

tainty of its results: for that is what, beyond almost all mental treasures, the human intellect craves for. Let us only be sure of *something*! More light, more light! Ἐν δέ φαει και ολέσσον. 'And, if our lot be death, give light and let us die!' This is the cry that, through all the ages, is going up from perplexed Humanity, and Science has little else to offer, that will really meet the demands of its votaries, than the conclusions of Pure Mathematics. Most other Sciences are in a state of constant flux —the precious truths of one generation being smiled at as paradoxes by the second generation, and contemptuously swept away as childish nonsense by the third. If you would see a specimen of the rapidity of this process of decomposition, take Biology for a sample: quote, to any distinguished Biologist you happen to meet, some book published thirty years ago, and observe his pitying smile!

But neither thirty years, nor thirty centuries, affect the clearness, or the charm, of Geometrical truths. Such a theorem as 'the square of the hypotenuse of a right-angled triangle is equal to the sum of the squares of the sides' is as dazzlingly beautiful now as it was in the day when Pythagoras first discovered it, and celebrated its advent, it is said, by sacrificing a hecatomb of oxen —a method of doing honour to science that has always seemed to me slightly exaggerated and uncalled-for.

Elsewhere he exalts even more unequivocally the absolute truth of mathematics—but here it is the logician speaking. I quote from one of his papers about the rotation of proctors:[16]

At least one may trust that no one will be led away by so flimsy a plea as that advanced by Mr. Pelham in the last debate—that 'what is mathematically true is usually found to be practically false'! Does Mr. Pelham suppose that Architecture, Engineering, Insurance, Land-surveying, Navigation, are not 'practical' sciences? Would he willingly take his passage in a ship, whose captain adopted this wild theory in calculating his latitude and longitude? If ever Mr. Pelham undertakes the management of a large School, I presume he will make some such speech as this to his boys. 'I have noticed, Boys, a great inequality in the distribution of food at dinner-time. The long table in the middle has

[16] "The Proctorial Cycle to be voted on in Congregation on Tuesday, Nov. 10, 1885," Oxford, 1885.

four times as much as the end one, and each sidetable has three
times as much. This was so arranged, I believe, for the ridiculous reason that the one contains four times as many boys as the
end-table, and the others three times as many. But this is merely
a *mathematical* truth, Boys, and is therefore *practically* false. The
new arrangement, which I am sure will commend itself to your
common sense, will be that of delivering the dishes to the separate tables *in simple rotation.* So remember, Boys, that in the
future the long table will not have its four dishes and the side
ones their three, but that there will be *one leg of mutton for each
table!'* (Cheers?)

If mathematical truth represented an absolute, we are
led to wonder whether it remained for him the stable, fixed
point in a world in which all other certainties might be
shaken. Given especially the attacks made on religion, was
mathematics a kind of court of last appeal? Despite the two
passages I have quoted, I see no reason to think that Carroll
ever attributed to it any such lofty role. He was immersed in
mathematics, yes, but he never worshipped it. Indeed, in his
intellectual activity, especially his work as a writer, it held a
lower place than logic. It was always a major constituent of
his work, and indeed of his personality, but it would be ridiculous to claim, as some people do, that *Alice*, the *Snark*, or
Sylvie and Bruno could have come only from the pen of a
mathematician.

Notables

When Collingwood speaks of the young Dodgson's physical toughness and ability to use his fists, he contrasts it with the more familiar memory of "the gentle and retiring don." And, indeed, that is how he seems to emerge from all the reminiscences people have left of him; it was the aspect of himself he cultivated most in the later years of his life. But it was far from being the only aspect. Though he never wanted to be lionized as the author of *Alice*, for a long time he sought (often assiduously) the company, however briefly, of the celebrities of the moment.

Tennyson

Most significant of all, undoubtedly, was his relationship with Tennyson. He seems always to have been one of Carroll's favorite poets, to judge both by the index Carroll made for *In Memoriam*—published with the author's blessing, but anonymously—and his parody of Tennyson's poem "The Two Voices," written in 1856, "The Three Voices." In 1857, he had the opportunity of photographing the daughter of Tennyson's sister-in-law, and a fortnight later, he heard that the poet had been impressed by the result. Carroll then left for a visit to Scotland, but on his way back, he decided to go by way of the Lake District, "intending at least to see Tent

Lodge (where Tennyson is staying) if not call" (*Diaries*, p. 124). Temptation overcame him: "When I reached it I at last made up my mind to take the liberty of calling." Tennyson himself was not there, but on Carroll's sending in his name as the photographer of their niece, Mrs. Tennyson welcomed him and introduced her two children:

> I saw also the two children, Hallam and Lionel, five and three years old, the most beautiful boys of their age I ever saw. I got leave to take portraits of them, in case I take my camera over to Coniston; she even seemed to think it was not hopeless that Tennyson himself might sit, though I said I would not request it, as he must have refused so many that it is unfair to expect it. She also promised that I should have an autograph of the poet's. Both the children proposed coming with me when I left—how far seemed immaterial to them.
> I mark this day with a white stone.

Four days later, he returned with his equipment, and having asked for Mrs. Tennyson, was shown into the drawing room:

> The door opened, and a strange, shaggy-looking man entered: his hair, moustache and beard looked wild and neglected: these very much hid the character of his face. . . . His manner was kind and friendly from the first: there is a dry lurking humour in his style of talking. (p. 125)

Conversation was easy. Carroll got Tennyson to explain the meaning of certain passages in his poetry, brought some of his photographs "to be looked at," joined the family for two meals, talked about Ruskin; altogether he spent eleven hours with the great man. He did not dare ask to photograph him, but his summing up of the day is clear enough: "*Dies mirabilis!*" (pp. 125–27). Six days later he was allowed to take a number of pictures of the whole family.

In 1859, he decided to spend a holiday in the Isle of Wight—where Tennyson had a house. Though, as he explained to one of his cousins:

> W. must have basely misrepresented me if he said that I followed the Laureate down to his retreat, as I went, not knowing

that he was there, to stay with an old college friend at Freshwater. Being there, I had the inalienable right of a free-born Briton to make a morning call. (*Diaries*, p. 144)

After a somewhat false start—Tennyson was in the act of mowing the lawn—Carroll was welcomed, invited to dine, and observed with curiosity everything of interest (Tennyson's choice of reading, for instance). It is possible that he was upset to find that Tennyson, seeming to know nothing of his literary work, even the parody of "The Two Voices," regarded him as purely and simply a photographer. There was a further meeting in 1862; in 1865, an inscribed copy of *Alice* was sent. In short, it was a relationship depending more on Carroll's persistence than any inclination on Tennyson's part.

Disaster supervened, however, in 1870, when Carroll wrote to ask permission to read and show to his friends a manuscript copy of one of Tennyson's poems which had come into his hands. Tennyson had apparently withdrawn the poem, and his wife wrote Carroll a stiff letter, bordering on rudeness. Carroll, offended, replied politely but firmly. There must then have been a none too pleasant correspondence, for Hudson reproduces a final letter of Carroll's[1] as follows:

My Dear Sir,
Thus it is, as it seems to me, that you first do a man an injury, and then forgive him—that you first tread on his toes, & then beg him not to cry out!
    Nevertheless I accept what you say, as being in substance, what it certainly is not in form, a retractation (though without a shadow of apology or expression of regret) of all dishonourable charges against me, & an admission that you had made them on insufficient grounds.

And on the back of the letter itself, there is a short but significant dialogue:

'Sir, you are no gentleman'.

[1] Hudson, pp. 109–11.

'Sir, you do me grievous wrong by such words. Prove them or retract them!'

'I reiterate them. Your conduct has been dishonourable'.

'It is not so. I offer a full history of my conduct. I charge you with groundless libel: what say you to the charge?'

'I once believed even worse of you, but begin to think you may be a gentleman after all'.

'These new imputations are as unfounded as the former. Once more, what say you to the charge of groundless libel?'

'*I absolve you.* Say no more'.

A chilly, though polite, letter from Tennyson two years later was to prove that the dispute was not forgotten.

The whole episode throws tremendous light on Carroll's personality. He, who was later to be so implacably hostile to autograph-hunters, had—however great and sincere his admiration for the most famous poet of the day—behaved in the very same way as those he castigated so fiercely when they pursued him. But at the same time, his keen sensitivity—plus, perhaps, a slightly guilty conscience—made him unsheathe his claws the moment he felt that he was being misjudged; he might be prepared to make some concessions to get what he wanted but was certainly not going to go down on his knees to anyone.

Further proof of this appears many years later, in reference to a visit by Cardinal Newman in Oxford. It was in 1880, and Newman, who had been one of the leading lights of Oxford in past years, had become a Cardinal—a dignity which to an Anglican was at once intriguing and alarming. We read this in the diary (p. 387):

Percival, President of Trinity, who has Cardinal Newman as his guest, wrote to say the Cardinal would sit for a photo, to me [which suggests that Carroll had indicated a desire to take such a portrait] at Trinity. But I couldn't take my photography there [for technical reasons, presumably, though, as we saw, he had lugged it up the hills of the Lake District to take Tennyson!], and he couldn't come to me; so nothing came of it. Percival had asked me to come and meet him on Saturday, but I didn't go.

Carroll's touchiness is clearly manifest in this to-ing and fro-ing of invitations, and the uncompromising final phrase.

Was He a Snob?

As with the Tennysons, it was generally Carroll's photography that served as an introduction to the celebrities of the day. But there were some other encounters. He met Ruskin, for instance, in the Christ Church Common Room in 1857; we read:

> I had a little conversation with him, but not enough to bring out anything characteristic or striking in him. His appearance was rather disappointing. . . .

Nonetheless, the entry concludes: *"Dies notabilis"* (pp. 128–29).

As the diary progresses, we find him being introduced to various artists of the period: the Rossettis, for instance; the painters, Holman Hunt and Millais; writers like Charles and Henry Kingsley and certain well-known playwrights; he also met some political figures, through the Oxford (Conservative) Member of Parliament, whom he knew fairly well. It is worth recalling that his talents and his tastes combined to enable him to gain introductions in at least three different worlds: the theatre; art; and up to a point, letters; to say nothing of the Anglican Church (he had occasion to meet and photograph more than one Archbishop). He never missed an opportunity, and the childlike delight he felt at meeting men like Tennyson and Ruskin is demonstrated by the diary—and the "white stone" that so often celebrated his meetings with the famous. So, when he was invited in 1875 to photograph one of Queen Victoria's sons, who was a student at Oxford, and to lunch with him, he wrote with some pride in his diary (p. 339):

> I found myself treated as senior guest, and had to sit next to my young host who was particularly unassuming and genial in manner: I do not wonder at his being so universal a favourite.

Sometimes, though there is no "white stone" mentioned, it is implicit in the length of a particular account; here, for instance, is a meeting with the Prince and Princess of Wales, when the young couple visited Oxford (pp. 197–98):

An eventful day. The Prince and Princess arrived at about one. I
was up in Bayne's rooms with a number of friends of his . . . ; I
had my telescope up there (for the accommodation of which he
broke out the pane of one window) and with it we managed to
see them wonderfully well. . . . I had intended to go only into
the gardens and not into the Bazaar itself, but when I got there
the Bazaar was not yet open, so I thought I would go in at the
back and make myself useful to the Liddells [sic]. After I had
helped them in their stall a short time, the Royal Party arrived:
there were very few admitted with them and the place was comparatively clear: I crept under the counter and joined the children outside, and the Prince (I don't know whether he knew
me) bowed and made a remark about a picture [a photo?]. The
children were selling some white kittens (like Persian) and as
Alice did not dare offer her's to the Princess, I volunteered to
plead further, and asked the Prince if the Princess would not
like a kitten—on which she turned round and said to me: 'Oh,
but I've bought one of those kittens already'—(which I record
as the only remark *she* is ever likely to make to me). . . . A day
to be remembered as unique and most interesting.

But there is one case in particular that pinpoints the
constant ambivalence of this snobbishness: Carroll's relations
with the Salisbury family. Lord Salisbury, a Marquis and
leading Conservative who was later to be Prime Minister, was
elected Chancellor of Oxford University in 1870. Carroll,
given his political views, was enchanted when a friend enabled
him to photograph the new Chancellor's children. He devotes
almost twenty lines of his diary to that first meeting (p.
288), of which he says, "I fancy *Wonderland* had a great deal
to do with my gracious reception." Once again photography,
coupled with his prestige as a writer (as he, for once, admits
himself!), provided a splendid passport to the world of high
society. For, from that meeting onwards, Carroll became a regular visitor to the Salisburys; the following summer, he was
invited to spend a few days at Hatfield House—when he
commented: "The family are really delightful—perfectly at
their own ease, and kindness itself, they make all their guests
feel at their ease also" (p. 301), and, the visit over, "One of
the pleasantest visits I have ever spent." He became great
friends with one of the little girls, and became a welcome vis-

itor; he was invited to spend New Year's there in 1872-73 (Christmas itself he always spent with his own family at Guildford). The same thing happened again in 1874–75 and 1875–76; then, after what seems to have been a break, we read on January 1, 1884: "Began the year with one of those visits I have always enjoyed so much—to Hatfield" (p. 422). But in the meantime, one of these little incidents occurred that are so revealing of the man's intense sensitivity. During his first New Year's visit, in 1873, he was invited to entertain the children by telling stories; on the third day, he notes (p. 317): "The appetite of the party for stories is insatiable." It was apparently the same in 1875; and the following New Year's Eve he notes: "I declined to undertake my usual role of story-teller in the morning, and so (I hope) broke the rule of being always expected to do it" (p. 348). He may have broken it a little too brusquely, for he seems not to have gone to Hatfield again until 1884, though Lady Salisbury invited him in a most friendly letter in 1878: "Though you have foresworn children's parties perhaps grave old folks may tempt you."[2]

This relationship seems in a general way to have followed the same pattern as that with the Tennysons: there was a snobbishness, certainly, which led him to act with less than his normal reserve; but the moment he felt, or believed himself to be, treated in a hurtful way, his sensitivity reasserted itself forcefully. However, Hatfield and the Salisbury circle gave him an introduction into British aristocratic life, and the impression he got of it was favourable enough to have inspired a very sympathetic picture of the Earl and Lady Muriel and the village of Elveston in *Sylvie and Bruno*.

A Solitary

In 1881, after an evening out, he wrote in his diary (p. 401): "The noise was too great for comfort. I weary more and more of dinner-parties, and rejoice that people have almost ceased to invite me." And three years later, we find an

[2] Hudson, p. 186.

entry that suggests his having made a final decision on the point:

> Wrote to Spooner (who had invited me to dine) to beg off, on the ground that in my old age, I find dinner-parties more and more fatiguing. This is quite a new 'departure'—I much grudge giving an evening (even if it were not tiring) to bandying small-talk with dull people. (p. 435)

Certainly he did not consider his little-girl friends (or even always their parents) dull people, for he went on entertaining them regularly and visiting them; but even with them, he sometimes had occasion to recall his resolution. On November 23, 1895, we read (p. 521):

> Broke the rule which I made some years ago, to decline *all* invitations, by going, at Enid's invitation, to have tea with her and her chief friend Margaret Mayhew. (However, she shall be the *only* exception).

Back in 1875, he had written to Beatrice Hatch's mother, in reply to her invitation to tea "from 4 to 6":

> What an awful proposition! To drink tea from 4 to 6 would tax the constitution even of a hardened tea-drinker. For me, who hardly ever touch it, it would probably be fatal—I must ask you to let me leave it quite doubtful whether I will look in or not.[3]

But what he was doing was simply refusing to attend formal social events; he was not turning wholly in upon himself. Outings to theatres and exhibitions continued as before; the vacations remained just as filled with encounters of all kinds; and he gave more sermons, which brought at least one further form of contact with people. But he ceased to hanker for new faces, especially for meeting celebrities. The somewhat childish love of mingling with the great that he had felt in youth and middle age, though it never totally disappeared, diminished considerably—in proportion to his growing irritation with the autograph-hunters who were now besieging him. This is clear from the following extract from a letter to Marion Richards's mother of December 11, 1885:

[3] E. M. Hatch, *Letters of Lewis Carroll to his Child-Friends*, p. 94.

It can only be as a 'Lion' he wants to know me, and a Lion is the *one* animal I *don't* want to be regarded as. It is hard work some-times—"checking off" the lion-hunters.[4]

Yet he never entirely lost his own fondness for the great; for in 1897, when the Prince of Wales came to visit Oxford again, Carroll wrote in his diary:

I went round to the Deanery etc. to invite them to come through my rooms up on the roof, to see the procession arrive. (p. 534)

And he afterward went to dinner in the hall in Christ Church and noted that he was sitting "almost *vis-a-vis* with the Prince." But then, admirer as he was of Queen Victoria and the Monarchy, he could hardly have stayed away from that particular social event.

[4] Letter in Yale University Library.

Occultism

Collingwood tells us that "Mr. Dodgson took a great interest in occult phenomena, and was for some time an enthusiastic member of the 'Psychical Society' " (p. 92). One sees this also from a perusal of the inventory of his books; at his death it contained some twenty to thirty works with such titles as *The Wonders of the Invisible World*, *The History of Apparitions*, *The Devil*, *A History of Sorcery and Magic*, *Stories of Witches*, *The Other World*, *The Truth about Mesmerism*, *The Philosophy of Magic*, *Superstition and Sorcery*, *The Vampire*, and so on. He seems to have developed this interest fairly early on, for Collingwood mentions it (p. 93) in introducing a letter Carroll wrote to his sister Mary in 1862:

> During my last visit to town, I paid a very interesting visit to a new artist, Mr. Heaphy. Do you remember the curious story of a ghost lady . . . who sat to an artist for her picture; it was called 'Mr. H.'s Story', and he was the writer. . . . He received me most kindly, and we had a very interesting talk about the ghost, which certainly is one of the most curious and inexplicable stories I ever heard. He showed me her picture (life size), and she must have been very lovely, if it is like her (or like it . . .).

A few years later, Carroll introduced ghosts into his writing for the first time, but humorously: a long poem, "Phantasmagoria"[1] recounts the unhappiness, disappoint-

[1] *Works*, p. 827.

ment, and inconvenience attendant upon being a ghost. But one should perhaps take more seriously what he was trying to do in *Sylvie and Bruno*. In the preface to *Sylvie and Bruno Concluded*, he states this clearly:

> It may interest some of my Readers to know the *theory* on which this story is constructed. It is an attempt to show what might *possibly* happen, supposing that Fairies really existed; and that they were sometimes visible to us and we to them; and that they were sometimes able to assume human form: and supposing, also, that human beings might sometimes become conscious of what goes on in the Fairy-world—by actual transference of their immaterial essence, such as we meet with in 'Esoteric Buddhism'.

It seems as though he was seeking to synthesize the fairyland of childhood with the beliefs of occultism. It is not surprising to find him writing this at about that time (December 4, 1882) to a friend:

> That trickery will *not* do as complete explanation of all the phenomena of table-rapping, thought-reading, etc., I am more & more convinced. At the same time I see no need as yet for believing that *dis*embodied spirits have anything to do with it. I have just read a small pamphlet, the first report of the 'Psychical Society', on 'thought-reading'. The evidence, which seems to have been most carefully taken, excludes the possibility that 'unconscious guidance by pressure' (Carpenter's explanation) will account for all the phenomena. All seems to point to the existence of a natural force, allied to electricity & nerve-force, by which brain can act on brain. I think we are close on the day when this shall be classed among the known natural forces, & its laws tabulated, & when the scientific sceptics, who always shut their eyes, till the last moment, to any evidence that seems to point beyond materialism, will have to accept it as a proved fact in nature.[2]

We need not, I think, see this interest in occult phenomena as anything more than evidence of a wide-ranging intellectual curiosity of a kind fairly common in the artistic and literary circles of the time. It would certainly not be enough to account for the origins of *Alice* or the *Looking-Glass*. But

[2] Hudson, pp. 227–28.

it does add a further complex detail to our picture of the
disembodied mathematician-cum-logician, as well as of the
austere and highly orthodox clergyman. As is evident from
Sylvie and Bruno, Carroll made every effort to integrate his
belief in the supernatural into his whole philosophy of aesthet-
ics; this indicates not only his concern to weld his life and his
writings into a unity, but also how little his life was actually
turned in upon the world created by his own imagination.

Oxford

The university, when Charles Dodgson came to it as an undergraduate in 1850, was coming to the end of its life under "the old system"—a system barely changed since the sixteenth century.

It contained some two thousand members: fourteen hundred students, five hundred Fellows, and twenty or so Professors.[1] These two last figures are in themselves an indication of one of the features over which outsiders so often complained: the advantageous position of the colleges as compared with the university. As regards entities, the university consisted of no more than six: a library (the Bodleian), a museum (the Ashmolean), a church (St. Mary's), a printer's (the Clarendon Press), and two buildings used for professorial lectures and ceremonies (the Clarendon Building and the Sheldonian Theatre). The Fellows (at Christ Church they were called Students) were teachers attached to a college, elected and paid by the college itself. In fact, it was they who actually taught the undergraduates (those who did so, for it was not obligatory, were called Tutors), while the Professors, appointed by the Crown and paid by the university, often gave their lectures to empty halls. There was a per-

---

[1] These are the approximate figures given for 1840 by John Sparrow in his book, *Mark Pattison and the Idea of a University*, Cambridge, England, 1967, from which much of the information in this chapter has been drawn.

fectly simple reason why this was so: "modern" subjects—i.e., everything other than theology, classics, and mathematics—were subject to no examination, and counted for nothing toward getting one's degree. On the other hand, the Tutors in each college taught all subjects to all students (with the help of an assistant, sometimes, in mathematics). They would do it by dividing sometimes the students, sometimes the subjects, amongst themselves, but all had to be prepared to teach virtually anything. Since, furthermore, they were chosen without any reference to their possible pedagogical, or even their intellectual, qualities, the system left a lot to be desired.

As an undergraduate, Carroll seems to have had no special problems. He did well, except in philosophy: in those days Aristotelianism still ruled supreme, and when later he wrote his own *Symbolic Logic*, he referred to Aristotelian logic as "an almost useless machine." He was fairly soon appointed a Student of the college and given the job of teaching mathematics—one sensible choice, at least. From 1855 onward, he found himself willy-nilly caught up in the whirlwind of disputes in which the university was to spend the next forty years. They were disputes of various kinds: political, religious, intellectual, and practical. Though we have no evidence of his having adopted a specific stance on these individually, we have, in his *Notes by an Oxford Chiel*, and a series of short pieces, some anonymous, others signed C. L. Dodgson, some sent to newspapers, others printed and distributed by himself, enough to give us a good idea of the path he followed.

Political Problems

These related specifically to the fact that the university, as such, had its own Member of Parliament and that the senior members of the university (though not, of course, the undergraduates) actually had to vote in Oxford. When Carroll got there, Gladstone had recently been elected (in 1847), and was to remain M.P. for Oxford until 1865. The name Gladstone aroused a storm of political passions, especially among Conservatives who saw him primarily as the renegade who had

left the Tory party for the Liberals. Here Carroll always stood
with the Conservatives. But since the period 1850–71 was the
time when changes were being introduced into the university
by act of Parliament, cleavages in party allegiance cut across
cleavages in university policy, and added to the complexity and
virulence of the disputes. In any event, between 1830—when
the Tutors were urged to patrol at night to contain the revolutionary threat feared likely to spread from the continent—and
the end of the century, liberalism, despite the removal of Gladstone, made considerable strides: the overwhelming Conservative majority, of which Carroll was a part when he first arrived,
had decreased enormously by the time of his death in 1898.

Religious Problems

These were to some extent indistinguishable from the
political ones, if only because one of the themes of liberal agitation, in the first half of the century, was the secularization
of the universities, and perhaps even the disestablishment of
the Church of England. Oxford was totally Anglican, for
non-Conformists, Catholics, and Jews were excluded by the re-
quirement to submit to the Thirty-Nine Articles. It was also
largely clerical: of the twenty-five thousand undergraduates
enrolled between 1800 and 1850, ten thousand took Holy Orders.[2] Hence the sense of a closed society, and the identification
with the Tory party (it was at that period that the Church
of England came so aptly to be described as "the Conservative
Party at prayer"). So cautious was Gladstone, so strong the
political power of the universities and their supporters, that it
was not until 1871 that the university at last allowed the
adherents of all faiths to take a university degree or a university post (though jobs attached to colleges remained subject
to the specific regulations of each college).

But two major religious disputes marked the life of
Oxford under Queen Victoria: the first ended for all practi-
cal purposes when Newman and several of his friends left the
Church of England for Catholicism; the second centred

[2] Sparrow, *Mark Pattison.*

upon Benjamin Jowett, the Professor of Greek and a friend of Liddell's, who was accused of heresy in 1855. He had only just been made Professor of Greek, and his opponents insisted that he be made to reaffirm his belief in the Thirty-Nine Articles (which he did), and that his emolument remain fixed at the £40 considered equitable by Henry VIII in the sixteenth century. It was to this last point that Carroll devoted his first anonymous pamphlet in 1865 (avoiding all reference to the religious aspect of the case). He called it *The New Method of Evaluation, as applied to* π. But it is clear from the diary that Carroll, apparently unlike his colleagues, was determined to see the two aspects as distinct:

> The speaking took up the whole afternoon, and the two points at issue, the endowing a *Regius* Professorship, and the countenancing Jowett's theological opinions, got so inextricably mixed up that I rose to beg that they might be kept separate.[3]

But Collingwood, who presumably knew the facts, comments sadly, "I am afraid that Mr. Dodgson, nothing if not a staunch Conservative, sided with the majority against him."

University Problems

Of all the various matters that preoccupied the Oxford Fellows, at least two attracted considerable attention from Carroll: the subjects to be taught for degrees, and the admission of women as resident undergraduates.

The problem of subjects was in essence that of adapting the examinations to suit the disciplines actually being studied. To do that meant reforming the system authorized in 1800 —a system that gave classics pride of place, to the detriment of the newer disciplines, and above all of the exact and applied sciences. For a long time people had been demanding reform, and in 1864 the university finally agreed to permit undergraduates to give up classics after their first year, if they wanted to get a science degree. Carroll wrote in his diary for February 25, 1864:

[3] Collingwood, p. 91.

The new Examination Statute . . . passed in Convocation by 281 to 243. I fear it is the beginning of very grievous changes in the University: this evening I have been seriously thinking about resigning my Examinership in consequence, and have written a sketch of a letter to the Vice-Chancellor on the subject. (pp. 210–11)

A few days later, he sent the letter, and had it printed and circulated; his central objection was to the surrender, which even though only partial, was "a step towards a total surrender, of the principle, hitherto inviolate, that the classics are an *essential* part of an Oxford education" (p. 211).

It is strange that this suspicion of scientific disciplines—which did not, of course, encompass mathematics—never left him. In 1874, when the Professor of Physics asked for money to supply all that was needed to teach his subject properly, Carroll responded with a burlesque letter, justifying the construction of enormous buildings and laboratories for the teaching of mathematics.[4]

Twenty years later, in the last piece he published about university matters, Carroll considered the admission of "Resident Women-Students." In 1896, women were still not allowed to take degrees at Oxford, but the proposal was being made, and Carroll felt that once that step had been taken—in fact, it never was during his lifetime—they would have to live in the colleges, which would not be a healthy situation, either for themselves or for the male students. (Even today there is a tremendous disproportion between the numbers of the two sexes in both Oxford and Cambridge, and only recently have colleges begun to accept students of both sexes.) In this short piece, then, Carroll tried to convince his readers, by logical argument, of the grave dangers that would flow from introducing any change:[5]

I

One of the chief functions, if not *the* chief function, of our University, is to prepare young Men—partly by teaching, partly by discipline, partly by the personal influence of those who have

[4] "The Offer of the Clarendon Trustees," *Works*, p. 1121.
[5] "Resident Women-Students," *Works*, p. 1185.

charge of them, and partly by the influence they exercise on one
another—for the business of Life.

> (This needs to be *specially* borne in mind in connection
> with the assumption, so constantly made in this controversy,
> that the *sole* meaning of the B.A. Degree is that it guaran-
> tees the possession of a large amount of *knowledge.*)

Consequently,

2

The first question to be asked, as to any Scheme proposed to our
University, is, 'How will it affect those for whose well-being we
are responsible?' When we have assured ourselves that it will not
exercise any harmful influence on our own Students, then, and
not till then, may we fairly proceed to consider those for whose
well-being we are *not* responsible.

3

Any Scheme for the recognition of Women-Students—whether
by a series of Certificates or a single Diploma—whereby those
who have resided here will have an advantage, in the keen com-
petition for educational posts, over those who have not, will
most certainly end in making residence *compulsory* on all.
Whether they wish it or not, whether they can afford it or not,
Women-Students will find that they *must* reside, unless they are
content to be hopelessly distanced in the race whose prize is
'daily bread'.

Consequently,

4

Any such Scheme is certain to produce an enormous influx of
resident Women-Students. Considering that we have over 3000
young Men-Students, and that the number of young Women,
who are devoting themselves to study, is increasing 'by leaps
and bounds', it may be confidently predicted that any such
Scheme will bring to Oxford at least 3000 more young Women-
Students. . . .

The main question before us is, 'Will the mutual influence,
of two such sets of Students, residing in such close proximity, be
for good or evil?'

Some Members of the Congregation will reply, 'For good',
some 'For evil'. By all means let each form his own independent

judgment, and give effect to it by his vote: but let him do it *deliberately*, and in the full light of *facts*.

What was Carroll's own suggestion? He wanted to set up a *women's* university: in a praiseworthy spirit of emulation, this would not take long to achieve results quite as good as those of the male Oxford. And he concludes:

> This proposal has been met by the plea that it is *not* what the Women themselves 'desire'. Surely no weaker plea was ever urged in any controversy. Even *men* very often fail to 'desire' what is, after all, the best thing for them to *have*. And those ancients, on whom the onerous task was laid, of weighing and, if reasonably possible, satisfying the claims of the horse-leech and her two daughters, had other things to consider than the mere shrillness of their outcries.

What can we deduce from all this about Carroll's own feelings toward Oxford?

First, that the university must inevitably have held a position of enormous importance in his life. After all, he lived there from 1851 until his death—that is, forty-seven years—leaving only during the vacations (though it is true that these made up about half of the year). For an academic, the closed world it represented from so many points of view must have been immensely satisfying: remember that the university even elected its own Member of Parliament. Yet, in Carroll's case, there is nothing to prove that he found it so. It is extraordinary that his diary (in which he would presumably have noted everything he felt strongly about) contains hardly a mention of Oxford "events"—except for the visit of the Prince and Princess of Wales in 1860. Even the defeat of Gladstone in 1865 does not appear, though he was a man Carroll hated! Jowett, the various reforms, controversies of all kinds—all these are mentioned, if at all, at the ends of paragraphs. In other words, though Oxford was certainly what we may call his natural habitat—Oxford, or rather, Christ Church, which no doubt reflects the comparative status of the university and the colleges—he never really became part of it. Certain events in Oxford stirred him into action: the downgrading of classics, the architectural modernizations,

for example; he protested violently against a plan to turn
some of the parks into cricket fields in a poem "The Deserted
Parks,"[6] parodying Goldsmith's "Deserted Village." But that
is about all. In every instance he took a fiercely conservative
stance; perhaps because of attachment to the memories of
his own student days; perhaps, too, because of the way the
stability of Oxford itself seemed symbolized in its buildings
and its traditions. But never for one moment does he seem
to have envisaged leaving the place like some of his colleagues.

Nor did he ever become an Oxford "character." He certainly became something of a legend in his own college, but
his reputation does not seem to have extended much further
than that. How many academics would have read—how
many today read—children's books? How many were interested in symbolic logic? In a period when people's private
lives were little intruded upon, hardly anyone would have
given a thought to all the little girls who used to walk around
the streets of Oxford with him. It might have been different
had Carroll taken an outrageous position in any of the great
debates of the time; but he never did, for he always aligned
himself with the exponents of common sense and respect for
tradition. That in his forty-seven years at Oxford he achieved
absolutely no celebrity was not a matter of chance, nor
should it be deplored: he wanted to pass unnoticed, and he
succeeded. Oxford, like everywhere else he lived, remained a
port of call rather than an anchorage. If the price he had to
pay for that was obscurity, there is no doubt that he paid it
gladly enough.

[6] *LCPB,* p. 92.

Papa and Mama

Though the third child of his parents, he was their first son; and it is not impossible that, as several of his biographers think, Charles was Mrs. Dodgson's favourite. But, unfortunately, we have no evidence on this point at all; even Collingwood has nothing to say about it. The only letter written by Charles's mother to her son that Collingwood reproduces is affectionate and indeed loving, but it was clearly addressed to him as the eldest of the boys, and for no other reason:[1]

> My Dearest Charlie,
>
> I have used you rather ill in not having written to you sooner, but I know you will forgive me, as your Grandpapa has liked to have me with him so much, and I could not write and talk to him comfortably. All your notes have delighted me, my precious children, and show me that you have not quite forgotten me. I am always thinking of you, and longing to have you all round me again more than words can tell. . . . It delights me, my darling Charlie, to hear that you are getting on so well with your Latin and that you make so few mistakes in your Exercises. You will be happy to hear that your dearest Grandpapa is going on nicely. . . . He talks a great deal and most kindly about you all. I hope my sweetest Will says 'Mama' sometimes, and that precious Tish has not forgotten. Give them and all my other treasures, including yourself, 1,000,000,000 kisses from me, with my most affectionate love. I am sending you a shabby note, but I cannot

[1] Collingwood, pp. 13–14.

Archdeacon Dodgson, father of Lewis Carroll.

help it. Give my kindest love to Aunt Dar, and believe me, my
own dearest Charlie, to be your sincerely affectionate

Mama

Obviously this letter itself gives us no reason to deduce
any special preference for "Charlie" on Mrs. Dodgson's
part.[2] But what Collingwood tells us about it certainly makes
clear Charles's own warm affection for her:

> He set much store by this letter, which was probably one of the
> first he had received. He was afraid that some of his little sisters
> would mess it, or tear it up, so he wrote on the back, 'No one is
> to touch this note, for it belongs to C.L.D.'; but, this warning
> appearing insufficient, he added, 'Covered with slimy pitch, so
> that they will wet their fingers'.

We also have one letter from his father, dating from the
same period—1840—but written in a very different tone:[3]

> I will not forget your commission. As soon as I get to Leeds I
> shall scream out in the middle of the street, *Ironmongers—Iron-
> mongers*—Six hundred men will rush out of their shops in a
> moment—fly, fly, fly in all directions—ring the bells, call the
> constables—set the town on fire. I *will* have a file & a screw-
> driver, & a ring, & if they are not brought directly, in forty sec-
> onds I will leave nothing but one small cat alive in the whole
> town of Leeds, & I shall only leave that, because I am afraid I
> shall not have time to kill it.
>
> Then what a bawling & a tearing of hair there will be! Pigs
> and babies, camels and butterflies, rolling in the gutter together
> —old women rushing up the chimneys & cows after them—
> ducks hiding themselves in coffee cups, & fat geese trying to
> squeeze themselves into pencil cases—at last the Mayor of Leeds
> will be found in a soup plate covered up with custard & stuck
> full of almonds to make him look like a sponge cake that he may
> escape the dreadful destruction of the Town. . . .
>
> At last they bring the things which I ordered & then I spare
> the Town & send off in fifty waggons & under the protection of

---

[2] As we shall see, Phyllis Greenacre attributes enormous importance
to the "1,000,000,000 kisses" Mrs. Dodgson sends. We must remember,
however, that they were to be divided among all the children!

[3] First published in Hudson, pp. 23–24.

10,000 soldiers, a file & a screwdriver and a ring as a present to Charles Lutwidge Dodgson from his affec^nte Papa.

It is hard to reconcile this letter with the seriousness generally attributed to Mr. Dodgson, described by Collingwood as "a man of deep piety and of a somewhat reserved and grave disposition"—though it is true that he goes on to add that "in moments of relaxation his wit and humour were the delight of his clerical friends, for he had the rare power of telling anecdotes effectively" (p. 8). But he would have nothing to do with the theatre, and "his reverence for sacred things was so great that he was never known to relate a story which included a jest upon words from the Bible" (*ibid.*). This mixture of gravity bordering on severity, with a sense of humour and even of nonsense, he transmitted to his son Charles—though perhaps in slightly different proportions.

So we see the two adult figures who dominated Carroll's childhood: a father who, though austere in some respects, had a considerable sense of fun; and a loving mother, of whom Collingwood tells us she was

> one of the sweetest and gentlest women that ever lived, whom to know was to love. The earnestness of her simple faith and love shone forth in all she did and said; she seemed to live always in the conscious presence of God. It has been said by her children that they never in all their lives remember to have heard an impatient or harsh word from her lips. (*Ibid.*)

Furthermore, until Charles was twelve, his father was also his teacher,[4] so the paternal influence must have been considerable. And it long remained so, since it was his mother who died first, in January 1851, just as Carroll was beginning his student life at Oxford. Of her death and its immediate effect upon him, we know nothing. However, almost twenty years afterward, he did make one comment in a letter he wrote to his sister Mary upon the birth of her son Stuart (the future biographer):

> God bless you & the little one now entrusted to you—& may

[4] Collingwood tells us that he was an accomplished Latinist who had translated Tertullian, but in later years he turned more to mathematics.

you be to him what our own dear mother was to *her* eldest son. I can hardly utter for your boy a better wish than that.[5]

His father died in 1868, and we read in his diary (p. 270):

Here the record broke off, and was not resumed till this day, Sunday the 2nd of August [1868]. On the evening of June 21, the day on which the above entry was made, it pleased God to take to himself my dear Father. Even in our sorrow may we be enabled still to say: 'Blessed be His holy Name for ever and ever'.

Many years later, he was to describe this as "the greatest blow that has ever fallen on my life."[6] And, on an earlier occasion, writing to his friend Edith Rix, he said:[7]

In those solemn days, when we used to steal, one by one, into the darkened room, to take yet another look at the dear calm face, and to pray for strength, the one feature in the room that I remember was a framed text, illuminated by one of my sisters, 'Then are they glad, because they are at rest; and so he bringeth them into the haven where they would be!' That text will always have for me a sadness and a sweetness of its own.

The depth of feeling apparent in both these extracts may have been due partly to the fact that Archdeacon Dodgson always took his parental role with the utmost seriousness, as is evident from the letters he wrote to Charles during his undergraduate years. Whether discussing his son's professional future or his financial situation, those letters make it clear that the Archdeacon never hesitated unreservedly to give his son what he believed to be the right advice, though he never sought to compel him to follow it. It is perhaps remarkable that the young man, in the face of this barrage of sensible suggestions, managed to preserve total freedom of judgment. Thus he writes in his diary on July 31, 1857 (p. 117):

Walked to Stapleton in the afternoon with my father. We discussed the subject of insurances. . . .
    My present opinion is this: that it will be best not to effect

[5] Hudson, p. 57.
[6] Collingwood, p. 131.
[7] *Ibid.*, p. 132.

any insurance at present, but simply to save as much as I reasonably can from year to year. If at any future period I contemplate marriage, (of which I see no present likelihood), it will be quite time enough to begin paying the premium then.

This is the only direct information we have as to the reactions of the young man to the father's advice. (An earlier letter, quoted in "Assets and Expenditure," receives no mention in the diary.) It demonstrates both how eminently practical were the problems discussed between the two, and how independent were the son's views. But it is not in itself enough to support the hypothesis of an out-and-out rebellion against parental authority, still less that of a total submission to it.

In short, the explicit statements made by Charles Dodgson give us very little to go on and absolutely no grounds for certainty as to his feelings for either of his parents. A father who was respected and perhaps feared but who could quite clearly communicate with his son; a mother who was loved and loving (perhaps a little cloying?): in other words, a straightforward, commonplace, thoroughly well-balanced family relationship.

The writings of Lewis Carroll alter this picture considerably, and in a somewhat surprising way. But before we consider how, let us pause briefly to recall how perfectly the foregoing description reproduces the traditional picture of the ideal Victorian family: the father manly, serious, and strict; the mother sweetness itself, giving her children all the love that the father, preoccupied with working and earning a living, can demonstrate only in terms of advice and authority. Dickens presents just such a portrait of the parental couple in *David Copperfield* (though the father there is a cruel stepfather); so does George Eliot in *The Mill on the Floss* and *Adam Bede*. The tradition from which it derived was that of a deeply Christian country upper middle class (Puritan at first, and often Methodist later on), and it was to be the model for the parents in all of Victorian literature. Only later, in the aristocracy, did there arise the by now more familiar fictional picture of remote parents who barely

deigned to converse with their children at all until they
reached adolescence, and who confided them in the meantime
to the care of an all-powerful, all-pervading nurse.[8]

But this traditional Victorian image is one that Carroll
destroys *completely* in his works. Though, here again, we
must make a careful distinction.

His "serious" poems, those published from 1856 onwards,
present a stylized, nostalgic vision of the child-mother relationship. This, for instance, comes from "Solitude," published
in 1856, but dated by Carroll March 16, 1853:[9]

> Here from the world I win release,
>   Nor scorn of men, nor footstep rude,
> Break in to mar the holy peace
>   Of this great solitude.
>
> Here may the silent tears I weep
>   Lull the vexed spirit into rest,
> As infants sob themselves to sleep
>   Upon a mother's breast.
>
> . . . .
>
> Ye golden hours of Life's young spring,
>   Of innocence, of love and truth!
> Bright, beyond all imagining,
>   Thou fairy-dream of youth!
>
> I'd give all wealth that years have piled,
>   The slow result of Life's decay,
> To be once more a little child
>   For one bright summer-day.

Similarly with the vision that appears at the end of
another poem, "Stolen Waters,"[10] another version of "La
belle dame sans merci," in which the hero sees his childhood
rise before him, a happy time marked by "The joy of hear-
ing, seeing / The simple joy of being," in connection with
the death of his mother:

[8] It is this image that Kenneth Grahame—the author of *Wind in the
Willows*—was to convey for the twentieth century in his term "The
Olympians."

[9] *Works*, p. 958.

[10] *Works*, p. 962.

An angel-child—
Gazing with living eyes on a dead face:
The mortal form forsaken,
That none may now awaken,
That lieth painless, moveless in her place,
As though in death she smiled!

Finally, let me quote a short extract from "An Easter
Greeting to Every Child Who Loves *Alice*,"[11] which was
composed in 1876, and inserted as a leaflet into *The Hunting of
the Snark*. Carroll thought it so important that it was repub-
lished and sold by itself up to the time of his death:

> Do you know that delicious dreamy feeling when one first wakes
> on a summer morning, with the twitter of birds in the air? . . . It
> is a pleasure very near to sadness, bringing tears to one's eyes
> like a beautiful picture or poem. And is not that a Mother's
> sweet voice that summons you to rise? To rise and forget, in the
> bright sunlight, the ugly dreams that frightened you so when all
> was dark. . . .

It is a curious passage: the Mother (always with a capital
M) is somehow held, wedged, so to say, between a bittersweet
feeling—loving and dying, or dying of love, perhaps—and
the terrors of the night. Only the Mother can bring reality
back, liberating from both imaginary fears and inexplicable
emotions; only she is the foundation of life in the workaday
world; only she assures and reassures. And to confirm what he
is saying, he brings the Mother in again at the end, in the
glory of death and salvation, evoking for his little (!) readers
that time

> when angel-hands shall undraw your curtains, and sweeter tones
> than ever loving Mother breathed shall wake you to a new and
> glorious day—and when all the sadness, and the sin, that dark-
> ened life on this little earth, shall be forgotten like the dreams
> of a night that is past!

All this, though not reproducing the conventional Victorian image in its entirety, does give the Mother one supreme

[11] Since reprinted in *Works*, edited by Green, London, 1965, pp.
226–27.

excellence: love, the basis of everything real and secure in a child's world.

But these are all "serious" pieces; they convey the author's conscious and explicit message to his readers, and need no interpreting. The world of nonsense is rather different; and there the maternal image splits—and the two parts are by no means equal. The form most often represented is that embodied in the queens Alice meets, and, of course, the Duchess; and, in *Sylvie and Bruno*, the wife of the Sub-Warden, Uggug's mother. Buffoons and shrews, heartless when not positively cruel (and remember, the Duchess's baby does change into a pig!) and a terror to everyone around them, they could not be more different from the loving mother Carroll describes elsewhere. So much so indeed that one may well be tempted to cry "castrating mothers" and leave it at that. The other kind of mother only appears once, in the rather complex figure of Lady Muriel, in *Sylvie and Bruno*. Of course, she is not actually a mother in the book (and indeed seems unlikely ever to become one), but that is the role she fulfils for Sylvie and Bruno when they venture out into the "real" world of Elveston. It is then that things become somewhat complicated, for she is actually taking a place that has been left empty: the two children seem to have lost their mother in the fairyland world in which Carroll puts them, and the only maternal figure in that world is Uggug's mother. Lady Muriel, though not really a mother, takes the place of one for children whose "real" mother could well have been more like the other, loving maternal figure. She could, that is, if she were not at the same time (as Carroll himself explicitly tells us) Sylvie grown up—who could hardly, without considerable confusion, be her own and her brother's mother.

If we cut our way out of this imbroglio, we actually end up with a very simple situation: in the world of imagination (a fusion of nonsense and "reality") the only maternal figure possible is an idealized little girl. In other words (but the concept is the same): the little girl can only be fulfilled as an asexual, virgin mother. I suspect that this point is essential to any understanding of one of Carroll's fundamental problems.

But, first of all, it explodes once and for all the falsity of Carroll's pious words about "the Mother." It would seem that
almost *because* the mother in his own life never spoke—nor
did he ever speak of her—except in a way that expressed or
asssumed the lovingness she represented, she had to be seen in
his fiction as omnipresent and omnipotent (or rather as
trying to be so—for Alice does, in fact, manage to thwart all
three queens). This contradiction is far from resolved by the
famous explanation given by Carroll in 1887, in the piece he
wrote for *The Theatre*:[12]

> I pictured to myself the Queen of Hearts as a sort of embodi-
> ment of ungovernable passion—a blind and aimless Fury. The
> Red Queen . . . must be cold and calm . . . the concentrated
> essence of all governesses! Lastly, the White Queen seemed, to
> my dreaming fancy, gentle, stupid, fat and pale; helpless as an
> infant. . . .

For we can see that not merely is each of these images he out-
lines different from the other two in some vital feature, but
all are the opposite of the ideal image exemplified by Sylvie-
Muriel. Carroll in 1887 could not actually contradict what he
had written from 1862 to 1872, but this attempt to replace
the Mother by the governess remains totally unconvincing—
especially in view of the close resemblance of that governess
to certain mothers![13]

The figure of "the Father" undergoes a similar transmu-
tation. Though in his son's life Archdeacon Dodgson held a
place that was important, and was ackowledged as such long
after the death of his wife, in Carroll's fiction the Father is
almost totally effaced. Indeed, he disappears altogether in
these serious and explicit pieces that salute the importance of
the Mother. But in the works of imagination, the forms he
takes may be divided, as it were, into one category: the absent
father. The kings in the Alice books are pale reflections, the

[12] "Alice on the Stage." Reproduced in *LCPB*, pp. 163–74, and
Works, edited by Green.
[13] If I might, for once, follow up the clues, I would like to suggest
that Mrs. Liddell was probably not far from his mind (see "The Liddells").

"negatives" if you like, of their wives; they tremble before them and, like the Sub-Warden in *Sylvie and Bruno*, they obey their slightest whim, or, like the Red King in the *Looking-Glass*, they escape into sleep and dreams of freedom. As for Sylvie and Bruno's father, his whole function is not being there: almost the entire story takes place, and could only take place, in his absence. He does, of course, put in an appearance at the end, but in an aura of quasidivinity that makes him even less real than his presence-through-absence. Most important of all, this character—the only good father figure in Carroll—is always referred to as an old man; and in the final scene everything seems more suggestive of a grandfather with his grandchildren than a father with his children, an impression amply borne out by the frontispiece of the book.

The image that prevails in Carroll's works of imagination, of a father who is either absent, emasculated, or replaced by an uncle or godfather (the Professor in *Sylvie and Bruno*, and perhaps also the White Knight in the *Looking-Glass*), is thus diametrically opposed to the Victorian family structure. The picture with which we started has been turned upside-down, and with it the sense of secure relationships. The question is, Why? The explanation put forward by Phyllis Greenacre, the author of the only thoroughgoing psychoanalytical work on Carroll, fits in with the traditional Oedipal pattern, but only in terms of a disconnected time scale (related no doubt to the late development of young Charles's affectivity):

> In the oedipal crime of the boy it is the father who becomes the feared rival who may punish the child by dismemberment [whereas in Carroll it is the queens who are "castrating"]. With love focussed so strongly on his mother as it seemed to be in the case of the little boy Charles, it might seem then that he would represent the King-father as the awesomely threatening one. It is necessary to realize, however, that Charles' love for his mother was . . . too much involved with the wishes of the earliest infantile period rather than having the fullest oedipal quality. It belonged rather to that period when the mother is nearly everything, good and bad, to the children of both sexes; and is the desired one for protection and nurture or the feared one whose anger or withdrawal is devastating. On such a state of emotional

development, the father may be somewhat awe-inspiring but is a peripheral and secondary figure at best, not very actively involved in the child's life.

This probably exaggerates but otherwise represents Charles L. Dodgson's relation to his father.[14]

This subtle explanation evinces the difficulty felt by the author faced with an insoluble problem: how to explain an anti-Oedipal situation in Oedipal terms. Anti-Oedipal, or rather, perhaps, an-Oedipal. We may allow that little Charles did not wish his father dead; but that he should have represented his mother for the most part as castrating seems to be going too far! For this crucial point must be stressed: despite the importance of Lady Muriel in *Sylvie and Bruno*, the first, most "spontaneous" works, these nearest in time to his own early life, contain no one at all like her; all the mother figures are hostile ones. Nor, in those earlier works, is it possible to transform the heroine into a mother figure, as we can with Sylvie.

Is the Oedipal triangle even thinkable? I think one can remain faithful to the family-centredness of Freudian analysis without having to resort to a pattern which, in this particular case, is totally inapplicable.[15] Freud's short piece on the "family romance" of neurotics[16] can help us here. He wrote it before his first formulation of the Oedipus complex, and it has the advantage of describing the child's family structure in more global terms, with the relationship to "the parents" preponderating over the relationship with each parent individually. Starting from the statement that every personality takes shape by rebelling against parental authority, Freud points out that some children fail to rebel successfully; those children who are, or will be, neurotics, rather than criticize their

[14] P. Greenacre, *Swift and Carroll: A psychoanalytic study of two lives*, p. 221.

[15] It would be more relevant if we could decide that little Charles was really a girl. But then that would complicate the business of his later relationships with prepubertal girls.

[16] Sigmund Freud, *Standard Edition of the Complete Psychological Works of Sigmund Freud*, translated by James Strachey, London, 1950, vol. IX, p. 236.

parents (when they have been punished, or treated in a way that seems unfair), seek flight into a world of imagination, and create what Freud calls a "family romance":

> A quite peculiarly marked imaginative activity is one of the essential characteristics of neurotics and also of all comparatively highly-gifted people. This activity emerges first in children's play, and then, starting roughly from the period before puberty, takes over the topic of family relations.

The imagination of such children usually follows a comparatively straightforward itinerary: they first achieve liberation from their parents by picturing situations in which the parents are replaced by people higher up in the social scale. Then, once a child has grasped the sexual identity of each parent, when, as Freud says, "*pater semper incertus est,* while the mother is *certissima,*" the family romance "contents itself with exalting the child's father, but no longer casts any doubt on his maternal origin, which is regarded as something unalterable." But at the same time, the child feels a "desire to bring his mother (who is the subject of the most intense sexual curiosity) into situations of secret infidelity." And Freud adds:

> Moreover the motive of revenge and retaliation, which was in the foreground at the earlier stage, is also to be found in the later one. It is, as a rule, precisely these neurotic children who were punished by their parents for sexual naughtiness and who now revenge themselves on their parents by means of phantasies of this kind.

Freud finally concludes his development with a reference to a variant of that romance: when the hero, almost always represented as a bastard (in search of his illustrious parents), becomes legitimate, while his brothers and sisters are got rid of by becoming bastards instead.

This schema is quite illuminating. Of course, it cannot be made to fit word for word the adventures of Alice, or of Sylvie and Bruno. But the child-parents relationship just described tells us a lot: a generalized rejection of both parents —the father dismissed to a position of distant splendour, the mother made to behave so atrociously as to be hateful—is very close to what we find in both *Alice* and *Sylvie and Bruno*. It would have been impossible for a Victorian writer of impeccable morality like Carroll to have depicted situations in which there could be any suspicion of conjugal infidelity; but it was perfectly possible to depict others in which his hostility could have equally free rein. It is somewhat difficult to think in terms of "exaltation" in relation to the kings in *Alice*, but we must remember that the process described by Freud starts with an increased distancing of the paternal figure; and though the situation of Sylvie and Bruno's father is the perfect model of this, the effacement of the other father figures is really a variant of the same thing: they may be made to look foolish, but they are not rejected altogether, as the mothers are.

Though certainly somewhat oversimplified, this is ultimately far more flexible than the Oedipal interpretation, which tends to become something of a Procrustean bed. And it has the further advantage of accounting for one (by no means "neurotic")[17] feature of Carroll's adult personality which I have mentioned before: his increasingly marked resemblance to his father. A puritan as well as a humanist, a raconteur as well as a preacher, Carroll came to adopt more and more of his father's ways. But there was one difference, and an essential one: physical fatherhood was replaced by fondness for children already born. Yet, even in this major respect, it is not impossible to see an effect of his father's influence: it may well be that with that particular model before him, Carroll simply could not manage to conceive of himself as ever becoming a father himself.

The father figure certainly holds a central place in Carroll's work, whether as invested with a quasidivine, though disembodied, power, or in the form of a temporary substitute

[17] I shall be coming back later to the problem of unfair punishments that may have been meted out to Charles by his parents. But it is important to remember that the birth of five younger sisters and three younger brothers must have seemed to him, as it would to any child, a torture inflicted specifically by his mother.

who in no way reduces the legitimate father's authority. But it is a central place in a clearly defined framework: that of Victorian society, and more precisely, the most traditional upper-middle-class family structure. Carroll's imagination was working within that particular framework, and it was in its context that he constructed his "family romance." And here we may note that his fictional parents—especially his fathers—are all socially superior to his own parents; they are kings and queens, people with authority. Only the "indulgent uncles" remain on the same social level: the White Knight, the Professor, and the narrator in *Sylvie and Bruno*. Actual paternity—and here I am making what seems to me an absolutely justified identification of paternity with the married state—is achieved only at the cost of distorting social reality. Thus, killing two birds with one stone, Carroll attacks the parental status so revered in his society by making his fictional parents either thoroughly unpleasant or ineffectual, while at the same time exalting bachelorhood, to which he attributes everything that is excellent, above all the ability to give affection. He is not attacking the middle class as such, but only the absolutely central ethos of the middle class whereby, just as the individual man derives his power from his situation as head of a family, so the legitimate structure of society as a whole is a familial one in which the head has complete authority over all the members. Carroll, in fact, managed to become the head of a family without ever having any children, simply because he was the eldest son. Procreation could thus be displaced in favour of the natural right of masculine primogeniture. This meant—only in Carroll's case, of course—liberating sexuality from the Judaeo-Christian command to "increase and multiply," and liberating authority from the structures superimposed on it by the social system, making it flow simply from goodness of heart. And goodness of heart is simply another form of sexuality—but a sexuality directed not to a particular or limited object. What we see in Carroll, then, as against a restricted sexuality centred on the relationships of marriage and the family, is a generalized, open sexuality, drawing people together without producing any new structure. And Sylvie and Bruno's song about "love"[18] is really a hymn to the universal power of sexuality, as the source of everything that exists:

> For I think it is Love,
> For I feel it is Love,
> For I'm sure it is nothing but Love!

This is a far cry from Oedipus. But it comes close to one of the central facts of Carrollian reality. His family romance is, not surprisingly, a social romance. He is rejecting not so much his father or his mother, as "Papa" and "Mama"; he is rejecting the institutionalized family, paradigm of all institutionalized social relationships. As a man and a citizen, he almost always supported the dominant class; he loved being near the great, whether with his photographic apparatus or without it. But in his writing, he was continually questioning the very foundation of their dominance. The royal personages encountered by Alice and by the Narrator in *Sylvie and Bruno* are portrayed in the image of the families she and he knew—artificial and insecure—and both due to be overthrown in the end. The overthrow of the familial and the social by the sexual: that is the core of the matter.

---

[18] *Sylvie and Bruno Concluded*, Chap. XIX, "A Fairy-Duet."

Photography

From the remarkable book by an English historian of photography, Helmut Gernsheim,[1] published in 1949 and presenting some of Carroll's portraits for the first time, we know that Carroll was not merely an enthusiastic photographer, but a pioneer and a considerable artist. More recently, the French photographer Brassaï has spoken of his talent with similar admiration.[2] I don't want to say over again what has been said by Brassaï and Gernsheim, but would like to stress a few points that seem of special significance.

The Story of a Passion

It began in 1855. One of Carroll's uncles, an enthusiast for this quite new hobby, introduced him to it in September. Ten days later, not content with having made at least one expedition with his uncle, Carroll wrote his first piece on the subject, for the *Comic Times*: "Photography Extraordinary";[3] in it, he applies the idea of photographic development to literature, suggesting that the more intense the pro-

---

[1] *Lewis Carroll, Photographer*, London, Max Parrish, 1949. Revised edn., published in New York by Dover, 1971.

[2] Brassaï, "Lewis Carroll photographe, ou l'autre côté du miroir," *Cahier Lewis Carroll*, Paris, 1971.

[3] *Works*, p. 1231.

cess to which it was subjected, the more tense or intense would
be the style of a given passage. It is three pages of typical
Carroll wordplay, in which photography is no more than a
pretext for producing some literary parodies. The following
year, we find Carroll visiting a photographic exhibition, and
then writing to his uncle to get him "a photographic apparatus" for use at Christ Church. In the end, he bought himself
the equipment he wanted.[4] It was all absolutely modern. As
Brassaï points out, Carroll was twenty-four years old, and
photography only seventeen; the collodion process had been
used for barely five years. In May 1856, within two months
of his purchases, Carroll was photographing the Liddell children.

For the next twenty-five years, he took his "apparatus"
with him wherever he went (except to Russia), and he was
constantly visiting, or being visited by, a multitude of potential sitters. It has proved impossible to discover just how many
photos he took, but the albums that have been discovered
contain some 720 that he thought worth preserving. In 1872,
to do the job better, he got permission to construct a studio
above his rooms in Christ Church, having tried in vain to
rent one either in London or in Oxford. In 1858, some of
his pictures were exhibited in London, including the famous
portrait of Tennyson's niece as Little Red Riding Hood. This
was the only time he ever allowed his work to be shown in
public, but we know that he had no hesitation in introducing
himself to possible sitters, using some of his earlier portraits to
support his claim upon their attention.

For twenty-five years, then, photography was the great
leitmotif; it even coloured his literary work, for as well as "Photography Extraordinary," he made it the theme of three other
pieces: a poem, "Hiawatha's Photographing" (1857)[5] and
two short stories, "The Ladye's History"[6] published posthu-
mously in 1899 but written in 1858, and "A Photographer's
Day Out"[7] (1860).

[4] *Diaries,* pp. 72, 74, 81.
[5] *Works,* p. 856.
[6] In *The Legend of Scotland, LCPB,* pp. 331–39; *Works,* p. 1111.
[7] *Works,* p. 1089.

"Hiawatha's Photographing" is another instance of combining photography with parody: it is, of course, Longfellow this time who is the victim. Carroll says in his introductory note:

> Any fairly practised writer, with the slightest ear for rhythm, could compose, for hours together, in the easy running metre of 'The Song of Hiawatha'. Having, then, distinctly stated that I challenge no attention in the following little poem to its merely verbal jingle, I must beg the candid reader to confine his criticism to its treatment of the subject.

The poem describes a photographic sitting, involving a father, his son who is a student at Cambridge, and his many daughters; the sitting is unsuccessful, and Hiawatha, abused by his victims, flees bag and baggage. Carroll uses this both to describe the various stages in a photographic session (and the risks to which it exposes the photographer!) and to present a cruel portrait of father, son, and eldest daughter—making a passing dig at Ruskin in the process.

"The Ladye's History" is a legend he wrote for the small daughters of the Bishop of Durham; it is in a supposedly Anglo-Saxon English, at least as regards the spelling. A "Ladye" recounts how an artist, with a "merveillous machine called by men a Chimera," wanted to take her picture, but failed, and "thereon I shut hym ynto the Cellar"; there he dies, and becomes a Ghost. Like Hiawatha—possibly because Carroll himself was still somewhat inexperienced in the photographic art—this hero, too, is unsuccessful with his camera.

In the third piece, "A Photographer's Day Out," the photographer fails yet again—this time not only in his technical and artistic endeavour, but also in the amorous enterprise that is linked with it. There are two rather interesting passages. One is satirical, in which the hero describes the beauty of his beloved in terms of photographic technique; in the other he defends his—and perhaps Carroll's own?—passion:

> They say that we Photographers are a blind race at best; that we learn to look at even the prettiest faces as so much light and shade; that we seldom admire, and never love. This is a delusion I long to break through.

Agnes Weld (Tennyson's niece) as Little Red Riding
Hood.

Certainly the photographs Carroll took, at least those of his little-girl friends, are proof enough of the admiration, the affection, indeed the love he felt for some of his sitters. The sheer number of photographs he took, the mass of references he makes in his diary to his hobby or art (and to him photography was both), to say nothing of the amount of money he spent, all demonstrate amply that it was a real passion with him.

Yet, without a word of explanation or a backward glance, Carroll suddenly stopped writing about photography completely, and apparently stopped taking pictures as well. Gernsheim was the first to discuss, and seek to discover the reason for, this curious fact. He rejects the "technical" one —the substitution of the dry-plate process for the collodion process—on the grounds that the older process is still in use today, and there was no reason why Carroll should not have continued with it. But the reason he puts forward[8] is, alas, not really convincing. He says that it was to devote himself wholly to writing that Carroll sacrificed this favorite hobby, in 1880, as he was the following year to sacrifice his Lectureship, and his dinner parties. Though not an adequate explanation, it is by no means a foolish one, for Carroll manifestly began withdrawing into himself around the year 1881. But adequate it is not. The Lectureship had never been a pleasure, and its relinquishment was no sacrifice; and his refusal of dinner party invitations would only have been a sacrifice had he at the same time given up going to the theatre, which he did not. Above all, the emotional charge photography held for Carroll—whether taking pictures of his little-girl friends or of the great—was quite unparalleled in either of the occupations he abandoned the following year.

Green is surely far closer to the truth. In his view,[9] Carroll's increasing interest in nude photographs (see further on this section) must have led to unfavourable comment, either from a little girl's mother or some other quarter:

[8] H. Gernsheim, *Lewis Carroll, Photographer*, pp. 81–82 (Dover edition).

[9] *Diaries*, pp. 388–89.

Maybe he realized that there might be some unconscious impropriety involved; certainly, it seems, he felt that, whether as a
mortification or as a safeguard, photography must be given up.

And Green comments (with a sureness that suggests that presenting this as merely a hypothesis may be something of a dip-
lomatic ruse) that Carroll at this time "dropped" a great
many of his friends in Oxford. This explanation seems all the
more probable in view of the fact that Carroll left instruc-
tions to destroy a number of negatives upon his death: "I
would not like (for the families' sakes) the possibility of their
getting into other hands."[10]

What I think we have to do is to combine the two
hypotheses, both Gernsheim's and Green's. The years 1880
and 1881 were decisive for Carroll, in that they marked the
end of a whole series of occupations, and an attempt (which
in the event he did not sustain for very long) to devote himself wholly to what seemed most essential. But photography
could not be sacrificed so completely without some more profound reason; and "What will people say?," along with a
sudden twinge of conscience, seems to constitute by far the
most likely one. Carroll's giving up of photography after
July 15, 1880, resulting probably from two impulses, one
deliberate, the other external, remains a significant event in
his life.

How to Make the Best Use of Photography

In fact, photography fulfilled two functions for Carroll.
First and foremost, it fed his passion for all things technical;
this propensity was clear in his choosing from the first the
most up-to-date and satisfactory process. But it further
enabled him to indulge his sometimes excessive love for meeting celebrities. We see him with Tennyson engineering a
meeting by means of the most skilful manoeuvres—in fact, a
series of portraits: the sister-in-law, the niece, the son, the
wife, and finally the man himself. Not all such attempts were
successful, however. When the Prince of Wales became a stu-

[10] Hudson, p. 270.

Alice Pleasance Liddell.

dent at Christ Church in October 1859, Carroll tried in vain
to get permission to photograph him. His first request was
met with: "His Royal Highness was tired of having his picture taken." Undaunted, he returned to the charge in
December 1860, when the Queen came to Oxford. Having
asked to be presented to the Prince, he apologized for having
been so "importunate" about the photograph the previous
year, and then talked for a while about photography, new
American photographic techniques, the pictures he had taken
of the Liddell children—to which the Prince replied that he
had seen Carroll's photographs of them—and offered to present him with copies. Then, seeing that the Prince seemed
unlikely to propose sitting for him, he finally asked for an
autograph, which he received some days later.[11] It is easy
enough to understand why, several months later, when the
Prince of Wales's brother-in-law, Prince Frederick of Den-
mark, readily allowed himself to be photographed, Carroll
wrote in his dairy (p. 207): "He conversed pleasantly and sensibly, and he is evidently a much brighter specimen of royalty
than his brother-in-law." The story of the missed sitting with
Cardinal Newman is very much the same. However, it may
be pointed out that, generally speaking, at a time when the
art of photography was still young, the notables of the day
may well have felt honoured to sit for a man whose work was
so evidently good, and who could also have been discreetly
introduced (after 1865, that is) as the author of *Alice's
Adventures in Wonderland*. Certainly, in ecclesiastical, aristocratic and artistic circles (I use "artistic" to include actors,
writers, and painters), Carroll had little trouble in immortal-
izing the features of many a celebrity. And in Christ Church
itself, he seems to have become more or less the official photographer: the college has a hundred or so photos of dons and
undergraduates (all seated in the same leather armchair)
taken by him.

   Though over the years he did certainly display a fondness for meeting famous people, contacts of this kind,
through the camera lens, were certainly not satisfying enough

[11] Gernsheim, *Lewis Carroll, Photographer*, p. 46.

to account for Carroll's consuming passion for photography. There very soon came a second, and quite different, reward: a prolonged contact with children, or rather, with little girls. The chronology of his apprenticeship he himself gives in his diary (pp. 81–86) speaks volumes: having gone with his friend Southey to buy his "apparatus" (March 17 and 18, 1856), the first thing he attempted to photograph—with Southey—was Christ Church Cathedral, with "the three little girls" who were playing in the Deanery garden (Alice and her sisters) in the foreground; three days later (April 28), he was with them again, though we do not know whether he actually photographed them or not. But once the rest of his equipment arrived (the chemicals needed to develop and print the photos), Carroll himself certainly took some successful pictures, and it was he who got Harry Liddell to come in and sit (Southey being apparently more interested in the adults). On June 3, Carroll could write proudly: "Spent the morning at the Deanery, photographing the children." Contact had been made.

From then on, photographs of children—and almost all of them were of girls—became for Carroll both an end and a means. He certainly wanted to take pictures, of that there can be no doubt, to capture on paper the looks that he found so enchanting in the flesh; but it was also a means of getting to know the sitters, since the idea of a photograph was one that attracted both child and parents. Gernsheim gives us an idea of the scale of the enterprise by telling us that in the diary for March 25, 1863,[12] he gives the names of 107 little girls "photographed or to be photographed"! Gernsheim adds:

> What makes this entry particularly characteristic is that the girls are grouped under their Christian names, all the Agneses and all the Beatrices etc. together, in many cases the date of birth is given in addition!

[12] *Ibid.*, p. 51. The published *Diaries*, edited by Green, do not contain the passage, nor any reference to it. Gernsheim may have mentioned it because, as a photographer himself, he understood Carroll's attitude.

Characteristic indeed! But characteristic of the collector not of photographs, but of little girls—for why else the date of birth? and why the Christian names, which can only refer to the flesh-and-blood children, rather than the type of portrait (full length, head and shoulders, vignette, etc.), or details about the faces or the clothes?

This makes it easier to understand the wily manoeuvres Carroll sometimes adopted in order to meet girls and get them to sit for him; he would ask a sister or cousin to approach the children of various of their acquaintances for him. In July 1863, for instance, when he met the sculptor Alexander Munro, "he promises to get me Mr. Tom Taylor," a well-known playwright of the day, who knew Ellen Terry and her sisters; and Carroll at once adds, "I think I must try to get *them* also as sitters" (*Diaries*, p. 200). Though in September, having as he hopes succeeded in his aim, he notes sadly, "All my photographic victims seem to be available but the Terrys, who are acting at Bristol" (p. 201). Note his amazed exclamation, on meeting a certain Colonel Holder: "his little girl joined us, Helen Agnes, a pretty little thing, whom he has never photographed!";[13] and this, from a letter to his sister Louisa,[14] written during the same holiday: "I called on Mrs. Cameron on Monday and told her I felt rather tempted to have my camera sent down here, there are so many pretty children about"; indeed, the next few lines of the letter make it evident that, when he felt an instant attraction, he at once thought of photography as a means of access:

> I asked if she would photograph for me . . . the prettiest one being a child of Mr. Bradley's . . . and the other, name unknown, but constantly to be seen about. . . .
>
> On Monday afternoon I was lounging about on the beach, and came on the same little unknown child—such a little gypsy beauty, rich brown complexion and black eyes.

And Gernsheim quotes an entry in 1866: "Never before in one week have I had such lovely children to photograph" (p. 65). We read in the diary in 1871:

[13] *Ibid.*, p. 59.
[14] *Ibid.*, p. 60.

On Sunday I added to my list of friends in Oxford by joining Arnold . . . where he was walking with his children . . . and going back with him to his house. Of course I arranged to photograph the children, Julia (8) and Ethel (6). (p. 296)

Finally here are three entries from the diary (pp. 359, 362) about one little girl:

The Harlequin was a little girl named Gilchrist . . . one of the most beautiful children, in face and figure, that I have ever seen; I must get an opportunity of photographing her.

Three months later:

I was decidedly pleased with Connie [Gilchrist] . . . who is about the most gloriously beautiful child (both face and figure) that I ever saw. One would like to do 100 photographs of her.

And five days after that:

Devised a plan which seems more feasible than any I have yet thought of, for getting photos of Connie Gilchrist:—to be staying in London, to bring her over to Oxford by the early train, and take her back in the evening. This would give me nine hours in Oxford, and cost little more than paying for her and an escort, who would be an encumbrance.

One cannot help speculating as to the ultimate goal of all these strategic manoeuvres, some of them quite complicated. There are many people who think, like Brassaï in the article I have mentioned, that Carroll's passion for photographing little girls led him quite naturally to photographing nudes. And this seems to be largely borne out by the way his work did, in fact, develop. We find him moving on from straightforward portraits, to posing his sitters in more elaborate *tableaux vivants* (in which costume came to be more and more important), until on July 8, 1866, he produced the photograph of "little Ella . . . with no other dress than a cloth tied round her, savage fashion" (p. 245). The following year, we have the first mention by Carroll of a nude photograph: "Mrs. L. brought Beatrice, and I took a photograph of the two; and several of Beatrice alone, 'sans habilement' [sic]";[15]

---

[15] This passage is quoted by Gernsheim, p. 65; it has been omitted by Green in his edition of the *Diaries*.

the use of a French phrase probably represented a euphemism
to salve Carroll's own conscience (rather than, as Brassaï suggests, to avoid upsetting anyone else who might read it).
From then on, photographs of naked children, often
described in veiled terms, become more and more frequent. In
May 1867, for instance:

> Since Commemoration I have been continually photographing
> and have done some beautiful ones of children—the Owens and
> the Max Müllers: the former in night-dress, with an actual bed,
> made several excellent groups.[16]

Beds and sofas figure more and more frequently, and night-
clothes, too:

> He [Henry Holiday] fetched Xie Kitchin to be photographed,
> and I did a large one, full length, lying on the sofa in a long
> night-gown, which H. arranged; about the best I have done of
> her.[17]

Holiday, the illustrator of *The Hunting of the Snark*, appears
to have given Carroll a great deal of help, and not only in
arranging the sitters for his *tableaux vivants*; we read in the
diary (p. 326):

> He showed me the drawings he is doing for me (suggestions for
> groups of two children—nude studies—for me to try to repro-
> duce in photographs from life).

Sometimes what he says is less explicit:

> A very dull afternoon, yet I got two good negatives of Lily—
> one seated on a low chair, and one standing with wand. . . . It is
> quite a new privilege to have a subject for photography so
> entirely indifferent as to dress: I have had none such since Bea-
> trice Hatch, July 30/73.[18]

A long entry for July 18, 1879 (omitted in the *Diaries*, but

---

[16] *Ibid.*, p. 65. (In the *Diaries*, p. 261, the entry ends with "the Max
Müllers.")

[17] *Ibid.*, p. 71; omitted from the *Diaries*.

[18] *Ibid.*, p. 76. The *Diaries*, p. 356, omit the precise date of the Beatrice Hatch sitting, obviously an important one for Carroll. And surely
"indifference as to dress" must be construed as meaning "as to lack of
dress."

reproduced in Gernsheim, p. 79) is in a similar tone; it refers to a mother who has brought her little girls to be photographed:

> I had warned Mrs. —— that I thought the children so nervous I should not even ask for 'bare feet' and was agreeably surprised to find they were ready for any amount of undress, and seemed delighted at being allowed to run about naked. It was a great privilege to have such a model as —— to take: a *very* pretty face, and a good figure.

And Gernsheim goes on to say:

> During this month there are many references to Oxford children being photographed in the artist's favourite dress of 'nothing', lying on a blanket, or on the sofa—'a kind of photograph I have often done lately'.

It is not really surprising to find Carroll suddenly giving up photography only a year after this. Whatever the conventions of the day in regard to children's photographs—and it would appear that Victorian families adored pictures of naked children—it was inevitable that some mothers would come to feel anxious over Carroll's propensity for undressing their small daughters. Gernsheim remarks (p. 70) that from 1873 on

> Lewis Carroll indulged ever increasingly in costume pictures, dressing up his child friends as Roman girls, in Greek dress, in Indian shawls, in Danish costume, as Chinamen, in South Sea Island costume, in beach dress, and occasionally still further undressing until there was no costume at all.

As long as Carroll found such delight in all this dressing up, the amount of undressing that it involved would cause no particular concern (at least to anyone not looking for ulterior motives). But all pleasures pall with time, and there seems no reason why Carroll should have been an exception to this rule. Furthermore, some mothers must have found it even more disturbing to discover that he kept in his possession the negatives of those artistic photos, which might well cause raised eyebrows.

For a man like Carroll, photography was bound to come

Alice Liddell as "the young beggar."

up against this particular obstacle. Everything indicates that, though his love of photography began with pleasure in mastering the technique, it only really found fulfilment in his photographs of children. The venture was thus doomed from the start. Carroll's degree of emotional investment was bound sooner or later to lead him to a form of fetishism unacceptable to others, and indeed to himself.

Despite his penchant for *tableaux vivants* and scenes of pathos ("The Elopement," "The Beggar Child," etc.), it was certainly fetishism rather than voyeurism. In those days, when poses had to be held for a long time, that time was inevitably one of enjoyment for a photographer who loved his sitter—remember "A Photographer's Day Out," quoted earlier —and once the sitter was gone, the enjoyment would be transferred to the photograph. Highly significant is the last reference to photography in his diary (quoted by Gernsheim, p. 82, but omitted from Green's edition of the *Diaries*). He records the death of the Reverend E. Hatch: "A friend of many years standing, whose daughter Beatrice, now grown up, was as a baby-child[19] a favourite photo subject of mine."

[19] "Baby-child" is misleading in the extreme: she was at least four or five years old.

Politics

Politics was never a major interest of Carroll's. At a time when a great many intellectuals[1] were debating with passion first the problems presented by English society in itself, and then the problems of England's role in the world, Carroll, like the majority of Oxford and Cambridge dons, was fully occupied with the internal debates of his university and the ways in which he felt it to be threatened by the government and society at large. He was not uninterested in social, economic, and political matters, but they represented some of the many provinces in which he knew (or thought he knew) he had no part to play. He makes this clear in his diary in January 1856 (p. 71):

> Finished *Alton Locke* [by Charles Kingsley]. It tells the tale well of the privations and miseries of the poor, but I wish he would propose some more definite remedy, and especially that he would tell us what he wishes to substitute for the iniquitous "sweating" system in tailoring and other trades.
>
> If the book were but a little more definite, it might stir up many fellow-workers in the same good field of social improvement. Oh that God, in His good providence, may make me hereafter such a worker! But alas, what are the means? Each has his own nostrum to propound, and in the Babel of voices, nothing is done. . . .

[1] This term, always difficult to use when speaking of England, must not be taken to include the teaching staff of the universities.

And nothing in his later life ever occurred to modify that initial pessimism.

Nothing, or almost nothing. Whatever he did, or tried to do, was always in the sphere of charitable activity. With regard to child actors, indeed, everything he did ran counter to the "progressive" movement of his day to regulate, if not abolish, child labour. On the other hand, he was always prepared to put his views into writing: he did so at length through the mouthpiece of Arthur Forester, the noble doctor in the *Sylvie and Bruno* books, and he sent a letter under his own name, C. L. Dodgson, to the *Pall Mall Gazette* in 1867, proposing the setting up of a "National Philanthropical Society" to coordinate all the various charitable activities in the country; this, he declared, would be

> a central point *to* which, and again *from* which, the streams of benevolence should flow; one where contributions could be received, by some simple process, from all quarters, and for all charitable purposes, and handed over again, *without deduction*, to the objects designated, and from which information should be circulated of the names, purposes, claims and progress of the various charitable institutions. Could such an object be attained, I believe that the giving of charity would be made so much more easy and attractive to those who, having abundance to give, need only information as to where and how to give it, that probably much more would be given . . .[2]

This makes it abundantly clear, and the arguments used by Arthur Forester make it even more so, that he saw charity as a duty, and that the only problem was knowing how to perform it. In addition, as he was not concerned over the traditional charity-or-justice dilemma, since for him true charity necessarily involved justice, all that mattered was to make it easy for people—that is to say, clear, evident, intelligible, logical—and the rest would follow with equal logic. Further than that he seems never to have gone; neither the social Christian teaching of F. D. Maurice and Charles Kingsley, nor the social prophecy of Ruskin (and he knew all three) ever managed to win him to the notion that other remedies or methods might perhaps be called for.

[2] *Diaries*, p. 250.

Politics in the narrower sense held a rather more important place in his life. But this statement too needs some
amplification. The Crimean War, for instance, merited only
three entries in the diary (at least as much of it as we have).
In June 1855, he notes: "Melancholy news of the repulse of
the Allies in their attack on the Malakoff tower; it looks very
bad for us" (p. 53), and then goes on to describe a museum
visit. On September 11, two and a half lines: "The glorious
intelligence arrived of the *fall of Sebastopol*: the whole town
is in the hands of the allies. The Russians still hold the batter-
ies on the North side" (p. 64), after which he goes on to
describe a little girl he has just met. Finally, on March 31,
1856, the peace gets two more lines: "*News of the signing of
Peace* came by telegraph. The cathedral bells were ringing
most of the day, and flags flying all over the town" (p. 82).
Only one other issue of the day attracted more references in
his journal: the Irish problem. But that was not so much for
reasons of high politics as for its repercussions on the life of
the university.

The fact of the matter was this: the university of
Oxford had its own Member of Parliament. From 1847 to
1865 that Member was Gladstone, who therefore became
involved in the heated disputes which racked the university.
Over this particular issue, the hostilities were almost always
absolute. They certainly were so for people who, like Carroll,
having taken no continuous action in politics, and still less
feeling any identification with either of the major parties,
approached each election with all the bitterness left by past
scars. Thus, even had the Anglican Church not for the most
part come gradually to make common cause with the Conservative party (led by Disraeli), Carroll would probably still
have voted against Gladstone. But this was an additional
reason for the unrelenting hostility of which we have abun-
dant evidence. Despite some commentators, that evidence is
not to be found in the Alice books: the graphic resemblance
between Tenniel's illustrations for them and his caricatures in
Punch are as unflattering to Disraeli as they are to Gladstone.[3]
But we do find it in the various anagrams Carroll made out of

[3] Especially in the pictures of the Walrus and the Carpenter, and the
Lion and the Unicorn.

the letters in Gladstone's name (William Ewart Gladstone);
he even sent one to the London *Times* when Gladstone was de-
feated in 1868: "Wilt tear down all images?" Later, he worked
out an even better one: "Wild agitator: means well."[4] This
being the tone, it is not surprising to find that Carroll associated
the Liberal Prime Minister and the Irish problem which had
become one of the symbols of his policies in the same hostility.
Thus Parnell gets three mentions in the diary. In October 1881,
Carroll writes (p. 400):

> Heard the welcome news of the arrest of Mr. Parnell: hope it
> may finish the 'Land League', but fear Mr. Gladstone has let
> things go too far, and that it *may* lead to actual fighting.

On June 7, 1886 (p. 442):

> The night was a memorable one: at 1.30 a.m. on Tuesday the
> great division took place on the Second Reading of Gladstone's
> Home Rule Bill, which was thrown out by 343 to 313. I trust
> the nation will never again be so near to a gigantic catastrophe.

And on November 29, 1890 (p. 481):

> History is moving briskly just now! First, Parnell's disgrace as
> co-respondent in a divorce suit. Then Gladstone's letter, calling
> on him to resign the leadership of the 'Home Rule' party. And
> this morning Parnell's Manifesto to the Irish People, revealing
> Gladstone's negotiations with him, and the sham 'Home Rule'
> Bill he proposed to bring in when next in power, offering Par-
> nell the Irish Secretaryship as a sop!

But, in fact, it was upon Oxford that Carroll's political
interests were concentrated. His commitment, though
restricted, was absolutely clear: he was anti-Liberal, pro-Con-
servative. The most explicit evidence we have of this is a
letter he sent to an Oxford newspaper in November 1868,
following an article that had appeared in another publication
describing a by-election near Oxford. He comments in his
diary (p. 275): "An account of the Woodstock Election has
appeared in the *Oxford Chronicle*—written by a Liberal, but
so charmingly candid as to the brutal behaviour of the Liberal
electors, that I thought it fair subject for a letter to the *Uni-*

[4] *Diaries*, p. 277.

versity Herald." The letter is ironic in tone throughout: signed "A Liberal of the Liberals," it is by way of highlighting the abominable behaviour of the Conservatives:

> We are told, Sir, that the successful [Conservative] candidate, Mr. Barnett, *'attempted in vain to address the crowd. Not a word was audible amidst the hootings and execrations which greeted him'.* I cannot, Sir, tell you how refreshing to my ears were those manly voices! Though Tory tricks, aristocratic art, and the brute force of numerical superiority, had turned the day against the noble and enlightened minority, I seemed to hear in those voices the knell of a dying monster, the crashing downfall of the rotten fabric of Conservatism!
>
> Mark, however, the contrast when the defeated candidate, Mr. Broderick comes forward. He *'was received with enthusiastic cheering and listened to in perfect silence'.* I do not, of course, suppose that the Conservative electors were hypocrites enough to join in the enthusiastic cheering; such depths of baseness have not yet, let us hope, been reached, even in degenerate Woodstock. But that he should be *'listened to in perfect silence!'* Sir, my blood boils within me at the thought. What! that a set of electors with lungs in their bodies and breath in their lungs, should listen to a political opponent *'in perfect silence!'* It is too mean, too pitiful for belief! (*Diaries*, p. 275–76)

Two years earlier, Carroll had produced an (anonymous) reply to a colleague who had written a letter deploring the fact that the university should have elected two Conservatives to the Hebdomadal Council, thus giving the Conservatives a majority, and proposing large-scale institutional reforms in order to put an end to such scandals in future. In a seven-page poem, with lengthy explanatory notes,[5] Carroll then used irony to flatten his opponent, concluding with this Liberal idyll of the Oxford of the future:

> Then, then shall Oxford be herself again,
> Neglect the heart, and cultivate the brain—
> Then this shall be the burden of our song,
> "All change is good—whatever is, is wrong—"
> Then Intellect's proud flag shall be unfurled,
> And Brain, and Brain alone, shall rule the world!

[5] "The Elections to the Hebdomadal Council," *LCPB,* pp. 81–89. *Works,* pp. 908–16.

Clearly, this was a vision in which political problems were narrowly bound up with the religious and philosophical disputes that divided innovators and traditionalists in the university.

However, his most typically "Carrollian" political attitude was also his earliest. In 1865, even before *Alice* had appeared, Carroll had distributed a little pamphlet called *The Dynamics of a Parti-cle*,[6] in which, spinning dizzily from one pun to another, he gave a "geometrical" account of the election then in progress, when Gladstone lost his Oxford seat to a Conservative, Gathorne Hardy; the two men are represented by two lines—WEG and GH. The election (the "Representation") is summed up in this proposition: "To remove a given Tangent from a given Circle, and to bring another Line into contact with it." This is how it is done:

> Let UNIV be a Large Circle, whose centre is O (V [Victoria] being, of course, placed at the top), and let WGH be a triangle, two of whose sides, WEG and WH are in contact with the circle, while GH (called 'the base' by liberal mathematicians), is not in contact with it. (see Fig. 1). It is required to destroy the contact of WEG, and to bring GH into contact instead.
>
> Let I be the point of maximum illumination of the circle, and therefore E the point of maximum enlightenment of the triangle. (E of course varying perversely as the square of the distance from O.)

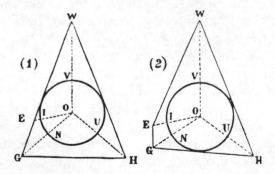

Fig. 1. *The Dynamics of a Parti-cle* (in *LCPB*, p. 73).

6 *LCPB*, pp. 58–75. *Works*, pp. 1129–39.

Let WH be fixed absolutely, and remain always in contact
with the circle, and let the direction of OI be also fixed.

Now, so long as WEG preserves a perfectly straight course,
GH cannot possibly come into contact with the circle, but if the
force of illumination, acting along OI, cause it to bend (as in
Fig. 2), a partial revolution on the part of WEG and GH is
effected, WEG ceases to touch the circle, and GH is immediately
brought into contact with it.

Q.E.F.

Once one grasps that O is Oxford; that "the illumination" is the light that the Liberals identify with progress, liberty, and their views in general; that the bending of WEG is
an allusion to the many political changes made by the Liberal
leader (which Carroll had explained, a few pages earlier, in
defining the word "Trilinear" as "a line which takes 3 different courses. Such a line is usually expressed by three letters, as
W.E.G.")—then the whole thing becomes quite clear.

After these early published attitudes, we scarcely find
Carroll nailing his colours in public to any political mast,
though no one was ever in any doubt as to his views. Even
Collingwood was obliged to recognize that his uncle was
"nothing if not a staunch Conservative" (p. 91). But the
picture of him that emerges from *Sylvie and Bruno* is considerably less fierce—and more disillusioned—at least if we take
it to be embodied in Mein Herr (the other figure of the Professor), who expounds his theory of the "Political Dichotomy" on which English society seems to him to be based: the
party in power, the "Ins," had to do "the best they could for
the national welfare," while the opposition, the "Outs," had
to try to prevent them from succeeding. Then, by a logical
reductio ad absurdum, Mein Herr/Carroll shows how that
principle can be applied to everything in life, thus reaching
total confusion.[7]

But he reserved his own energies for another matter, one
in which it seemed to him that party prejudice must yield to
the certainty of logic and mathematics: the introduction of
proportional representation in political elections. In 1884 and

[7] *Sylvie and Bruno Concluded*, Chap. XIII.

1885, he wrote two letters (published in the *St. James's Gazette*), and no fewer than four pamphlets on the subject. His overriding concern was to "purify" elections. As early as 1881 he had suggested putting an end to elections that lasted for several days—which had led to some minor scandals in Oxford itself—for the sake of public honesty. He declared that

> so long as general elections are conducted as at present we shall be liable to oscillations of political power, like those of 1874 and 1880, but of ever-increasing violence—one Parliament wholly at the mercy of one political party, the next wholly at the mercy of the other—while the Government of the hour, joyfully hastening to undo all that its predecessors have done, will wield a majority so immense that the fate of every question will be foredoomed, and debate will be a farce. . . .[8]

His solution was, first, to keep the results of the voting in each constituency secret until the whole election was completed. He then wanted to ensure that the voting process itself was made absolutely equitable by a series of simple measures: making all constituencies equal in numbers; allowing the minority some representation; simplifying the ballot papers "to meet the case of voters of the very narrowest mental calibre"; simplifying the process of vote counting. Then comes a plan for proportional representation whereby there would be one seat not directly elected, for which the *elected* candidates would give their surplus votes (i.e., over and above the "quota" fixed for election) to the candidate(s) of their choice.

As with social problems, we find Carroll gradually modifying his political animosities in favour of his concern for arithmetical equity and practical clarity, the latter obviously going hand in hand with the preoccupation with logic that was absorbing more and more of his attention. When he talked of the two parties as though they were parallel, he was speaking as a mathematician and logician, rather than as a voter—for his own tendency was always Tory. A technocrat before his time, Carroll was henceforth to concentrate on the

[8] Collingwood, pp. 233–34.

forms and structures that moulded the political life of the period. Everything else was simply a game, as he had shown earlier in the fight between the Lion and the Unicorn: when Alice asked him whether "the one that wins gets the crown," the White King was horrified: "Dear me, no! . . . What an idea!"[9]

[9] *Through the Looking-Glass*, Chap. VII.

Priest or Layman?

The Dodgson family had a solidly clerical tradition. Charles's great-grandfather, Charles Dodgson, was an Anglican clergyman in Yorkshire, and later became a Bishop. His eldest son, Charles, was never anything but a soldier; but that son's eldest son, Lewis Carroll's father, Charles Dodgson, renewed the tradition and took Holy Orders. Consequently, when young Charles Lutwidge Dodgson had to decide on a course of studies to pursue, the path to ordination seemed the normal one to follow.

The word *decide* is perhaps deceptive, in the sense that we find no trace of any doubt or discussion prior to his committing himself to that course. And in fact, at Oxford, preparation for Holy Orders simply involved following a university course; there was not even any obligation to make theology one's major subject of study. When he received his first official appointment in 1855 as Mathematical Lecturer, it was conditional upon his ultimately taking Holy Orders, though his diary at no point suggests any such intention. However, his father clearly expected it, for we have a letter sent by him to Charles that year, which includes the following suggestions:

> I will just sketch for you a supposed case, applicable to your own circumstances, of a young man of twenty-three, making up his mind to work [i.e. teach at the university] for ten years . . . on an Income enabling him to save £150 a year. . . . Suppose him at

the end of the ten years to get a Living enabling him to settle
[i.e. to marry]¹. . . .

We do not know Charles's response, but at the end of 1856,
he noted certain resolutions in his diary: "I want time for
some Divinity reading, which is at present entirely dropped"
November 12 (p. 95); and on December 31, "11:30 p.m.," he
writes "As to the future:—I may lay down as absolute
necessities *Divinity Reading* and *Mathematical Reading*" (p.
99).

This strange hanging back is confirmed, a month later,
by a comment susceptible of many subtleties of interpretation, but also totally negative:

> This also suggests to me grave doubts as to the work of the min-
> istry which I am looking forward to—if I find it so hard to
> prove a plain duty to one individual [his brother Wilfred], and
> that one unpractised in argument, how can I ever be ready to
> face the countless sophisms and ingenious arguments against
> religion which a clergyman must meet with! (p. 102)

However, six days later, "Went to Chapel in surplice for
the first time since 14th October, 1855" (p. 103).

On September 1, 1857, he writes: "I am now settled into
a tolerably regular habit of three or four hours' work every
morning, Divinity and Mathematics alternately" (p. 119);
and on December 31 of that year:

> What do I propose as the work of the New Year?
> (1) Reading for Ordination at the end of the year—and settling
> the subject finally and definitely in my mind. (p. 136)

At that time, then, he was still hesitating.

He was to reach a decision during the next few years,
but as to how he reached it we know almost nothing, for it is
that period for which several volumes of his diary are missing.
His nephew (who had consulted them) tells us that his hesitation basically arose from two difficulties:

> He was not prepared to live the life of almost puritanical strict-
> ness which was then considered essential for a clergyman, and he
> saw that the impediment of speech from which he suffered

¹ Collingwood, p. 61.

would greatly interfere with the proper performance of his clerical duties.[2]

That "puritanical" life seems to have involved chiefly giving up the theatre, at least in the Oxford diocese, a pleasure Carroll was to continue to the end of his life. On the other hand, certainly at least up to that date, before Carroll had had any of the rebuffs I have mentioned elsewhere from his young friends' mamas, he certainly had no sense of the slightest impropriety, even in intention, in his rather special relationships with little girls. On the contrary, everything indicates his satisfaction in those friendships, which obviously gave great pleasure on both sides.

The arguments given by Collingwood are fairly convincing:

> Not only was this step [ordination] necessary if he wished to retain his Studentship [at Christ Church], but also he felt that it would give him much more influence among the undergraduates, and thus increase his power of doing good.

And he concludes:

> He discussed the matter with Dr. Pusey, and with Dr. Liddon [the friend with whom he went to Russia]. The latter said that 'he thought a deacon might lawfully, if he found himself unfit for the work, abstain from ministerial duty'. (p. 74)

This would also make it possible not to have to worry about contravening the wishes of the Bishop of Oxford as far as the theatre was concerned. Having clarified his mind thus far, Carroll was ordained Deacon on December 22, 1861.

But this did little to resolve the problem. The diaconate had become, by modern times, no more than a step on the way to the priesthood, usually preceding it by about a year. For Carroll to decide not to go further, there must have been strong reasons. The explanation he gave to his godson, William Wilcox, toward the end of his life, is not very illuminating:

> When I reached the age for taking Deacon's Orders, I found myself established as the Mathematical Lecturer, & with no sort

[2] *Ibid.*, p. 74.

of inclination to give it up & take parochial work: & I had grave doubts whether it would not be my duty *not* to take Orders. . . .

And a further doubt occurred—I could not feel sure that I should ever wish to take *Priest's* Orders—And I asked Dr. Liddon whether he thought I should be justified in taking Deacon's Orders as a sort of experiment, which would enable me to try how the occupation of a clergyman suited me, & *then* decide whether I would take full Orders. He said "most certainly"—& that a Deacon is in a totally different position from a Priest: & much more free to regard himself as *practically* a layman. So I took Deacon's Orders in that spirit. And now, for several reasons, I have given up all idea of taking full Orders, & regard myself . . . as practically a layman.[3]

However, it would seem that this choice was settled as early as 1862, to judge from the diary (p. 188):

Oct. 21. Called on the Dean [Liddell] to ask him if I was in any way obliged to take Priest's Orders—(I consider mine as a Lay Studentship). His opinion was that by being ordained Deacon I became a Clerical Student, and so subject to the same conditions as if I had taken a Clerical Studentship, viz: that I must take Priest's Orders within four years from my time for being M.A., and that as this was clearly impossible in my case, I have probably already lost the Studentship, and am at least bound to take Priest's Orders as soon as possible. I differed from this view, and he talked of laying the matter before the electors. Oct. 22. The Dean has decided on not consulting the electors, and says he shall do nothing more about it, so that I consider myself free as to being ordained Priest.

("Free" here must obviously be taken to mean "under no constraint," rather than "authorized.")

"For several reasons": that is as much as we know of Carroll's motives! Some biographers have suggested his stammer as a reason—but it did not prevent his preaching to children, to the servants at Christ Church, and even, though only on two occasions, in St. Mary's Church, Oxford. For the reasons I gave earlier, it does not seem to me legitimate to adduce a sense of sin Carroll may be supposed to have felt in connection with his complicated emotional problems. As for doctrinal

[3] Hudson, p. 117.

difficulties, they never amounted to more than slight questioning—and the Anglican Church has always been well able to allow for hesitation in matters of belief.

The only explanation that seems to me likely—and it would also account for others of Carroll's choices—is his reluctance to commit himself, to become in any way tied down. No doubt his wish to remain free was a selfish one, but it was due also to his determination to be honest: what point was there in promising to do something that he knew he could not do properly? Carroll's faith was too strict to allow for half measures or falsehoods—even if only by omission. The resulting situation was one in which, in a sense, he "had it both ways"; through the half-open door of Holy Orders he could talk with a certain clerical authority, yet he never went far enough to jeopardize his freedom of action.

The Preacher

That freedom did not stop him from preaching, as we know. But it was only towards the end of his life that he did it. In Guildford, where his family lived, he preached at least once a year, from 1887 onwards, generally the last Sunday in December. At Christ Church he was for several years responsible for preaching to the college servants, and in 1896, we find him concerned over not having been asked to do so for two and a half years. In 1887, he was asked to give a sermon in a girls' school in Oxford. And during the last few years of his life, and in particular in 1896 and 1897, he actually dared to preach in St. Mary's, the "University Church" of Oxford, to a congregation mainly composed of undergraduates. Of this he writes:

> Dec. 6. Preached at St. Mary's at the evening service. One of our Chaplains . . . is curate in charge, and had asked for my help. It was indeed a privilege to be thankful for—but a formidable task. I had fancied there would be only a small audience, and the church was *full.* . . . The sermon lasted about eighteen minutes. March 7. There is now a system established of a course of six sermons at St. Mary's each year, for University men *only*, and specially meant for undergraduates. . . . This evening ended the

course for this term, and it was my great privilege to preach. It
has been the most formidable sermon I have ever had to preach:
and it is a *great* relief to have it over. . . . It lasted about three
quarters of an hour. (*Diaries*, pp. 531, 533)

He notes himself that his stammer was a handicap, but
that by a tremendous effort of will and concentration, he
managed to overcome it. As a consequence, he was even able
sometimes to agree (notably in 1895) to preach before a
totally different audience, during his vacation at Eastbourne.
The Vicar gave this description to Stuart Collingwood (pp.
328–29):

On Sunday our grand old church was crowded, and although our
villagers are mostly agricultural labourers, yet they breathlessly
listened to a sermon forty minutes long, and apparently took in
every word of it. It was quite extempore, in very simple words,
and illustrated by some delightful and most touching stories of
children. I only wish there had been a shorthand-writer there.

And he himself gives this description of a sermon given
to an audience of children in 1897:

Last Sunday week I tried a novel experiment. For the first time
in my life I was asked to address *children*—it was an extremely
interesting task. I took no text, but merely told them a story (an
allegory I devised years ago,) with a *very* few words of explanation. It took about twenty minutes.[4]

I will conclude with the following extract from a newspaper article at the time of Carroll's death:

He knew exactly what he wished to say, and completely forgot
his audience in his anxiety to explain his point clearly. He
thought of the subject only, and the words came of themselves.
Looking straight in front of him he saw, as it were, his argument
mapped out in the form of a diagram, and he set to work to
prove it point by point, under its separate heads, and then
summed up the whole.[5]

What are we to make of all this? First, it was only
toward the very end of his life that he was prepared to strug-

[4] *Diaries*, p. 538.
[5] Collingwood, p. 76.

gle against the natural handicap that he had given as one of his chief reasons for refusing to take priest's Orders: this seems to show that he was perfectly sincere at the time, and that once he had overcome his fear of making himself ridiculous, there was nothing to stop his endeavouring to carry out the functions he had always wished to fulfil.

Second, preaching was never a thing he enjoyed—except perhaps to the audience of children—but once having agreed to do it, he devoted himself to the work with absolute seriousness and conviction. People listened to him (though this may have been only because they knew he was Lewis Carroll). This partial ministry was therefore yet one more of the things he could do well, but since he only fulfilled it for ten years or so, it never became his life's work. In short, the priestly calling, which he only partly accepted, represented at once an ideal he felt to be inaccessible, and a conscientiously performed, though brief, duty.

It is also perhaps worth pointing out that a Church that does not demand, or even encourage, celibacy in its priests is all too likely to produce priestly dynasties. This was the case in England, at least up until the nineteenth century; a clergyman's sons would look upon Holy Orders in the same spirit —neither of ardent longing, nor of keen distaste—as the sons of soldiers or teachers who wanted "to be like Papa." To use the term *vocation* is as misleading in those circumstances, as in the case of the younger sons of the French nobility in the *Ancien Régime* who became priests in order to receive wealthy bishoprics.

In Dodgson's case, it seems fairly clear that this sort of family conditioning worked not so much to force him into the Church as to make the clerical state seem the most normal one to choose. On the other hand, it is quite clear that there was no pressure on him from home. But he wanted to remain faithful to that "non-choice," and it is this that explains his increased commitment toward the end of his life.

Profession: Teaching

Carroll's relationship to teaching poses the same questions, and produces very much the same answers, as his relationship to Holy Orders. Why did he choose it in the first place? And why did he then give it up halfway? But it does also throw light on one important point: Dodgson's attitude to boys.

The Initial Choice

We have no information as to the precise circumstances that drew young Charles to university teaching. Possibly the letter sent to his father in 1845 by his first headmaster at Richmond, served as a pointer to Archdeacon Dodgson, indicating that a university career—and with it, the clerical state —would be the natural one for Charles, like his other sons, to adopt. What Mr. Tate wrote was this:

> He has passed an excellent examination just now in mathematics, exhibiting at times an illustration of that love of precise argument, which seems to him natural. . . . You may fairly anticipate for him a bright career.[1]

And by the time he left Rugby, he was considered outstandingly capable in three directions: mathematics, classical humanities, and divinity (this last was what we should call religious instruction, rather than theology proper).

[1] Collingwood, p. 25.

Though there was nothing at Oxford to suggest any particular predisposition to teaching on his part, everything led inexorably to it. The subjects in which he had shone at Rugby made it possible for him to be a success at the university, though the stress came more and more to be on mathematics. At the end of his first year he won a Boulter Scholarship, and this was followed at the end of 1852 by his being nominated a Student (a full member of the college—equivalent to a Fellow in other Oxford colleges), with some responsibility for teaching, but precisely *what* was not defined.

His career was thus laid out for him, and Roger Green has no hesitation in saying: "In short, Charles Dodgson worked hard and conscientiously at Oxford, with an academic career as his goal."[2] The only explicit mention he makes of any intention to "teach" relates to his very short attempt at *school* teaching in 1855–56. His diary describes it for us (p. 55):

> July 5. I went to the Boys' School in the morning to hear my Father teach, as I want to begin trying myself soon. . . .
> July 8. I took the 1st and 2nd class of the Boys' School in the morning. . . . I liked my first attempt in teaching very much.
> July 9. Took the first class alone in the Old Testament.

All this took place at Croft, where his father was Rector, during the university vacation; Archdeacon Dodgson had also begun at Oxford, and moved on to take up parish work and religious instruction.

In January 1856, Carroll had his first experience in an Oxford school, teaching "sums." He was given a group of eight boys (they tried combining them with a group of seven girls, but after one attempt, that was given up). At first, he found the work pleasant; the boys seemed "tractable and in good order," and he had some stimulating ideas: he tried using a story to introduce the arithmetic he wanted them to do (the idea he later used in *A Tangled Tale*), and painting magic lantern slides to use like a marionette theatre. But his fourth visit was disappointing:

[2] *Diaries*, p. 33.

> The school class noisy and inattentive—the novelty of the thing is wearing off, and I find them rather unmanageable.

The following week (the sixth visit) is worse:

> School class again noisy and troublesome—I have not yet acquired the art of keeping order.

And on the ninth visit he considers giving it up:

> Class again noisy and inattentive—it is very disheartening, and I almost think I had better give up teaching there for the present.

Which he then does:

> Left word at the school that I shall not be able to come again for the present. I doubt if I shall try again next term: the good done does not seem worth the time and trouble. (pp. 75–78)

Though it may sound strange to modern ears, it is only this experience that Carroll ever calls "teaching." His university work is always called "lecturing," even the individual tutoring he did at Christ Church. But, as regards his feelings, it is all of a piece: in November of that same year, he writes of his work at Christ Church:

> I am weary of lecturing, and discouraged. . . . It is thankless, uphill work, goading unwilling men to learning they have no taste for, to the inevitable neglect of others who really want to get on. (p. 96)

This discouragement he felt in 1856 was to continue to haunt him. And when he decided to resign his Lectureship in 1881, he could only express the most formal regret at giving up that "thankless, uphill work":

> November 30. I find in my journal that I gave my first Euclid Lecture in the Lecture-room on Monday Jan: 28, 1856. It consisted of twelve men, of whom nine attended. This morning I have given what is probably my *last*: the lecture is now reduced to nine, of whom all attended on Monday: this morning being a Saint's Day, the attendance was voluntary, and only two appeared, E. H. Morris and G. Lavie. I was lecturer when the *father* of the latter took his degree, viz. in 1858. There is a sadness in coming to the *end* of anything in Life. Man's instinct clings to the Life that will never end. (p. 402)

Yet burdensome though he found it, he did, in fact, continue lecturing at Christ Church until 1881, whereas he never again tried school teaching. It would seem that other aspects of his character entered into this distinction: he certainly felt no love for little boys.

Dodgson the Lecturer

Collingwood tells us how the young Charles loved inventing things and organizing games for his brothers and sisters. His Lectureship may well have provided an opportunity for continuing to satisfy his fondness for stimulating others and suggesting leisure-time activities. Certainly his earliest experience at Oxford would tend to confirm this hypothesis. We have a letter he sent his family in 1853, shortly after being nominated Student:

> My one pupil has begun his work with me, and I will give you a description how the lecture is conducted. It is the most important point, you know, that the tutor should be *dignified* and at a distance from the pupil, and that the pupil should be as much as possible *degraded*.
>
> Otherwise, you know, they are not humble enough.
>
> So I sit at the further end of the room; outside the door (*which is shut*) sits the scout [college servants are called scouts in Oxford]: outside the outer door (*also shut*) sits the sub-scout: half-way downstairs sits the sub-sub-scout; and down in the yard sits the *pupil*.[3]

He then describes the dialogue that takes place in these conditions (rather like a game of "Pass it on") which enables him to produce some fine wordplay.

But, quite aside from his wish to entertain his correspondents, he was aware very keenly of the gulf, the very real distance of which his students were unhappily also fully conscious. One of them recalled in 1932:

> Very few, if any, of my contemporaries survive to confirm my impression of the singularly dry and perfunctory manner in

[3] *LCPB*, pp. 198–99.

which he imparted instruction to us, never betraying the slightest
personal interest in matters that were of deep concern to us.[4]

And one critic has collected even clearer evidence from
among his former pupils:

> I asked one of them if Carroll's lectures were bad. He said they
> were as dull as ditchwater. I asked another if he was a poor
> tutor. He said that he and others once signed a round robin to
> the head of the college, asking to be transferred to other hands.[5]

But Green quotes another witness to show that Carroll
was capable of giving very clear explanations of Euclid, with
the help of comparisons borrowed from his pupils' daily life:

> He took me last, and, glancing at a problem of Euclid which I
> had written out, he placed his finger on an omission. 'I deny
> your right to assert that'. I supplied what was wanting. 'Why
> did you not say so before? What is a corollary?' Silence. 'Do you
> ever play billiards?' 'Sometimes'. 'If you attempted a cannon,
> missed, and holed your own and the red ball, what would you
> call it?' 'A fluke'. 'Exactly. A corollary is a fluke in Euclid. Good
> morning'.[6]

It is not that he was indifferent to his students' working
conditions. Far from it. *Sylvie and Bruno* contains long passages in which he attacks the whole system of examinations
and competitions:

> Oh this Upas tree of Competitive Examinations! Beneath whose
> deadly shade all the original genius, all the exhaustive research,
> all the untiring life-long diligence by which our fore-fathers
> have so advanced human knowledge, must slowly but surely
> wither away, and give place to a system of Cookery, in which the
> human mind is a sausage, and all we ask is, how much indigesti-
> ble stuff can be crammed into it! . . .
>
> Of course, as the Examination was all in all, we tried to put
> in just what was wanted—and the *great* thing to aim at was, that
> the Candidate should know absolutely *nothing* beyond the needs
> of the Examination! I don't say it was ever *quite* achieved: but
> one of my own pupils . . . came very near it. After the Examina-

[4] F. B. Lennon, *Victoria Through the Looking-Glass*, p. 159.
[5] *Ibid.*, p. 274.
[6] *Diaries*, p. 67.

tion he mentioned to me the few facts which he knew but had *not* been able to bring in, and I can assure you they were trivial, Sir, absolutely trivial! . . .

As it was, we made our unfortunate pupil into a Leyden-jar, charged him up to the eyelids—then applied the knob of a Competitive Examination, and drew off one magnificent spark, which very often cracked the jar! What mattered *that*? We labeled it 'First Class Spark', and put it away on the shelf.[7]

On at least two occasions, in 1877 and 1882, he protested publicly against the anomalies of the results in Responsions (the first examinations at Oxford). Here are some extracts from his letter to the Vice-Chancellor, April 18, 1877:

It seems to me that the result of the examination of last Term was so anomalous that it ought to be brought before the notice of the University, and some means adopted to prevent its recurrence. . . . It is not, of course, to be expected that the same standard should be accurately maintained in different examinations, or even in the two sections into which the candidates in each examination are divided; and it will be seen that the percentage passed varied, during the years 1875 and 1876, from a *minimum* value of 54 to a *maximum* value of 69, the average being 61. But in the recent examination, while the percentage passed in one section reached the *maximum* value of 69, that in the other suddenly sank to 46, far below the *minimum* value. The anomaly is even more startling if we take the difference between the percentages passed in the two sections in any one examination, which averaged 5½ during the previous two years, but suddenly rose to 23 last Term.

No accidental circumstance can possibly account for so large a discrepancy: and the conclusion seems inevitable that the candidates in the first section were judged by far too high a standard, and that many failed in consequence who would have passed if they had happened to be in the other section. . . .[8]

There speaks the mathematician, perhaps even the hair-splitting statistician; but there speaks, too, a man who cared about his students.

[7] *Sylvie and Bruno Concluded*, Chap. XII.
[8] This letter, "Responsions, Hilary Term, 1877," was printed in Oxford, at the University Press.

The solution to this apparent contradiction must, I think, be this: Carroll's reaction to the problems of teaching, as to every other problem, was *first of all* that of an intellectual (usually a logician) who questions whether the system is coherent, efficient, and sound. From this point of view, his vision is amazingly clear, and no flaw escapes him. One has only to recall the astonishing rewards he promises to those who have mastered logical reasoning in the introduction to his *Symbolic Logic!*[9] Hence the analysis, the criticism, the sarcasm. But teaching is also a matter of human contacts, and in this sphere Carroll was totally different: he did not like boys, and his experience of teaching the pupils at St. Aldate's School was a failure; he felt no affinity with young men, and his university teaching was also a failure. But he did like girls, little and big; and it seems hardly possible that it was chance alone that led him to start teaching again later on (in 1886, for instance) in a girls' school in Oxford, and in one of the women's colleges, Lady Margaret Hall—logic, in this case. For here at last he could combine both aspects of teaching, and both elements of his own personality in the intelligent communication of knowledge, and in a relationship with the kind of human beings he liked best. But to have achieved such a perfect balance earlier on, he would have had to break through the constructions of the system, flout the traditions of his profession, and for once, act freely.

Once more, comparisons are revealing: he began preaching once it was quite clear that he was under no obligation to do so; and he only really taught after having given up working within the university system, and when no one was requiring him to do it. To him, both teaching and preaching were conceivable only in a context of absolute freedom.

[9] *Symbolic Logic*, New York, Dover, 1958, p. xvii.

Prudery

———◆———

Prudery is perhaps too strong a word, but by using it I want
to draw attention to one curious aspect of Carroll's personality. Though he always refused to "see evil" where it seemed to
him there could be none—as in photographs or drawings of
nude children—and though he adored the theatre, including
everything that went on backstage, Carroll seems to have
been excessively preoccupied with the moral dangers to which
children might be exposed. Ellen Terry records one significant incident. He had taken one of his little-girl friends to see
Faust (in which Terry was playing), and apparently when
Margaret began to undress, the child had said, "Where is it
going to stop?" On his reporting this to Ellen Terry, she must
have felt he was blaming her, for she replied tartly, "I thought
you only knew *nice* children."[1]

But, as we know, he was always highly sensitive regarding the theatre, and would even leave before the end of a
play when he thought it really objectionable. In 1889, we
read in his diary (p. 475):

> [*The Middleman*] is not a *healthy* play. Seduction is too plainly
> put into the plot; and the man's sin is too lightly treated. I am
> sorry that I took Kitty to see it.

The word "wholesome" often recurs in his summing-up of

[1] Hudson, p. 197.

evenings at the theatre, as does the phrase "unobjectionable."
One play, on the other hand (*Diaries*, p. 520) "is not a nice
one, being spoiled by the regular *French* element of making
love to another man's wife." In each of these cases, then, it is
sexual morality (whether of society or of the individual)
that causes the trouble. Carroll looked to the theatre to provide a positive education in that respect. Of one famous
singer, he wrote: "I am very glad to be able to think that his
influence, on public taste, is towards refinement and purity"
(p. 500). Anything that went in the other direction he condemned. He disapproved of transvestite parts, though only
when it involved a man's being dressed as a woman: Isa
Bowman tells[2] how one day "he walked out of the theatre
when the comedian . . . entered, dressed as a woman. . . . He
could not tolerate the idea of a man in petticoats."

Hence his wish (otherwise so out of character) to "mor-
alize" Shakespeare. This was a project dear to his heart, to
which he refers several times. Thus we read in his diary (p.
405), in April 1882:

> Began sending round printed request, to lady-friends, for lists of
> plays of Shakespeare suitable for girls.

In June of the same year, a short piece "to my lady readers" appeared in a magazine to which he contributed, and
Carroll later had it printed separately:[3]

> The Editor kindly allows me a little extra space to make a
> request to my lady readers. I am thinking of trying whether a
> selection of Shakespeare's plays can be produced, in which many
> of the beauties should be preserved, and yet the whole made so
> absolutely free from objectionable matter, whether in plot or in
> language, that any English mother might, without scruple, put it
> into the hands of her daughters from the age of 10 or 12 up to
> 16 or 18. Younger girls would not be likely to understand or
> appreciate the greatest of poets: and older ones may be safely
> left to read Shakespeare in any edition, unexpurgated or not,
> they may prefer: but it seems a pity that so many children should

[2] *Diaries*, p. 525.
[3] The text is in the Bodleian Library in Oxford; it is signed "Lewis
Carroll."

be debarred from a great enjoyment for want of an edition suitable to them. Neither Bowdler's, Chambers's, Brandram's, nor Cundell's 'Boudoir' Shakespeare seems to me to meet the want: they are not sufficiently expurgated to suit children.[4]

I hope to produce a cheap and handy volume, containing about 15 plays, and shall be much obliged to any lady who will send a list (founded on recollections of her own girlhood or on observation of her daughters' reading) of the plays she thinks suitable—when there are several girls in one family, if each would draw up an *independent* list, each list would have its own value as a separate piece of evidence. And a list arranged *in order of merit* would be even more useful: but this, I fear, would entail some trouble. Mistresses of girls' schools could give, probably, more information than any private individual as to which plays are most liked by girls.

It would seem that replies were few—perhaps the work proved too onerous—for in 1885, Carroll notes in his diary (p. 434), among various literary projects, "*Girls' Own Shakespeare*," adding "I have begun on *The Tempest*." By the time *Sylvie and Bruno* came out in 1889, the plan had gone no further, for he says in the preface (*loc. cit.*):

The resulting book might be slightly fragmentary: but it would be a real treasure to all British maidens who have any taste for poetry.

In any case, nothing more was done about it. Needless to say, it is no great loss. But this urge to "purify" is an interesting indication of the ambiguity of Carroll's position: as a writer, he would find it painful to mutilate Shakespeare, even though, as an educator, he would feel justified in doing so. Yet even here, the offhand way in which he dismisses all objections to older girls reading Shakespeare unexpurgated, shows that his concern was to protect the young rather than to enforce a rigid moral standard. Obviously, however, what he was protecting them against was anything that might—unpleasantly

[4] In the preface to *Sylvie and Bruno*, Carroll was to say of the edition so famous that it has given us the verb to "bowdlerize": "Bowdler's is the most extraordinary of all: looking through it, I am filled with a deep sense of wonder, considering what he has left in, that he should have cut *any-thing* out!"

or too soon—undermine the moral rigour he and his contemporaries believed to be necessary in the upbringing of children —of little girls, that is. It was not only that the Victorians always exaggerated and idealized the myth of feminine purity; but also, for Carroll personally, boys were essentially always bordering on the impure.

His "prudery" then, is simply one more way in which his personal problems found expression, as is plain from his attitude to transvestites: the central difficulty was the ambiguity of his feelings for little girls.

Pseudonym

———◆———

It was in 1856 that Dodgson, who had already published some poems in a small magazine, the *Comic Times,* and some in another review, *The Train,* was urged by the editor of the latter paper, Edmund Yates, to choose a pen name instead of using the initials "B.B."

He at first suggested "Dares," from Daresbury, the village where he was born, but Yates replied that it sounded "too much like a newspaper signature." Shortly afterward, we read:

> Feb. 11. Wrote to Mr. Yates sending him a choice of names: 1. *Edgar Cuthwellis* (made by transposition out of 'Charles Lutwidge'.) 2. *Edgar U.C. Westhill* (ditto). 3. *Louis Carroll* (derived from Lutwidge = Ludovic = Louis, and Charles [Carolus]. 4. *Lewis Carroll* (ditto). (*Diaries,* p. 77)

A few days later, as we know, Yates chose the last.

In the few days this exchange took—the first suggestion was on February 8—we witness Dodgson passing from the level of the subjective, the thing signified (I am tempted to call it the thematic level) to that of the abstract sign. "Dares" is in the realm of personal history; Lewis Carroll (and the other variants) is a play on the history of language, a play on letters, of the sort that was later to develop into *Doublets* and *Syzygies.*

From 1856 on, there was to be a division in Carroll's published works: the mathematical work, which developed out of his functions at Christ Church, was published under his real name; the work for another kind of reader—mainly the young—under his pen name. But there were exceptions within this schema.

a. A third alternative presented itself: anonymity. As early as 1857, Carroll sent a letter to the *Illustrated London News* entitled: "Where does the Day Begin?," which he signed, "A Mathematical Tutor, Oxford." The following year a piece appeared in Oxford on "The Fifth Book of Euclid," signed, "A College Tutor." Then, in total anonymity, he published the rules of a new game ("Rules for Court Circular," 1860) and an index for Tennyson's *In Memoriam* (1862). After that, anonymity was reserved for two types of publication: mathematical pieces expected to attract only a very narrow readership, and still more, writings dealing with internal Oxford affairs, in which he turned polemicist. Finally, at the very end of his life, Carroll once more resorted to anonymity for some short pieces on points of logic.

b. His letters to newspapers, of which he wrote quite a number (mainly to the *Pall Mall Gazette* and the *St. James's Gazette*) might be signed either Dodgson or Carroll, though there are slightly more signed by the former during the earliest days of Carroll's literary career.

c. Most significantly, Carroll soon discovered that his pen name carried infinitely more weight than the name of an obscure Oxford mathematician. Therefore, he used it whenever he was writing to support a cause about which he felt strongly, even though it had nothing to do with his nonsense writings: vivisection, for instance, from 1875 on, internal politics after 1881, and finally, after 1886, logic, too.

From very early on, Carroll refused to allow Dodgson to be confused with the author of *Alice* in Oxford, even though it was an open secret. The procession of children whom he took to have tea parties in his rooms in Christ Church could hardly have passed unnoticed; and the way in which he used to hand out endless inscribed copies of *Alice* on his train journeys to London must have meant that he was recognized from time to time.

This makes it all the more remarkable that he insisted on

keeping the two identities apart. Collingwood records two incidents:

> On [one] occasion, when he was dining out at Oxford, and some one, who did not know that it was a forbidden subject, turned the conversation on 'Alice in Wonderland', he rose suddenly and fled from the house. (pp. 272–73).

> On one occasion the secretary of a 'Young Ladies' Academy' in the United States asked him to present some of his works to the School Library. The envelope was addressed to 'Lewis Carroll, Christ Church', an incongruity which always annoyed him intensely. He replied to the Secretary, 'As Mr. Dodgson's books are all on Mathematical subjects, he fears that they would not be very acceptable in a school library'. (pp. 273–74)

As time went on, his attitude hardened, and he made his position official. In 1890 he asked the editor of the *St. James's Gazette* to publish nothing that would make it possible to identify Lewis Carroll and Charles L. Dodgson, "it being my earnest wish to remain, *personally*, in the obscurity of a private individual. In fact it is for that very purpose that I continue to use that 'nom de plume'."[1] The same year, he had a leaflet printed with the following short statement:

> Mr. Dodgson is so frequently addressed by strangers on the quite unauthorized assumption that he claims, or at any rate acknowledges the authorship of books not published under his name, that he has found it necessary to print this, once for all, as an answer to all such applications. He neither claims nor acknowledges any connection with any pseudonym, or with any book that is not published under his own name. Having therefore no claim to retain, or even to read the enclosed, he returns it for the convenience of the writer who has thus misaddressed it.[2]

And, on November 8, 1897 (he was to die the following January 14), he wrote in his diary:

> A letter came, addressed to 'L. Carroll, Christ Church, Oxford'. So many such now come, that I have decided to *refuse* them, and gave it, unopened, to Telling, to return to the Post Office. All such will now go back to the writers, through the Dead Letter Office, with endorsement 'not known'.

[1] *Diaries*, p. 481.
[2] "The Stranger Circular," *Handbook*, p. 155.

Religion

There is no mention of God in either of the *Alice* books. This may well have been intentional, as the following anecdote seems to suggest. Its author had occasion to meet Carroll several times, and made so bold as to question him:[1]

> Everybody remembers the triumphant conclusion of 'Alice in the Looking-Glass'. . . . All this, ever since my first perusal of the book, has reminded me of the closing scene of that favourite of my boyhood, "The Pilgrim's Progress". I mentioned this association of ideas to Dodgson; and I let him divine my curiosity to know whether the coincidence was undesigned. . . . With evident annoyance, he assured me that the thought of imitating Bunyan had never occurred to him; such trespassing on sacred ground would have seemed to him highly irreverent; and sooner than be guilty of that irreverence, he would have re-written this portion of the book.

We learn two things from this anecdote: first, that there is no justification for any, even indirect, "Christian" interpretation of Alice's adventures; second, and I shall be returning to this, that Carroll had an extraordinary sensitivity about all things religious. In any case, at least at that stage, the kind of nonsense represented by those first works seemed to him wholly incompatible with serious religious thinking, let alone edification. This was not always to be the case. In

[1] Lionel A. Tollemache, "Reminiscences of Lewis Carroll," *Literature*, February 5, 1898. See also "Priest or Layman?"

1876, when *The Hunting of the Snark* first appeared, Carroll had a leaflet inserted into it, which he later published separately: "An Easter Greeting to Every Child Who Loves *Alice*." On sending it to Macmillan's, he noted in his diary (p. 350):

> I am afraid the religious allusions will be thought 'out of season' by many, but I do not like to lose the opportunity of saying a few serious words to (perhaps) 20,000 children.

Indeed, earlier, in 1871, he had taken the opportunity of a reprint of *Alice* to insert a Christmas letter "To all Child-readers of *Alice's Adventures in Wonderland*," beginning in much the same vein:

> Dear children,
>   At Christmas time a few grave words are not quite out of place, I hope, even at the end of a book of nonsense.[2]

But the Easter greeting, considerably longer (two pages), is also more interesting, for it presents, and tries to resolve, a problem that evidently gave Carroll some concern—the split between his literary work and the religious message he wanted to give. The whole thing is written on a defensive note, as one might expect from the reference to it in the diary:[3]

> Are these strange words from a writer of such tales as 'Alice'? And is this a strange letter to find in a book of nonsense? It may be so. Some perhaps may blame me for thus mixing together things grave and gay; others may smile and think it odd that any one should speak of solemn things at all except in church and on a Sunday. . . . I do not believe God means us thus to divide life into two halves—to wear a grave face on Sunday, and to think it out-of-place to even so much as mention Him on a weekday.

At the time he wrote *Alice*, and even before, Carroll might well have found himself guilty of having two faces—grave for Sunday and gay for the rest of the week. For though his diary always bears traces of piety at the end of every year—on December 31, 1863, for instance, he says,

[2] E. M. Hatch, *Letters to Child-Friends*, p. 246.
[3] *Works*, edited by Green, pp. 226–27.

"How much of neglect, carelessness and sin have I to remember!" (p. 208)—it was not until 1871 and the Christmas letter that he first used literature as a means of expressing his religious convictions.

But here again there are subtle distinctions to be made. Until *Sylvie and Bruno*—and though he would have denied the fact hotly—Carroll proved unable to do more than *juxtapose* the religious and the secular (or frivolous). The two pieces I have just mentioned, as well as the letters to newspapers in which he used his pseudonym in the service of edifying causes, stood alongside his nonsense work without ever influencing its character. But he seems gradually to have become aware that, if he were to practice what he preached, the name and the prestige of the author of *Alice* must be used not merely in support of the occasional pious bromide, but to serve some rather loftier purpose. Hence the project he entertained for so long—indeed, so long that he never actually achieved it—of a book of selected Bible passages for old people "printed in large *readable* type—such passages as would do to say over to oneself in sleepless nights, etc."[4] In the same year as this entry, 1889, he spoke in the preface of *Sylvie and Bruno* of another project: a child's Bible, with "carefully selected passages, suitable for a child's reading, and pictures." Neither plan came to anything, and indeed Carroll may have foreseen that they would not even as he spoke of them to his readers; this would explain why he used the *Sylvie and Bruno* books to make his literary talent serve his religious convictions in the way they do.

The form he gave this work made it easier to introduce a religious element without its seeming incongruous: one of the two plots unfolds entirely in "this world," among upper-class English people, Victorians, in fact, for whom it is quite natural to discuss problems of faith and morality. Nevertheless, in the same breath as he announces in the preface his intention to introduce "along with what will, I hope, prove to be acceptable nonsense for children, some of the graver thoughts of human life," he repeats the very error he condemns of fail-

[4] *Diaries*, p. 468.

ing to integrate the religious element into the nonsense. The novel itself, however, by its very construction, enables him to go further along the road he wishes to take. For alongside the lengthy conversations of Arthur, Muriel, Eric, and the Earl —which range over such matters as theism and Christianity, respect for the Sabbath, Old Testament reading, the idea of fate, the value of prayer, hell, the quality of sermons, a respect for sacred things—Carroll gives us glimpses, in the adventures of Sylvie and Bruno, of a Christian, or Christian-ized, world. Thus, in Chapter IV, Uggug is unequivocally condemned for his cruel behaviour in pouring a jug of water over an old beggar who begs for a crust of bread; that the beggar turns out to be, in fact, the father of Sylvie and Bruno is important to the plot, of course, but this particular episode is a more broadly moral one. In the following scene, which takes place in the real world, we find Lady Muriel being kind to the same old man on the station platform, and in the one after that, Sylvie and Bruno are giving him cake. In a sense, the whole of the fairy plot is woven around the theme of charity—"love," in Carroll's terms—as is clear from the locket Sylvie is given by her father, on which the words "Sylvie will love all" naturally—or perhaps one should say, "Christianly"—turn into "All will love Sylvie." Is it possible to say, without stretching a point, that *Sylvie and Bruno* is a religious novel? Even apart from the ambiguity of such a description, I think it doubtful: charity is not the same thing as faith, and the sense of duty that leads Arthur to devote himself to the sick during an epidemic would hardly have been enough to convert Eric Lindon. Of course, there are the discussions, some learned, some impassioned, upon so many of the matters of conscience that racked the Victorian age: but it is clear that these are in the nature of condiments—in gen-erous dollops, perhaps!—rather than the main course of the novel. One has only to compare *Sylvie and Bruno* with any of the novels of George Eliot (who did not consider herself a Christian at all) to see how pervasive was the religious sense of the time. Carroll succeeded no more here than he did in any of his other literary works in combining the separate pieces: faith and nonsense were always to remain distinct.

Carroll's Religion

As we saw in relation to ordination, it was not problems of faith that stood in the way of Carroll's becoming a priest. His religious doubts, if he had any—and he probably did in that turbulent period of Christianity—were not such as to make him reject his convictions and his commitment, either explicitly or implicitly. I do not think one can argue anything from what he says in the introduction to Part II of *Curiosa Mathematica*[5] about the troubled insomniacs for whom that collection of mathematical problems is intended, referring, among others, to "sceptical thoughts, which seem for the moment to uproot the firmest faith." As Roger Green sensibly points out,[6] "any Christian reader, going to bed in that overtired condition which stings the mind into morbid over-activity, must have experienced them also." Similarly, the self-reproaches which crop up in his New Year resolutions are only in the most general tradition of Christian spirituality, and have nothing of the confessional about them. In short, there seems no external evidence for doubting Carroll's faith; and it is sheer waste of time to lament his not having had the burning intensity of a Newman or a Charles Kingsley.

Yet he himself sought to make his faith just as militant. That is the only possible explanation for the various endeavours we have been discussing; nor are these the only indications. Carroll left at least one relevant text, a "Draft for a Letter to an Agnostic"[7]—interesting not so much for the originality of its argument, as for its dense, logical rigour. We find this same characteristic in another piece, this time on the subject of eternal punishment (a phrase that involved the notion of some form of hell). It was a favorite theme of Carroll's; Collingwood tells us that he made it the subject of one of the very few sermons he preached in the Oxford university church. Toward the end of his life, he wrote the text in ques-

[5] *Pillow Problems*, New York, Dover, 1958, introduction, pp. xiv–xv.

[6] *Diaries*, p. 151.

[7] *Diaries*, pp. 569–71.

tion,[8] intending it, Collingwood tells us, to be the first of a series of essays on the difficulties of faith. Collingwood firmly assures us (p. 77), "It is hardly necessary to say that he himself did not believe in eternal punishment, or any other scholastic doctrine that contravenes the love of God." But, apart from the subject matter, what is most striking here again is the clarity of the reasoning. He says: "In conclusion, I will put together in one view the various modes of escape, from the original difficulty, which may be adopted without violating the inexorable laws of logical reasoning." Collingwood summed up his uncle's fundamental position very well by that stress on the supremacy of the love of God: God in his infinite goodness could not wish to punish even the most hardened sinner forever. Yet that conviction—whose consequences in human terms are expressed in the "fairy duet" about love whose theme runs right through the *Sylvie and Bruno* books—accords ill with the "inexorable laws of logical reasoning"; for the position Carroll explicitly made his own (the only one he did not see as fraught with dangerous consequences) is the following:

> I believe that God is perfectly good. Also I believe that such infliction of [eternal] punishment would be wrong. Consequently I believe that God is not capable of acting thus. I find that the Bible, in the English Version, seems to tell us that He *is* capable of acting thus. Yet I believe that it is a book inspired by God, and protected by Him from error in what it tells us of the relations between God and Man, and therefore that what it says, according to the real meaning of the words, may be relied on as true. Consequently I hold that the word, rendered in English as 'eternal' or 'everlasting', has been mistranslated, and that the Bible does not really assert more than that God will inflict suffering, of unknown duration but *not* necessarily eternal, punishment for sin.[9]

This unlimited trust in God's goodness undoubtedly accounts for Carroll's own immense tolerance (though tolerance is, of course, also a well-known feature of the Anglican

[8] "Eternal Punishment," *LCPB,* pp. 345–55.
[9] *Ibid.,* p. 355.

Church, with its ability to embrace almost every variety of religious and theological position). When one of his former child-friends wrote to tell Carroll of her conversion to Catholicism, he replied in a letter in 1890:[10] "More and more I am becoming content to know that Christians have *many* ways of looking at their religion, and less confident that my views must be right and all others wrong." Similarly, Lady Muriel and the Narrator can console themselves for Eric Lindon's agnosticism: "I feel sure, now, that the most absolute Atheist *may* be leading, though walking blindfold, a pure and noble life."[11] He was always offended by intolerance, even in the theatre, as we know from a letter to Ellen Terry[12] in which he discusses with abhorrence the duty laid upon Shylock at the end of *The Merchant of Venice* to become a Christian:

> It is a sentiment that is entirely horrible and revolting to the feelings of all who believe in the Gospel of Love. . . . To all Christians now (except perhaps extreme Calvinists) the idea of forcing a man to abjure his religion, whatever that religion may be, is (as I have said) simply horrible.

As the letter goes on, he tries to show that it is not only his faith that prompts this view, but also his artistic sense, since the condemnation turns Shylock suddenly into a religious victim. But that is really begging the question, for he only becomes a "victim" because Carroll sees enforced conversion as so appalling.

The law of love is also at issue in one of the demands made by Arthur in *Sylvie and Bruno*: that children be permitted to play on Sundays. Carroll touches on this in the preface, and in Chapter XXIV he uses a child's letter read by Lady Muriel to describe the oppressive dreariness of the English Sunday in families that observed the Sabbath strictly. But though we may attribute Carroll's protests against this to his fondness for children—"Why make the day irksome to their restless natures?" asks Arthur—they also represent a more

[10] Roger Lancelyn Green, *Lewis Carroll, A Monograph*, London, 1960, p. 15.
[11] *Sylvie and Bruno Concluded*, Chap. II.
[12] Collingwood, pp. 182–84.

general desire to make the law flexible; for Arthur also says: "I hold that Christians are freed from the *literal* observance of the Fourth Commandment." Was this, like his fondness for the theatre, simply the protest of a man jealous of his own freedom? It was that, certainly, but it was also a refusal to see human freedom in general constrained by a mechanistic law. All the more surprising, then, to find Carroll's religion marked by another dominant feature which is the very opposite: a positively fetishist reverence for sacred things, and mainly in relation to the spoken word. In the preface to *Sylvie and Bruno Concluded*, he puts it thus:

> There is, I fear, at the present time, an increasing tendency to irreverent treatment of the name of God and of subjects connected with religion. Some of our theatres are helping this downward movement by the gross caricatures of clergymen which they put upon the stage.

There are at least two other pieces of written evidence of this preoccupation of his. One is a letter written in 1894 to Mrs. Ben Greet, manager of a London theatre, after seeing a play there that had scandalized him.[13] He begins by pointing out that he writes, not knowing whether she herself is a Christian or not, but representing the view of most of the audience; he goes on to say:

> In any case, you will admit that the large majority of your audience believe in a life after death, in the immortality of the soul, & in a judgment to come, and recognise (in their better moments) the infinite seriousness & importance of such subjects, & that they are not things to be played with and treated as themes for laughter.
>
> Then, most certainly, a large number of your audience believe that He, who died for our sins, left us the Sacrament of Baptism: & that this also, is no fit subject for jesting on.
>
> To all in the audience, to whom these subjects are real and solemn, the passages in your play, which treat them as material for comedy, can give nothing but real *pain*: to *me*, I can assure you, it gave *great* pain to hear such flippant talk, about baptism & the soul, put into the mouths of those two dear children [Isa Bowman and a friend of hers].

[13] *Diaries*, pp. 562–65. See also "Prudery."

And he concludes:

> If you could see your way to striking out . . . all jesting allusions
> to baptism, & to the soul, you would, I am sure, relieve the feel-
> ings of very many, to whom your play must cause pain. . . .

The letter is signed "Lewis Carroll."

Earlier, in 1888, in an article published in *The Theatre*,[14] he had set out his views on this subject. And between
1888 and 1894, no fewer than *three* solemn pronouncements,
all signed "Lewis Carroll" appeared to reaffirm this profound
preoccupation. This is a little surprising. Obviously, the third
commandment—"Thou shalt not take the name of the Lord
thy God in vain; for the Lord will not hold him guiltless
who takes his name in vain"—which appears in full in the
Anglican catechism, is a law binding upon all Christians. But
it seems curious that a man who could find good reason to
take liberties with the fourth commandment could not do the
same for the third! Curious, too, that the same article could
contain the passage quoted elsewhere on the great relativity
of language ("a word means what the speaker intends by it,
and what the hearer understands by it, and that is all") and
then go on to argue that, as a logical conclusion, all the words
used in the language of piety must be restricted to that language alone.

There seem to me to be two possible explanations. The
first follows from Carroll's attitude to language: while continually stressing the difference between the meaning
intended and the meaning understood, and showing how
words are empty forms that one can play about with and not
worry about the "sense" one may arrive at, he also makes the
word the basic unit around which the whole universe of significance comes into being. Words, which he does his best to
destroy (with puns, plays on words, word games, etc.), also
take on a certain almost magical value as objects of supreme
enjoyment. Hence, to use certain words "wrongly" is to
endanger that enjoyment, unless it be an intentional and conscious wordplay on the part of the speaker. The second
explanation is related to the first in that it, too, represents a

[14] The Stage and the Spirit of Reverence," *LCPB*, pp. 175–95.

certain emotional block: it was not accidental that Carroll, in practice, when criticizing the irreverence of the age, placed sexual immorality on a par with mockery of the sacred. Puritanism (in the wider sense of the word) is a single whole, and to flirt with any form of profane frivolity is to open the door to every one. Ridiculing a clergyman, condoning adultery, jesting with the name of God or the damnation of the soul, are all ways of failing to take God's law seriously, of lightly accepting the transgression of the divine command. Sunday observance was not the same kind of immediate issue, since the rule was originally made for the Jewish Sabbath and applied less rigidly to the Christian Lord's Day. Though even here he was stricter with himself. He wrote to the artist Gertrude Thomson:

> Would you kindly do *no* sketches, or photos, for *me*, on a Sunday? It is, in *my* view (of *course* I don't condemn any one who differs from me) inconsistent with keeping the day holy. I do *not* hold it to be the Jewish 'Sabbath', but I *do* hold it to be 'the Lord's Day', and so to be made very distinct from the other days.[15]

The door must be shut fast against temptations of all sorts, and one of the best fastenings was the Ten Commandments; for the Anglican and the logician, they had the particular advantage of being clearly stated, in words to which one could easily refer, so that any transgression could at once be recognized for what it was. Words were an absolute barrier, for they were the very foundation of logical reality. Carroll's belief was such, harkening back perhaps to the Jewish sense of the name of God being ineffable, as to make it intolerable to profane the name of divine things, which would at the same time be profaning the laws of language.

Compared with these two basic—and in practice contradictory—features of Carroll's religion, other elements pale into insignificance. Most striking, however, is the almost total absence of any reference to the great religious controversies of the Victorian age. We read, of course, in Collingwood, that Carroll was a resolute conservative in this sphere, as in so

[15] Collingwood, p. 317.

many others; but that tells us little of the polemics raging around Benjamin Jowett at the time, of the repercussions of Kingsley's "social Christianity," and indeed of the impassioned religious climate that prevailed throughout the century. The *Sylvie and Bruno* books, of course, contain some comments on church services[16] in which Carroll tries to find a *via media* between ritualism and the austerity of Calvinism—but that is about the sum total of what he wrote about the religious issues of the nineteenth century. He did, however, witness with regret the decline in religious practice in Oxford: on June 19, 1894, he notes in his diary (p. 512): "Morning chapel had a congregation of *four*; the Dean, myself, and two under-graduates!" And, a year and a half later (p. 521): "A quite unique experience in my life of more than forty years in Christ Church. I went to morning chapel, and was *the only person there!*" It was in these last years of his life, too, that he adopted the custom of preaching. But that was a matter of personal behaviour, and though it contained an element of "testifying," it was the testimony of a man, and not of the apologist he must have hoped to be when he wrote to a fellow cleric in 1892:

> In 'Sylvie and Bruno' I took courage to introduce what I had entirely avoided in the two 'Alice' books—some reference to subjects which are, after all, the *only* subjects of real interest in life, subjects which are so intimately bound up with every topic of human interest that it needs more effort to avoid them than to touch on them.[17]

Do we detect a certain loss of impetus? A delayed, but grateful, recognition that, for all his anxieties and scruples, this was not his calling? It is certainly true that though his practice of religion became more devout in the latter years of his life, religious problems appeared more and more extraneous to his literary work. And, despite the statement I have just quoted, it was that literary work which remained the central reality in his life. It is certainly an enigma. It seems to

[16] *Sylvie and Bruno*, Chap. XIX; and the preface to *Sylvie and Bruno Concluded*.
[17] Collingwood, pp. 308–9.

me, quite simply, that Carroll's faith was not so much tepid as perfectly straightforward; having missed the cataclysm of the "Oxford movement" (he came to the university several years after Newman's conversion to Rome), and coming from a family where there was never any great discussion of religious problems, his life was, in that respect, untroubled. He preserved his certainties *and* his uncertainties (as to the existence of hell, for instance) as a middle-of-the-road Christian, an honest but never a fervid Anglican. Though there was a time when he believed that a man in his circumstances had a duty to use his *nom de plume* in the service of religion, he discovered fairly rapidly that his capacities were suited to nothing more ambitious than the Sunday sermon. And his sensitivity to irreverence may well have amounted to no more than the last gasp of his effort to establish a coherent link between his faith and his work in the field of logic: a fruitless effort that might well have endangered that faith, and whose only result (not really surprisingly) was to produce one more contradiction between reality and dream, between the material order and the intellectual.

Rugby

———◆———

Carroll was fourteen years old when, after two years at school at Richmond, where he seems both to have been happy and to have impressed his teachers favourably, he was sent by his father to Rugby. The famous Dr. Arnold who had reformed the school had died four years earlier, but his mark was left on everything. It was especially noticeable in the importance attributed to sport and physical exercise in education—necessary, in Arnold's view, as a balance to the intensity of intellectual work. It seems, though, that Carroll was not a games enthusiast; that in itself was a disadvantage.

Furthermore, though he had done well at Richmond, Carroll had had problems with Latin and Greek; when he left the school, the headmaster wrote to Archdeacon Dodgson:

> He is, moreover, remarkably ingenious in replacing the ordinary inflexions of nouns and verbs, as detailed in our grammars, by more exact analogies, or convenient forms of his own devising.[1]

Hence the many impositions he was now given in classics, of which he was later to write:

> I spent an incalculable time in writing out impositions—this last I consider one of the chief faults of Rugby School.[2]

It was a different aspect of his time there, however, that

[1] Collingwood, p. 25.
[2] *Ibid.*, p. 30.

was to leave the most permanent memory. In 1857 Carroll went with some friends to see another public school and wrote in his diary (p. 107):

> I was particularly struck by the healthy happy look of the boys and their gentlemanly appearance. The dormitory is the most unique feature of the whole: in two large rooms, by a very tri-fling expense in woodwork, every boy has a snug little bedroom secured to himself, where he is free from interruption and annoyance. This to little boys must be a very great addition to their happiness, as being a kind of counterbalance to any bully-ing they may suffer during the day. From my own experience of school life at Rugby I can say that if I could have been thus secure from annoyance at night, the hardships of the daily life would have been comparative trifles to bear.

We have no details (either from Carroll himself, his fellow scholars, or the school) about the years he spent at Rugby. We can only conjecture, therefore. But we must set them against the background of the very strong comments Carroll made about that period in his life:

> I cannot say that I look back upon my life at a Public School with any sensations of pleasure, or that any earthly considera-tions would induce me to go through my three years again.[3]

There are other indications to corroborate this painful recollection, in particular the total failure of his own experi-ment in teaching at a boys' school; and the whole thing must be set in the context of his fundamental dislike of boys. I think we can say that the most likely conjecture is that this period of early puberty, always a difficult time and especially so for a sensitive boy from a background in which moral rules were immensely important, was made even more painful by the peculiar methods in use at Rugby and the Spartan educa-tion introduced there by Arnold; this time, therefore, for Charles, represented a most painful apprenticeship to a com-munity whose overriding aim was virility (with all the osten-tation and at times hypocrisy that that word suggests) but whose cumulative effect was more like brutality. It is hardly

[3] *Ibid.*, p. 30.

surprising that he suffered more than most people (from
bullying in all its forms, an experience for which he was
totally unprepared, and also perhaps from anti-intellec-
tualism). That the resulting block was largely a sexual one
there can be no doubt; but that is about all one can say.

Russia

In 1867, never having up to then travelled further than Scotland, Carroll decided to spend the summer abroad with a colleague of his own age, Henry Liddon:

> Received my passport from London. During the last few days Liddon has informed me that he can go abroad with me, and we have decided on Moscow. Ambitious for one who has never yet left England. (*Diaries*, p. 261)

The trip took just two months, from July 12 to September 13. Aware that this was a most unusual kind of holiday, Carroll decided to keep his diary for those two months in a separate book—with the result that the family afterward sold it separately to a collector; in 1898, Collingwood wrote (pp. 111–12):

> In later years it did occur to him that others might be interested in his impressions and experiences, though he never actually took any steps towards putting them before the public.

And immediately goes on:

> Perhaps he was wise, for a traveller's diary always contains much information that can be obtained just as well from any guide-book.

On reading the forty-odd pages in question, one does certainly get this feeling: there is a straightforward description of every stopping place—Dover, Brussels, Cologne, Berlin,

Danzig, Königsberg, St. Petersburg, Moscow, Warsaw, Bres-
lau, Dresden, Ems, and Paris—with some stress on the pictur-
esque elements of each, but nothing very outstanding. In the
main his interest lay in visiting churches, museums, and mon-
asteries—as one might expect from a man with a strong religious sense who also loved painting. Similarly, it was completely in character for Carroll to go to the theatre whenever
possible (though Liddon, a more austere man, only went with
him once, to see *Mignon* at the Opéra Comique in Paris); in
Moscow, Carroll saw *Aladdin and His Wonderful Lamp*.

Derek Hudson says that this trip may have been under-
taken less purely for pleasure on Liddon's part, being something of a goodwill mission to the Patriarch of Moscow. His
aim was both to strengthen the contacts between the Anglican and Orthodox Churches, and to help undo the bitterness
of the Crimean War. Hudson records (p. 165) that

> Liddon reported the interview [with the Patriarch] to Bishop
> Wilberforce and to Bishop Hamilton of Salisbury, urging them
> to write letters congratulating Philaret on the fiftieth anniversary
> of his consecration as bishop. Altogether, the two envoys from
> Oxford played a useful part in improving Anglo-Russian rela-
> tions, though in this respect Liddon was the main agent. Dodg-
> son remained the conventional tourist.

But we do find some surprising reactions from this particular tourist. First of all, his emotion at seeing Cologne
cathedral: we read in his Russian journal:[1]

> It was the most beautiful of all churches I have ever seen, or can
> imagine. If one could imagine the spirit of devotion embodied
> in any material form, it would be in such a building.

Indeed, we have this from Liddon:

> I found him leaning against the rails of the Choir, and sobbing
> like a child. When the verger came to show us over the chapels,
> he got out of the way. He said that he could not bear the harsh
> voice of the man in the presence of so much beauty.[2]

---

[1] This and subsequent quotations from the journal are taken from the
Works, edited by Green.

[2] F. B. Lennon, *Victoria Through the Looking-Glass*, p. 146.

There is a descriptive sense we should not have expected from our reading of *Alice*. Here, for instance, are some comments on the Belgian countryside:

> The chief feature I remarked in the scenery was the way the trees were planted, in straight lines miles in length: as they generally all leaned one way, they seemed to me like long files of wearied soldiers marching hither and thither across the plains: some were drawn up in square, some standing at 'Attention!', but most of them were plodding hopelessly on, bending as they went, as if under the weight of ghostly knapsacks.

Or this very intense description of a picture in the Hermitage Museum:

> Perhaps the most striking of all the Russian pictures is a sea-piece, recently bought and not yet numbered: it represents a storm, the mast of a foundered ship, with a few survivors clinging to it, floats in front—behind, the waves are beaten up into mountains, & their crests shivered into driving showers of spray, by the fury of the wind—while the low sunlight shines through the higher waves with a pale green lustre that is perfectly deceptive in the way in which it seems to come *through* the water. I have seen the thing attempted in other pictures, but never so perfectly achieved.

Nor is there any lack of what we think of as Carrollian humour: in Danzig, we read:

> on our way to the station, we came across the grandest instance of the 'Majesty of Justice' that I have ever witnessed—A little boy was being taken to the magistrate, or to prison (probably for picking a pocket). The achievement of this feat had been entrusted to two soldiers in full uniform, who were solemnly marching, one in front of the poor little creature, and one behind; with bayonets fixed, of course, to be ready to charge in case he should attempt an escape.

And in Berlin:

> In fact the two principles of Berlin architecture appear to me to be these—'On the housetops, whenever there is a convenient place, put up the figure of a man; he is best placed standing on one leg. Whenever there is a room on the ground, put either a

circular group of busts on pedestals, in consultation, all looking
inwards—or else the colossal figure of a man killing, about to
kill, or having killed (the present tense is preferred) a beast; the
more prickles the beast has, the better—in fact a dragon is the
correct thing, but if that is beyond the artist, he may content
himself with a lion or a pig'.

Or, again:

The 2 things most sold in Königsberg *ought* to be (as they
occupy about half the shops) gloves & fireworks. Nevertheless, I
have met many gentlemen walking about without gloves: perhaps they are only used to guard the hands when letting off fireworks.

His comments about the people are less entertaining,
suggesting something of the "Cook's tours" becoming popular at the time. Here, for instance, he describes the journey
into Prussia:

It was pleasant to see the country growing more & more inhab-
ited & cultivated as we got further into Prussia—the fierce,
coarse-looking Russian soldier replaced by the more gentle &
intelligent Prussian—the very peasants seemed to be of a higher
order, more individuality & independence: the Russian peasant,
with his gentle, fine, often noble-looking face, always suggests to
me a submissive animal, long used to bearing in silence harsh-
ness & injustice, rather than a man able & ready to defend himself.

By then the journey was nearing its end, and the last
lines of the journal are by no means surprising:

We had a beautifully smooth passage, & a clear moonlight night
to enjoy it in—the moon shining out with all its splendour, as if
to make up for the time lost during the eclipse it had suffered
four hours earlier—I remained in the bow most of the time of
our passage, sometimes chatting with the sailor on the lookout,
& sometimes watching, through the last hour of my first foreign
tour, the lights of Dover, as they slowly broadened on the horizon, as if the old land were opening its arms to receive its home-
ward bound children—till they finally stood out clear and bold
as the two lighthouses on the cliff—till that which had long been
merely a glimmering line on the dark water, like a reflection of

the Milky Way, took form & substance as the lights of the shore-ward houses—till the faint white line behind them, that looked at first like a mist creeping along the horizon was visible at last in the grey twilight as the white cliffs of old England.

He never travelled abroad again, nor did he ever again write about his journey to Russia.

Sexuality

———◆———

If we try to assemble the partial conclusions, or rather the hypotheses, suggested by the various aspects of Carroll's sexuality, they seem to form a pattern of which the outline, or frame, is best represented by characters in his fiction. There are four cardinal points at the centre: Alice, Bruno, Sylvie, and Uggug. Distinct from these four, and yet connected, are the White Knight in *Through the Looking-Glass*, and Lady Muriel in *Sylvie and Bruno*.[1] I will try to explain this, though of course I am using the names of these characters only insofar as their "adventures" or their "personalities" express dimensions of Carroll's sexuality.

The Characters

Alice is, above all, determination and aggression; there is no gentle, passive femininity about her. She knows where she wants to go, and it is none of her doing that she is not getting there quicker. Whenever she has to deal with gentle characters, whether masculine or feminine, she at once takes the initiative and rapidly assumes command of the situation: we see this with the White Rabbit, the White Queen (when

[1] It is not really surprising that most of these characters are from *Sylvie and Bruno*, since that was the last work of fiction Carroll wrote.

she is on her own), and the White Knight. Whatever concessions she may make to "good manners," she always "answers
back." In this she is a strong feminine figure, similar to the
Queen of Hearts or the Red Queen; and when dealing with
masculine figures older than herself, she becomes more like a
praying mantis or a castrating mother.

    This becomes even more evident when one compares her
with Sylvie. Alice is seven and a half in *Through the Looking-
Glass,* Sylvie is about ten. Sylvie is protective, but only towards her little brother; with other people, she tends to be in a
strange position: she is not exactly ignored, but remains on the
sidelines. Conversation generally takes place with Bruno, and she
contributes only an occasional significant, but elliptical, "Oh
Bruno!" Only Lady Muriel takes an active interest in her, and
she herself is interested in no one but her brother; Uggug
makes her the victim of his first "joke" not because he considers her dangerous, but because she represents a world so
different from his. She never loses her temper, she blushes
easily, is "sweet" and "lovely," and is somehow separate—not
exactly inaccessible, but not really inviting contact either.
The fact that she is interchangeable with Lady Muriel, being
her fairy- and child-double, throws further light on these
traits: she is the virginal, and ultimately the maternal, figure,
but her motherhood is a kind of universal one; she is the
"Lady" of tales of chivalry, so beloved of the pre-Raphaelites,
for whom the only possible love is a courtly one.

    Uggug is the absolute opposite. Violent, cruel, and cun-
ning, his only contact with others is by way of aggression.
His final transformation into a porcupine is the logical conclusion of the two actions we see him performing at the start-
—his "birthday present" to Sylvie, and the way he treats the
beggar.[2] From the first he appears as a "bad boy"; he is hateful, he is everything that is detestable in (developing) virility. His behaviour to Sylvie represents a sexual attack, at once
sly and brutal, the virgin raped by bestiality. He stands for
virility at its blackest, destroying the whiteness of the lily.

    A final, crucial point: though Bruno does not represent

[2] *Sylvie and Bruno,* Chap. III and IV.

virility, he remains a character whom his author intends to be masculine. He has all the vivacity, the impudence, and the self-assurance of Alice. But there is no aggression in his dealings with other people; instead his approach is one of seduction. Yet it is primarily an *intellectual* seduction, and he arouses admiration (at least in the characters presented as "nice") rather than affection. It is Bruno's mind to which people respond rather than his heart. Bruno's position is thus *sui generis*: he is the opposite of Uggug in having absolutely no aggressive virility, but he is also the opposite of Sylvie in being so impoverished emotionally. It is Alice whom he is most like in behaviour; he differs from her only in sex. Thus he is a kind of hybrid figure—masculine and active, but not sexualized.

In more explicitly sexual terms, these four major characters may be interpreted something like this: Alice represents an active and conquering female sexuality; Sylvie a negative, if not actually desexualized, female sexuality; Uggug a conquering male sexuality; and Bruno an absence of sexuality, or if you like, a hermaphrodite sexuality.

There is another character who must be associated with these four—the White Knight. He is a male figure, but devirilized both by age and by helplessness,[3] and needing both physical and emotional support from Alice: unless someone can revive his wavering strength, he must remain a powerless old man. The narrator of *Sylvie and Bruno* represents a more tranquil variant of the same character; his affectivity is directed not to a little girl, but to a young woman, and he brazenly transforms his need to receive into a need to give, becoming a protector rather than a protégé—a "kind uncle."

I set this fifth form of sexuality apart from the others for it presents one major difference: whereas all the rest are depicted in the characters of children, this one takes adult form. This is of vital significance in any consideration of Carroll's sexuality. It was not just coincidence that most of

[3] I refer readers to my *Lewis Carroll*, Part II, chap. III. Though the word *helplessness* has no directly sexual connotation, remember that it is also a synonym of the word *impotence*.

Illustration by Harry Furniss from his *Confessions of a Caricaturist.*

the vehicles through which he expressed it belong to the world of childhood: it was the result both of the total blockage of his own sexual life, and of his inability to present any possible solution at an adult level. I shall have more to say about this. For the moment what matters is to recognize that this kind of hovering among four or five forms of sexuality is precisely what Carroll did in his own life in respect to his own sexual problems.

The Uggug solution he rejected totally, probably while still at boarding school, certainly from his earliest time at Oxford. Indeed, it is the only solution his books present in a totally negative manner. There is no such thing as a virile hero in his particular world. We may recall what one of his most faithful friends, Isa Bowman, said:[4]

[4] Isa Bowman, *The Story of Lewis Carroll*, pp. 9, 12.

He had a curiously womanish face, and in direct contradiction to
his real character, there seemed to be little strength in it. . . . In
the society of people of mature age he was almost old-maidishly
prim in his manner.

The terms that strike us here, despite the care with which
they are qualified, are "womanish" and "old-maidish." We
find them expressed pictorially in Furniss's caricatures. But
the same negation of virility can also be found in Carroll's
writings, above all in *Sylvie and Bruno*. One of the adult
characters who could quite easily play the part of a virile hero
is Eric Lindon, Lady Muriel's soldier cousin—a young officer,
who carries all before him, and as Arthur's rival, narrowly
misses snatching away his beloved. But he fails, and for a
very good reason: his contact with Lady Muriel (and the
fairy children?) leads him from agnosticism to a rediscovery
of his faith, and that rediscovery coincides with his abandoning the attempt to win her. There could hardly be a clearer
expression of emasculation, and the fact that it is accompanied by conversion to a more Christian way of life fits neatly
into the whole picture. Eric Lindon is saved at the moment
of losing his virility: and here endeth the lesson. To make it
clearer still, Carroll brings in the mad Gardener, whose wild
behaviour, as Phyllis Greenacre points out, can only be an
expression of sexual excitement.

   This rejection achieved, there remained (to Carroll)
three, and then four, possible positions. But these, too, were
subject to rearrangement; we must recall that, in the first
place, two feminine figures are suggested, of far from equal
weight. Sylvie was the possible *partner* image, corresponding
to the avuncular figure of the narrator in *Sylvie and Bruno*,
or even perhaps the White Knight. Their partnership is the
perfect representation of his relationship with all his little-
girl friends: a union of hearts and souls in a totally aseptic—
that is to say asexual—world. And though it may be at first
surprising to realize that he was occasionally prepared to continue a friendship with this or that little girl after she was
grown up, it becomes less so when we recall the kind of identity he established between Sylvie and Lady Muriel. Alice, on

the other hand, was not someone external to himself: *she was inside him*. Alice is one of the direct figures of his sexuality, because she is one of the explicit expressions of his childhood and his own childhood personality. In other words, where Sylvie is a complementary figure, Alice is a figure of identification.

On another level, however, Bruno can be connected with the uncle figure. Alice and Sylvie have one thing in common: for Carroll, as a masculine being, they are possible representations of sexual desire; the difference is the direction of the desire—it is directed toward Sylvie, whereas it orginates in Alice. Bruno and the uncle, on the other hand, are two forms of the negation of sexual desire—Bruno because he is asexual, and the uncle because he has been desexualized. Masculine sexuality has been abolished and condemned in the rejection of Uggug. But it is a sexuality that could be envisaged in a different way if one were to place oneself at different points on the plane of reality to Carroll, the stage director, presenting them simultaneously (since both appear in the same story). Bruno can only represent a fiction at one remove, whereas the uncle could be simply a portrait. In other words, the uncle may be the figure in whom Carroll sees (and shows) himself, while Bruno is what he would like to be (once again). If this is so, then the fantasy to which the two figures respond becomes clearer still: if the uncle is the existing Carroll as age has changed him, Bruno is the result of an attempt to mutilate him in the most total way possible—i.e., *ab initio*. Rather than a gradual abandonment, or fading away, of sexual desire, it is suppressed from the first by excluding virility altogether.

Thus the contrast between Bruno and Uggug becomes even more marked. Uggug is what Bruno will never be, for he will do what Bruno never will: "I always loved Sylvie, so I'll never get prickly like that," Bruno says.[5] His castration is no longer merely implicit, but clearly stated; it is the only possible response of Bruno/Carroll to the revulsion aroused in him by the image of virility. But the contrast does not stop

[5] *Sylvie and Bruno Concluded*, Chap. XXIV. I have discussed the word "prickly" in my introduction to the French translation of the book.

with the external attributes of Bruno and Uggug, for Carroll takes every opportunity to put the "love" upon which Bruno prides himself in place of Uggug's "prickles." (His love is for Sylvie, but in fact it is not the object that matters, for as the Elfin King says, what is wrong with Uggug is that he is "loveless.") Bruno and the Elfin King coalesce in their use of the word "love," and thereby become part of a wider group that obviously includes the Narrator, but also the Professor, the couple, Lady Muriel and Arthur, and of course, Sylvie herself. "Something-that-is-not-sexual" is thus the mark of the legal couple (which tells us a lot about Carroll's conception of marriage), but it is also the mark, above all, of *old men*—and the illustrations to *Sylvie and Bruno* certainly depict the Professor and the children's father as elderly. This brings the wheel full circle: there is nothing to separate the asexual Bruno from the desexualized old men; for though Bruno is presented as man before the fall, he has already acquired the knowledge of good and evil, and unlike Adam, has decided to choose the good—in this case virginity —albeit at the cost of his own mutilation.

Carroll's Itinerary

One can hardly base a description of Carroll's sexual development solely on his literary development. Yet what is expressed in his fiction is extremely informative. What does it in fact tell us if we place it in the perspective of its development in time?

In the first story, as we have seen, Alice is totally dominant. (The earlier writings of Carroll's youth, though offering a number of indications, do so in such a fragmented way as to make it impossible to draw them into a coherent whole.) Her figure is one of active, almost aggressive, feminine sexuality; in *Through the Looking-Glass* her presence is balanced by that of the White Knight, the first forerunner of the avuncular figure of virility overcome. But he is no more than a forerunner, for Alice remains the dominant figure, and their relationship is still a markedly sexual one. Not until fifteen years later did the final configuration emerge, showing a clear and total rejection of conquering virility and a call to castration, and, its corollary, the idealization of woman, not as a mother, but as an angel. At the explicit level, all sexuality is banished. But we are left with the fact that Uggug is banished only to be put into a cage immediately—which seems to show that virility cannot be destroyed merely by being rejected. It would appear, then, that the patterns of sexuality as they appear in Carroll's fiction developed in the following order in time:

  1. the emergence of conquering feminine sexuality;
  2. the appearance of conquered masculine sexuality;
  3. the incomplete expulsion of conquering masculine sexuality, achieved only by the destruction of sexuality altogether.

Though it is easy enough to see how (2) developed into (3), the passage from (1) to (2) is a leap impossible to explain. At least, it would be so were we not obliged to recognize that the progressive eclipse of conquering feminine sexuality in (2) and (3) is actually the essential element in both stages. The eclipse is not total in (2), since Alice remains the dominant figure; but she is no longer the only one, and the pathos enveloping everything to do with the White Knight makes it clear that he has already been appointed to succeed her. His figure is overwhelming in stage (3), not merely by his own omnipresence (the Narrator, the Professor, the Warden), but even more by the removal of the one thing that counterbalanced him in stage (2): Alice. In the final stage, then, we witness *two* rejections, one explicit, the other concealed: virile sexuality *and* feminine sexuality. The very care taken to conceal this last rejection is evidence of how absolutely central it is: what must not appear, what must never again appear, is Alice.

Why not? For the reason I indicated earlier—that the first story, because of the circumstances in which it was composed, is the one in which Carroll's unconscious spoke most clearly, the one in which there was the freest identification; it is the one in which Carroll looked at himself, and the image he saw reflected in his mirror was the face of Alice (or he looked at Alice and saw the reflection of his own face). It

could not go on. Not because of any moral law—the law that
forced Carroll to desexualize man into an old man, and
woman/girl into an unattainable virgin—but because of an
even more powerful law which forbade enjoyment in the very
act of designating the only form of enjoyment possible. For
the castration that matters, at least to the extent that Carroll
himself is the subject in *all* his fiction, is not the obvious castration of Uggug or of Bruno, but the castration whereby
Alice disappears. For what vanishes with Alice is the subject
of the book. As I have said elsewhere:[6] *Sylvie and Bruno* is a
novel of the wrong and the right way around, of the image
and its reflection: Bruno and the old man, Sylvie and Muriel
—both are echoes of one another. But Uggug remains the
mirror image of "something beyond reach in the mirror."[7]
Beyond reach, because it is itself the Other. The demand for
love with which *Sylvie and Bruno* is filled no longer has any
specific object. The need for a concrete object—which Carroll satisfied in his relationships with little girls—has now disappeared. What now appears is desire.

    And my readers will have grasped that, to my way of
thinking, the desire of Carroll is the desire of Alice.

    [6] See "Coda."
    [7] Jacques Lacan, 'Subversion du sujet et dialectique du désir,' *Ecrits,*
p. 818.

Sickness and Health

———◆———

Carroll seems to have taken excellent care of his health. Not until 1888, when he was fifty-six, did he first note in his diary a definite abnormality in his vision (p. 459):

> This morning, on getting up, I experienced that curious optical effect—of 'seeing fortifications'—discussed in Dr. Lathan's book on 'bilious headache'. In this instance it affected the *right* eye only, at the outer edge, and there was no head-ache.

Six months later it happened again, this time to the left eye. It occurred again the following year, when as well as having eye trouble, he had various other ailments, including "synovitis," an inflammation of the knee. In 1890, he notes "a combination of ague, cystitis and lumbago" lasting for a week (p. 481). And in 1891 he talks of headaches, and of fainting one morning in the college chapel. After this, apart from bad influenza, he seems to have been free of ailments. However, when his brother-in-law died suddenly on January 5, 1898, Carroll wrote to his sister:[1]

> I would certainly have come to you, if I could have done so with reasonable prudence: but, with a feverish cold, of the bronchial type, and the risk of ague (a form my colds usually take), Dr. Gabb forbids me to risk it.

[1] *Diaries*, p. 543.

This illness developed rapidly:

> At first his illness seemed a trifle, but before a week had passed
> bronchial symptoms had developed, and Dr. Gabb, the family
> physician, ordered him to keep his bed. His breathing rapidly
> became hard and laborious, and he had to be propped up with
> pillows. . . . 'Take away those pillows', he said on the 13th, 'I
> shall need them no more'. The end came about half past two on
> the afternoon of the 14th.[2]

Dying thus suddenly, of a perfectly straightforward illness, was all of a piece with the style of life he had chosen.

For the fact that he remained in excellent health till he
was nearly sixty was due to a way of life which, though never
austere, was far from being sybaritic. Having decided fairly
early on to refuse invitations to dinner, he used to eat lightly
in the evening—a meat course and a dessert, when his young
friends came to dine, and a little port—and, like so many
English people, ate virtually no lunch. This may well be why
such culinary references as we find in his work are so bizarre:
for instance, the White Knight's recipe for a pudding made
of blotting paper, gunpowder, and sealing wax, and later on,
Alice's misadventures with the Leg of Mutton and the Pudding placed before her at the banquet in the last chapter of
Through the Looking-Glass.

Most important, between his wish to live a healthy life
and his fondness for long walks, Carroll took a great deal of
exercise. In the last ten years of his life, he seems to have
tended more and more in this direction; we find him in his
diary dwelling on the distances he has walked, as though
determined not to be dictated to by his own body. In 1897 he
wrote to his sister Louisa:

> My eighteen mile walk to Hastings is becoming quite a common
> thing now; not long ago I walked there on a *Thursday*, and
> again on the *Saturday*! I hardly feel tired now, when I get
> there.[3]

It usually took him five hours and twenty-five minutes

[2] Collingwood, pp. 347–48.
[3] *Diaries*, p. 538.

to cover the eighteen miles "making exactly an average pace of 3¾ miles in the hour" (p. 458)—quite a good pace! And in the last year of his life, in 1897, he decided to install a "Whiteley exerciser" in his room, to develop his arm muscles. He was, in fact, only sixty-five.

This concern over his health, involving a way of life without excesses or any concession to "debilitating" comfort (though he was always on the watch for any invention that might cause a saving in physical effort), was probably related to the moral strictness he demanded of himself, if not of others. Rather like Swedish gymnasts in our own day, Carroll saw physical exercise as representing a sensible way of life, without either softness or affectation. In this respect he was very English, and very Victorian: he believed in standing up straight, and disapproved as much of interminable meals as he did of vulgarity and irreverence. But when, also in 1897, he proudly boasts of not feeling the cold—("December 15. 10 a.m. I am in my large room, with no fire, and open window. Temperature 54°")[4]—we must beware of construing this as a mortification. He was not trying to subdue his body, still less punish it. All (all!) that his regime aimed at was a respect for the "natural" life, at making the best possible use of the body one has been given, and a demonstration of the power of the human will.

[4] *Diaries*, p. 543.

Theatre

With Carroll the theatre was a pastime, and indeed a passion, throughout his life. As a child, he used to organize not only games of all kinds for his brothers and sisters, but also plays. We know the titles of at least two of these: *The Tragedy of King John* (drawing freely upon Shakespeare), and *La Guida di Bragia*, a comic opera based on Bradshaw's railway guide —trains were another of Carroll's lasting interests. But these two short plays[1] were especially interesting in that they were written for a marionette theatre which Charles had constructed at the age of eighteen, "with the assistance," Collingwood tells us (p. 20), "of various members of the family and the village carpenter." In fact, somewhat later (1855) we find in his diary a detailed reference to these theatrical experiments:

> As our own family are all at home now, and likewise the Webster boys, we got up an entertainment for the assembled party with the Marionette Theatre. I chose 'The Tragedy of King John', which went off very successfully. . . . A Christmas book for children that would sell well:—Practical hints for constructing Marionettes and a theatre (we have managed to get up the whole thing with about twenty figures, for a very few shillings).

[1] The *Diaries* (p. 55) mentions a third, *Alfred the Great*, which seems never to have been written, but of whose intended hero Carroll says: "His adventures in disguise in the herdsman's hut, and in the Danish camp, will furnish two very effective scenes."

This might be followed by several plays for representation by Marionettes or by children. All existing plays for such objects seem to me to have one of two faults—either (1) they are meant for real theatres, and are therefore not fitted for children, or (2) they are overpoweringly dull—no idea of fun in them. The three already written for our theatre have at least the advantage of being tested by experience and found to be popular. (p. 46)

Archdeacon Dodgson was firmly opposed to all professional theatre. But from Carroll's diary, which begins in 1855, we can see that young Charles Dodgson went regularly to plays in London from the time he took his degree. In February, having been to hear a great actress reading *Henry V*, he wrote: "I can hardly criticise her performance, as I never heard anything of the kind before, nor any Shakespeare on the stage" (p. 41). But during that year's summer vacation he discovered both opera (Bellini's *Norma*, and *The Barber of Seville*, which he found very tedious) and *Henry VIII*, played by the greatest actor of the day, Charles Kean, with his wife, Ellen Tree. His account of the latter is lyrical:

> The evening began with a capital farce. . . . And then came the great play *Henry VIII*, the greatest theatrical treat I ever had or ever expect to have—I had no idea that anything so superb as the scenery and dresses was ever to be seen on the stage. . . . Oh! That exquisite vision of Queen Catherine! I almost held my breath to watch; the illusion is perfect, and I felt as if in a dream all the time it lasted. It was like a delicious reverie, or the most beautiful poetry. This is the true end and object of acting—to raise the mind above itself, and out of its petty everyday cares— never shall I forget that wonderful evening, that exquisite vision. . . . I never enjoyed anything so much in my life before and never felt so inclined to shed tears at anything fictitious, save perhaps at that poetical gem of Dickens, the death of Little Paul [Dombey].

Though the tone is indeed lyrical, the comments are far more appraising than descriptive. One of the passages I have omitted, however, gives a lengthy description of one feature of the production: some angels being lowered to the stage on a sunbeam. It is hard to know whether what enchanted him was the technical feat or the depiction of the sacred. . . . But this first of Carroll's theatrical experiences is markedly different from those he describes later: though always aware of the physical beauty of the cast (especially of the younger actresses), he was in future to give far more thought to the plot and its "purity" than the emotional impression it made.

In any case, from 1855 on, the diary is strewn with references to the theatre which continue, without any notable gaps, right up to the last months of his life—the last play he saw being on November 20, 1897. It is impossible to work out just how many plays Carroll saw during those forty-two years as a theatre-goer. The diaries mention almost three hundred. What is noteworthy, though I doubt that any decisive conclusion can be drawn from it, is that he seems to have gone to the theatre oftenest during the years 1864–65, when *Alice in Wonderland* was being written, and 1888–92, when he was working on *Sylvie and Bruno*.

His excursions can also be related to his child-friendships, for they followed a fairly regular plan. First, chronologically: Carroll went to the theatre mainly during university vacations, for the theatre meant London. His visits were therefore concentrated around Christmas and Easter and the months of July and October; August and September were spent partly with his family at Guildford and partly at the seaside. But there is the further fact that the Christmas holidays represented a definite peak, for the simple reason that, in England, December and January are the season for "pantomimes"—plays for children (and their families), generally based upon traditional fairy tales, in which the leading actors of the moment are quite willing to appear. This was therefore *the* season when Carroll could safely take his little-girl friends, and he took full advantage of it.[2]

However, his taste appears to have been pretty catholic. There was no really great writer for the stage in the Victorian age—in its final decade, George Bernard Shaw was a critic rather than a playwright—but operas by Gilbert and Sullivan, and plays by Tom Taylor, H. J. Byron, Dion Boucicault, and Arthur Pinero, appeared regularly, and Carroll

[2] The outings were facilitated by the fact that his publisher was prepared, at his request, to get the tickets for him! See also "Girl-Friendships."

seldom missed anything by any of them. Apart from Boucicault, whose special feature was his effort to transfer the
problems of Ireland to the London stage, it cannot be said
that any of the playwrights of the period were deserving of
immortality. But that was not what Carroll was looking for.
Of Boucicault's Irish play, *Arrah na Pogue*, he said: "A very
effective drama" (*Diaries*, p. 229); of *Caste* by T. W. Robertson:

> The third act, in which Miss M. Wilton, as 'Polly', in order to
> break the news to her sister that her husband, supposed to be
> dead, has returned, rehearses part of an operatic scene, is far the
> best bit. Hare, as Sam Gerridge, a gas-fitter, and Honey, as the
> drunken old father, were excellent. (p. 258)

Actors

Generally speaking, what Carroll was most interested in
was the acting. Of another of Robertson's plays, *Ours*, he
wrote: "The whole play was a treat of uniformly good
acting: Marion [Ellen Terry's sister] showed depths of pathos,
and of fun, beyond what I had thought her capable of"
(p. 384). Certainly, with so marked a taste for comedy ("excellent farce" is a comment that occurs regularly), he was
concerned with the general impression made by each play, and
we find a number condemned for immorality (see later this
chapter). But most of the time his interest focused on the
acting of the women, and even more of any children in the
cast.

For—another somewhat surprising point about Carroll
—not only did he encourage all his child-friends to go to the
theatre with him, but quite a number of the little girls who
became his friends were drawn from stage families and
included some young actresses: the Terry sisters are the most
famous instance, for Carroll became friends not only with
Ellen, but also with her sisters Kate and Marion, who were
also on the stage; there were also Irene Vanbrugh (from
another famous acting family), Isa Bowman (who was to
play Alice in the stage version of Carroll's book in 1888),
Vera Beringer, who played *Little Lord Fauntleroy* for several

years; and many more. Understandably, then, he stood out against the reformers who wanted to see the work of children in the theatre brought under more supervision. He entered the lists twice, actually under the name of "Lewis Carroll," in 1887 and 1889. Of his first sally we read in the diary:

> The St. James's Gazette has an account of a large ladies' meeting 'to prevent children under 10 acting in theatres'. Whereupon I wrote a letter to the Editor, with an account of yesterday. (p. 452)

Here are some extracts from that letter:

> I spent yesterday afternoon at Brighton where for five hours I enjoyed the society of three exceedingly happy and healthy little girls, aged twelve, ten and seven. We paid three visits to the houses of friends: we spent a long time on the pier, where we vigorously applauded the marvellous under-water performances of Miss Louey Webb, and invested pennies in every mechanical device which invited such contributions and promised anything worth having, for body or mind, in return. . . . I think that anyone who could have seen the vigour of *life* in those three children—the intensity with which they enjoyed everything, great or small, which came their way—who could have watched the younger two running races on the Pier . . . would have agreed with me that here at least was no excessive 'physical strain', nor any *imminent* danger of 'fatal results'!
>
> But these, of course, were *not* stage children? They had never done anything more dangerous than Board school competition? Far from it: all three are on the stage—the eldest having acted for five years at least, and even the tiny creature of seven having already appeared in four dramas!
>
> But, at any rate, it is their holiday time, and they are not at present suffering the 'exceedingly heavy strain' of work on the stage? On the contrary, a drama, written by Mr. Savile Clarke, is now being played at Brighton; and in this (it is called *Alice in Wonderland*) all three children have been engaged, with only a month's interval, ever since Christmas [the letter is dated 16 July] . . . They had been acting every night this week, and *twice* on the day before I met them, the second performance lasting until after half past ten at night—after which they got up at seven next morning to bathe![3]

[3] That is, in the sea. *Diaries*, pp. 452–53.

However, his protests against attempts to "protect" stage children seem to have been to no avail, for in August 1889 a bill was passed in the House of Commons forbidding children under ten to act in theatres; and Carroll sent another letter, to *The Sunday Times,* in which, after urging that the employment of children should be so regulated and planned as to enable child actors to get some education, he concludes:

> But I do not believe that the law can absolutely prohibit children under ten from acting in theatres without doing a cruel wrong to many a poor struggling family, to whom the child's stage salary is a Godsend, and making many poor children miserable by debarring them from a healthy and innocent occupation which they dearly love.[4]

The argument drawn from the poverty of the families was one much in favour at that time with employers who wanted to make use of a cheap child-labour force. And it is all the more misplaced in that Carroll, in his letter, makes no suggestion of fixing a fair wage for such work. But the argument of the enjoyment of the children themselves, though to some extent objectionable on similar grounds, does at least indicate his awareness, through his many friends in the theatrical world, of what a world of families it was, with actors' children generally making their first stage appearances alongside their parents. So, though his attitude in this regard may not have been unexceptionable politically, it does at least reflect the depth of his interest in the theatre.

That interest is also clear from an account he gives of a visit backstage in a theatre where a children's play was being performed:[5]

> I had expressed a wish to see some of the mechanism, so [my friend] began by sending me round with one of the under officials to see below and above the stage, the painting-room, etc. after which I went to the green-room to wait for him. . . . The rest of the company soon assembled, many of the little actresses being carried downstairs, I suppose to keep them from the dust

[4] *Diaries*, p. 473.
[5] *Diaries*, pp. 251–53.

of the narrow staircases. I was agreeably surprised to see how pretty some of them were, even with all the disadvantages of daylight and rouge. Mr. Coe put me into the prompter's box: (there was no prompter at all—none needed, he said). I did not stay there for long at a time, but wandered about behind the scenes, to the green-room etc. . . . One of the best hits, from the front, is the snowstorm during which the fairies, in grey cloaks and hoods, enter the cottage, singing 'Home, sweet home'. The snow was very simply done by a man on the top of a tall pair of steps with a basket of cut up paper. . . . I am very glad I took the opportunity, probably the last I shall have [Carroll was only thirty-five!], of seeing the working of a theatre.

On reading such a passage, one can well understand how one of his former child-friends could write, long after his death:

> Side by side with this narrowness of outlook in one direction, was a certain strain of what can only be called Bohemianism, manifested in his love of the theater, his enjoyment and pride in the friendship of distinguished theatrical artists such as the Terry sisters, and more particularly perhaps in his love of child actresses.[6]

I would add, "and child actors," for it seems that in his devotion to the theatre, Carroll was able to overcome his dislike of little boys sufficiently to write, or rather outline, a play for one young actor whom he especially admired. This was, however, his only essay into that field, and soon met with discouragement. He says in his diary (pp. 240–41):

> Called on Tom Taylor, to have a talk about the sketch I sent him for *Morning Clouds*; he has read it and shown it to Miss Terry, and their opinion seems to be that it is impracticable—even my favourite ending. The public taste demands more sensation. He mentioned as a minor flaw the bringing in of the husband (who ought to have a leading part) so late in the piece.

The following year (1867), another theatrical manager was to approve of his outline, but in the end nothing came of it. There can be no doubt that, with his sense of dialogue, Carroll could have written magnificently for the stage: one

[6] Ethel H. Arnold, "Reminiscences of Lewis Carroll."

has only to read Alice's conversations with the three queens to realize that. Yet it may be, as the plot of *Sylvie and Bruno* would lead one to suppose, that he would have chosen the sort of sentimental or melodramatic theme which, though so fashionable at the time, we should find tiresome today. In any event, he was content with sending Ellen Terry a number of thoughtful comments on her acting and the production of various plays[7]—comments that she treated with the utmost seriousness.

The Theatre and Its Message

Despite Carroll's interest in the work, and the looks, of child actresses, the theatre was also for him a means of communication, and even more—perhaps because he so often went there with children—a means of *education*. As we have seen, he would often label plays as "wholesome," "without danger," or "unhealthy." He was never free of such moral preoccupations, and even in comedies, which he seems to have enjoyed more than anything, he was always attentive to the "purity" of the message. In 1882 he sent a circular to a number of his friends, giving his reasons:

> The stage (as every playgoer can testify) is an engine of incalculable power for influencing society; and every effort to purify and ennoble its aims seems to me to deserve all the countenance that the great, and all the material help that the wealthy, can give it; while even those who are neither great nor wealthy may yet do their part. . . . (Collingwood, p. 181)

It was because the effect of the theatre was so powerful that Carroll adopted such a censorious attitude to its treatment of two subjects in particular: social morality and a proper respect for religion.

His concern for morality caused him to condemn as "unhealthy" any play that, either from vulgarity or in an effort to "copy the French," contained improper situations, above all if it condoned adultery.

[7] See Langford Reed, *Lewis Carroll*, London, 1932, p. 80 ff.

Here, for instance, is an extract from a letter written to a theatrical manager, Mrs. Ben Greet:

> As you name 'The Second Mrs. Tanqueray', [a play by Arthur Pinero about a marital situation], I will add that I have not seen it, & do not mean to. The reviews are enough to settle that point. Friends have urged me to go: but I answer 'No, I consider it is a play that ought not to be acted'. And what ought not to be acted I feel that one ought not to witness.[8]

The same author, enormously popular at that date, drew Carroll's wrath for another of his plays:

> In the evening I went to the St. James's to see *The Squire*. It is the first distinctly objectionable piece I have known Mrs. Kendal produce: and I can no longer take a young friend with confidence to her theatre, but I must always ask about the character of the play. I was so displeased with it that I came out after the second act.[9]

But, still worse than this lowering of moral tone in the theatre was the loss of respect for sacred things. This he felt to deserve a full-length article: "The Stage and the Spirit of Reverence," which appeared in 1888.[10] Signed by "Lewis Carroll," the article, which he said was "not going to be a sermon in disguise," sets out to show that the normal purpose of the theatre is to present vice and virtue in such a recognizable way that the audience knows when to hiss or clap:

> When the gentlemanly scoundrel . . . sent the coarser scoundrel who served as his tool on the hateful mission of turning out of doors the poor mother whose child was dying, it was good to hear the low fierce hiss that ran through the audience.

But, alas, it was not always like that. Religious matters, especially, were sometimes presented in a manner to be deplored. This occurred even at the level of the use of words; sacred words were sullied and perverted by being used in a profane context. For, says Carroll:

> No word has a meaning *inseparably* attached to it; a word means

---

[8] *Diaries*, p. 565.
[9] *Diaries*, p. 462.
[10] In the review, *The Stage*; it is in *LCPB*, pp. 175–95.

what the speaker intends by it, and what the hearer understands by it, and that is all.

I meet a friend and say 'Good morning!' Harmless words enough, one would think. Yet possibly, in some language he and I have never heard, these words may convey utterly horrid and loathesome ideas. But are *we* responsible for this? This thought may serve to lessen the horror of some of the language used by the lower classes, which, it is a comfort to remember, is often a mere collection of unmeaning *sounds*, so far as speaker and hearer are concerned.

At all costs, then, the name of God must not be taken lightly—as was done far too often in "good" society. Hence his horror, upon finding Gilbert, in *H.M.S. Pinafore*, using the swear word "Damme!," which was then (in the production he saw) repeated by a chorus of children:

> I cannot find words to convey to the reader the pain I felt in seeing those dear children taught to utter such words to amuse ears grown callous to their ghastly meaning. . . . How Mr. Gilbert could have stooped to write, or Sir Arthur Sullivan could have prostituted his noble art to set to music such vile trash, it passes my skill to understand.

Worse still, ministers of religion were sometimes ridiculed. W. S. Gilbert was again attacked, this time for the "Pale young curate" in *The Sorcerer*—and compared to Goldsmith who, in *The Vicar of Wakefield*, was able to depict a gentle and lovable old clergyman (in an earlier age, of course).

These few extracts taken from a twenty-page article should not provoke too much mirth. On careful reading, it becomes clear that Carroll is quite the opposite of a fanatic on the subject: he explains, for instance, that when in *David Copperfield*, Steerforth is once called "a damned villain," anyone who would object to this as irreverent "attaches a meaning to the word 'irreverence' with which I have no sympathy." But, as he explains in more detail in the preface to *Sylvie and Bruno Concluded*, there is great danger, just because the theatre is so powerful a medium (and the novel, too, if it comes to that), that the harm done by irreverence of this kind is incalculable. His attitude is really the traditional attitude of the religious-minded, except that Carroll, because he loved the theatre and knew it well, could allow for a certain flexibility where realism demanded it and excuse the natural exaggeration of the dramatic.

It would hardly be possible to overestimate the part played by the theatre in his life—which makes it all the more surprising that he should have called on a playwright to transfer *Alice* to the stage. Presumably his failure with *Morning Clouds* had convinced him that he was incapable of doing it himself; the same thing had happened with his attempts to illustrate the book. Savile Clark's stage version is, in fact, a kind of operetta, and Carroll would certainly have had difficulty in writing lyrics. Nevertheless, it still seems a pity.

Trains

The railway, which actually made its first appearance in England during Carroll's childhood, had great significance in his life. Indeed, the first of young Charles's inventions described for us by Collingwood (pp. 19–20) involved a railway:

> He constructed a rude train out of a wheelbarrow, a barrel and a small truck, which used to convey passengers from one 'station' in the Rectory garden to another. At each of these stations there was a refreshment-room, and the passengers had to purchase tickets from him before they could enjoy their ride.

And Hudson (pp. 34–35) gives an extract from Carroll's "rules for the railway":

> Station master must mind his station, and supply refreshments: he can put anyone who behaves badly to prison, while a train goes round the garden: he must ring for the passengers to take their seats, then count 20 slowly, then ring again for the train to start. . . . Passengers may not go on the line on any pretence: parents responsible for their children: may not get in or out of the train when moving. . . .

It is hardly surprising, then, that one of the magazines to which he contributed as a young man was *The Train*. This was a small, short-lived comic paper, founded by Edmund Yates after the early failure of a previous magazine, the *Comic Times* (founded in August 1855, and dying in November of that same year). *The Train* survived somewhat

longer (January 1856–June 1858), and Carroll's last contribution was published in it in December 1857, his first having
appeared in March 1856. The most noteworthy thing about
this collaboration was not so much the pieces themselves, but
the fact that it was the occasion of his deciding to publish
under a pseudonym; and the name chosen by the editor of the
magazine was "Lewis Carroll."

Trains became a very important factor in Carroll's life
because his frequent journeys from Oxford to London gave
him an opportunity—and, at least until he started taking holidays by the seaside at Eastbourne and on the Isle of Wight, his
only opportunity—for getting to know enormous numbers
of children:

> Many of his friendships with children began in a railway car-
> riage, for he always took about with him a stock of puzzles when
> he travelled, to amuse any little companions whom chance might
> send him. Once he was in a carriage with a lady and her little
> daughter, both complete strangers to him. The child was reading
> 'Alice in Wonderland', and when she put her book down, he
> began talking to her about it. The mother soon joined in the con-
> versation, of course without the least idea who the stranger was
> with whom she was talking. 'Isn't it sad', she said, 'about poor
> Mr. Lewis Carroll? He's gone mad, you know'. 'Indeed', replied
> Mr. Dodgson, 'I had never heard that'. 'Oh, I assure you it is
> quite true', the lady answered. 'I have it on the best authority'.
> Before Mr. Dodgson parted with her, he obtained her leave to
> send a present to the little girl, and a few days afterwards she
> received a copy of 'Through the Looking-Glass', inscribed with
> her name, and 'From the Author, in memory of a pleasant
> journey'.[1]

All his encounters did not lead to quite such ludicrous
situations—though his passion for secrecy made this kind of
thing almost inevitable—but the pattern tended to be the
same: encounter—conversation—the sending of an auto-
graphed book. For instance (*Diaries*, p. 282): "I have today
sent off a copy [of *Alice*] to my railway-companions of yesterday, three children named Drury . . . on their way to
Blackwater." And (p. 355):

[1] Collingwood, pp. 407–8.

I made friends with my fellow-travellers from Oxford, a Mrs.
Dixon, and her daughter, Emily Phyllis (aged 12). The adventure had the usual ending—of my promising to send the child a
copy of *Alice*.

Evelyn Hatch describes how Carroll would provide himself
before setting out on a journey with the weapons he needed
for his conquests: his black travelling bag always contained "a
small collection of pencils, notebooks and puzzles."[2]

> If he took you up to London to see a play at the theatre, you
> were no sooner seated in the railway carriage than a game was
> produced from his bag, and all occupants of the compartment
> were invited to join in playing a kind of 'halma' or 'draughts' of
> his own invention, on the little wooden board that had been spe-
> cially made at his design for railway use, with 'men' warranted
> not to tumble down, because they fitted into little holes in the
> board.[3]

I believe that it was these, usually fleeting, always totally
chance, encounters that explain why railway journeys are
so important in Carroll's writings. There are two major
incidents, of which the first occurs in Chapter III of
Through the Looking-Glass ("Looking-Glass Insects"), when
Alice, having jumped a stream, suddenly finds herself in a
railway carriage: the guard asks for her ticket, and when she
admits that she hasn't got one, he replies: "You should have
bought one from the engine-driver." There follows a typical
nonsense conversation between Alice and the other passengers
in the carriage: a Goat, a Beetle, a Horse, a gentleman dressed
in white paper, and a Gnat; finally the train jumps over the
next brook and the episode ends abruptly. It is not an essential incident in Alice's adventure, but it has the advantage of
making it quite clear that she is making a journey, and at this
stage, a modern journey: not for nothing is the last stage
taken at the slow and medieval pace of the White Knight; the
train is fine for making a beginning, but it does not lead anywhere.

In *Sylvie and Bruno*, however, its role has grown, for it

[2] E. M. Hatch, *Letters to Child-Friends*, p. 207.
[3] Beatrice Hatch, "Lewis Carroll," *Strand Magazine*, April 1898.

is in a railway carriage that the Narrator meets Lady Muriel
—in other words, Sylvie, the little girl who is the model for
Carroll's child-friends. The conversation between them,
interrupted as it must be by incursions into the world of
"Outland"—the home of Sylvie and Bruno—also suggests
something of the disconcerting quality that his real-life fleeting encounters sometimes presented.

And when, in *A Tangled Tale*, the subject of the puzzle
to which Clara is subjected in Knot III turns out to be trains,
it is far more complex than the kind of classic problem about
trains that had (already!) become part of the teaching of
arithmetic. Clara, evidently a young girl, is set the test, significantly by her aunt, Mad Mathesis, who obviously represents Carroll himself (the other "problem setter" is Balbus,
who cannot be Carroll, for he is in charge of two young
boys). And the way the trains run—endlessly going around
in a circle, one set always starting by going east, the other west
—and the way the station functions, with the passengers shot
into and out of the trains from springboards, is reminiscent
both of the *Looking-Glass* train and *Sylvie and Bruno*. It
seems clear that for Carroll trains are not so much the means
to a journey as the substitute for one.

Tristan da Cunha

This was a characteristic episode—characteristic both of what Carroll conceived to be his duty and of the rather disconcerting forms it might take. Is *disconcerting* the right word? Would it not be enough to call the forms eccentric, with overtones of Phileas Fogg? I'd say not. Anyway, what happened was this:

One of Carroll's younger brothers, Edwin Dodgson, a clergyman like himself, had for some years been carrying out his ministry on the island of Tristan da Cunha. Thinking that his eighty-or-so parishioners were altogether too isolated, he resolved to get them moved either to South Africa or to Australia. He decided to appeal for help to the energy (and fame?) of his brother Charles; and Charles worked unstintingly for this cause: he visited a most impressive number of highly placed people, and got Sir George Baden-Powell, M.P. (brother of the man who founded the scout movement), whom he knew slightly, to bring the matter up in Parliament. Baden-Powell wrote of the incident:

> At his instance I brought the matter before Government and the House of Commons, and from that day to this frequent communication has been held with the islanders, and material assistance has been rendered them—thanks to the warm heart of 'Lewis Carroll'.[1]

[1] Collingwood, p. 345.

But the proposed transfer never took place.

It sounds like a fairly commonplace story of an English-man taking a sudden violent interest in a somewhat offbeat cause. And so it no doubt was. But it is hard not to believe that what first attracted Carroll was the actual idea of the transfer: it would be an operation very much in keeping with the kind of things done by the "aged aged man" in the White Knight's song: obviously the best way to deal with the isolation of an island is simply to transport it to a continent! And when that island, and its potential recipient, were at "the antipodes," i.e. upside-down, the prospect was clearly more enchanting than ever.

Uggug

◆

"A hideous fat boy, about the same age as Sylvie, with the expression of a prize pig": these are the terms, and it is in this relationship to a little girl, that the first small boy Carroll depicts between the covers of a book makes his first appearance—Uggug, in *Sylvie and Bruno*.[1] Even his name sounds repulsive—Phyllis Greenacre says it "sounds like a combination of burp or gulp and the sound of fecal dropping."[2] And all the situations Carroll puts him in combine to increase the overall picture of unpleasantness.

In fact, Uggug seems to represent Carroll's quintessential boy. Everything we know, whether from Carroll himself or his friends and acquaintances, shows the author as having had a fundamental dislike of boys. To Mrs. Richards, for instance, he wrote:[3]

> I wish you all success with your little boys [her pupils]—To me they are not an attractive race of beings (as a little boy, I was simply detestable), and if you wanted to induce me, by money, to come and teach them, I can only say you would have to offer more than £10,000 a year! I hope you won't get a black sheep among your flock—One bad boy, in a *small* number, has a terrible power of evil. . . .

[1] Chapter II.
[2] P. Greenacre, *Swift and Carroll: A psychoanalytic study of two lives,* p. 194.
[3] E. M. Hatch, *Letters of Lewis Carroll to his Child-Friends,* p. 177.

And Evelyn Hatch describes in a footnote to this letter how:

> Mr. Dodgson once made friends with a little girl on the sands at Eastbourne whose father was the headmaster of a preparatory school. When invited to go and stay with them, he declined, with the explanation: 'As a salmon would be on a gravel path, so should I be in a boys' school'.

Here is another letter, which says it even more clearly:

> I *do* sympathise so heartily with you in what you say about feeling shy with children when you have to entertain them! Sometimes they are a real *terror* to me—especially boys: little girls I can now and then get on with, when they're few enough. They easily become 'de trop'. But with little *boys* I'm out of my element altogether. I sent 'Sylvie and Bruno' to an Oxford friend, and, in writing his thanks, he added, 'I think I must bring my little boy to see you'. So I wrote to say '*don't*', or words to that effect: and he wrote again that he could hardly believe his eyes when he got my note. He thought I doted on *all* children. But I'm *not* omnivorous!—like a pig. I pick and choose. . . . [4]

The following anecdote is more interesting still, in that, like the quotation from *Sylvie and Bruno*, it shows clearly the contrast Carroll made between small boys and small girls when he saw them together. This is recounted by a little girl who was travelling with her brother in the same railway compartment as Carroll:

> Then followed a journey I shall never forget and a time which might have been boring became entrancing. For kind 'Lewis Carroll' took me on his knee and told me stories and drew pictures for me. I had the luck to be called Alice and to have a quantity of fair hair, so he took a fancy to me, while my poor brother, who knew 'Alice' almost by heart, gazed at its author with adoring eyes but had no notice taken of him. [5]

And Hudson goes on to recall two decisive phrases of Carroll's: "I am fond of children (except boys)"; and "Boys are not in my line: I think they are a mistake."

These reactions, whether in Carroll's own words or recorded by witnesses, seem pretty unambiguous. And Coll-

[4] Collingwood, pp. 392–3.
[5] Hudson, p. 260.

ingwood, who had as a small boy himself known Carroll, summed up his uncle's attitude in equally decisive terms: "an aversion, almost amounting to terror" (p. 109). Such a very extreme feeling seems to demand some explanation.

The letter to Mrs. Richards, with its reference to teaching, suggests one possibility. Though written in 1882, it appears that his schoolmaster experience of 1856 was still vivid in his mind. That year young Dodgson decided to take a class of boys in Oxford. After the first day, which was satisfactory, he was soon disenchanted, and by the end of four weeks (and a dozen or so classes), he gave up, saying in his diary (p. 78): "The good done does not seem worth the time and trouble." But this first indication leads us on, by association, to a second: that of the time when Carroll himself was at school (i.e., when he was a small boy). What he says of himself is also significant: "as a little boy I was simply detestable." This does not, in fact, seem to be what other people felt about him: neither his relatives nor his teachers provide the smallest confirmation for his saying that about himself; and his headmaster, when Charles was a young pupil at Richmond School, said the opposite, describing him as "gentle and cheerful in his intercourse with others" (Collingwood, p. 25). In view of the stress always laid on character training in English boarding schools, there seems no reason to doubt the truth of these words. Collingwood does certainly tell us that Charles was "a boy who knew well how to use his fists in defence of a righteous cause" (p. 23), an inference he draws from an early letter: but that incident could well have been simply an unpleasant memory for Carroll, even in old age.

Therefore, if he did have a traumatizing experience, it was something he alone experienced, and probably cannot even be described in terms of objective reality at all. But one may at least suggest a hypothesis, which would tally with Carroll's memories of his second boarding school (Rugby): that is, the communal living he found utterly unbearable, and worst of all was the dormitory at night. In other words, the bullying of the small boys by the bigger ones, of which he describes one instance during his time at Richmond, and still more the sexual experiences, actual or potential, of boarding school life, undoubtedly left a very strong impression on him. Should he have attempted any homosexual activity, or found himself the victim or unwilling witness of it, everything in his family upbringing would certainly have made him react with horror. That some such incident occurred seems all the more likely when one considers that Uggug is represented as a school-age child, like the boys he tried to teach, and that what distinguishes Uggug from his cousin Bruno, the adorable, cherubic, but asexual child, for whom Carroll has nothing but praise, is everything aggressively virile that Uggug represents.[6]

It seems difficult—to a layman at least—to go back from hypothesis to hypothesis to an even earlier period of Carroll's life. Phyllis Greenacre stresses the importance of the age four to five, a phase of genitality when "the increased genital sensations accompanying tumescence and detumescence become bewildering and frightening rather than invigorating."[7] Lacking any positive evidence, I am reluctant to agree with her that this is what actually happened in Carroll's case; but, if it did, then obviously the renewal of that alarm and fear in the prepubertal period could only have reinforced the effects of that experience. Collingwood's choice of the word "terror" to describe Carroll's aversion for boys would be all the more justified if so.

So, though we may wonder what the very first causes of that aversion were, there can be no doubt as to the circumstances that made it a permanent element in his life. Clear evidence can be found in his writing, for Sylvie and Bruno, with the figure of Bruno, represents, in Collingwood's phrase, "the only act of homage Lewis Carroll ever paid to boy-nature" (p. 109). But it is hardly a homage we can take at face value, for Bruno's "boy-nature" is reduced to the absolute minimum—as is clear from the comment he makes when his father explains Uggug's turning into a porcupine as "the fate of a loveless life": "I always loved Sylvie," he says, "so I'll

[6] On this point, see "Sexuality"; also my introduction to Sylvie et Bruno, pp. 18–19.

[7] Greenacre, Swift and Carroll: A psychoanalytic study of two lives, p. 217.

never get prickly like that!" In this context, that can only be
a categorical rejection of virile sexuality. And when he talks
about boys in his early verse, Carroll is far from wearing
rose-coloured glasses. In "The Two Brothers," for instance,
which dates from 1853,[8] Carroll tells the story of two young
boys, one of whom impales the other on a hook as a bait for
his fishing, and then runs away never to return; their sister
arrives at the end of the poem, and ends it with these words:

> One of the two will be wet through and through,
> And t'other'll be late for his tea!

Despite this deep-seated aversion, however, there were
occasions when Carroll did speak favourably of certain boys.
In fact, there were two families with whom this was especially
the case: the Tennysons and the MacDonalds. With both of
these, he took pains to stress in his diary how delighted he was
by the boys. For instance, of the little Tennysons, he wrote
(p. 124): "I saw also the two children, Hallam and Lionel,
five and three years old, the most beautiful boys of their age I
ever saw." And of one of George MacDonald's children, he
wrote at some length:

> They were a girl and a boy, about seven and six years old—I
> claimed their acquaintance, and began at once proving to the
> boy, Greville, that he had better take the opportunity of having
> his head changed for a marble one. The effect was that in about
> two minutes they had entirely forgotten that I was a total
> stranger, and were earnestly arguing the question as if we were
> old acquaintances. (Collingwood, p. 83)

Which they seem to have become, to judge from what Greville MacDonald wrote later in his life:

> One annual treat was Uncle Dodgson taking us to the Polytech-
> nic for the entrancing 'dissolving views' of fairy-tales, or to go
> down in the diving-bell, or watch the mechanical athlete, *Leo-
> tard*. There was also the Coliseum in Albany Street. . . . And
> there was Cremer's toy-shop in Regent Street . . . all associated in
> my memory with the adorable writer of 'Alice'.[9]

[8] *LCPB*, p. 18; and *Works*, p. 799.
[9] Hudson, p. 114.

Finally, there was Bertie—almost certainly the child
actor Bertie Coote, for whom Carroll seems to have tried to
write a play—the only boy we know of who could boast
having received a letter from Carroll, and even that ended
with the words: "Have you any sisters? I forget. If you have,
give them my love."[10]

Certainly all this cannot be said to outweigh the evidence we looked at earlier. Especially as, in the case of the
Tennyson children, and indeed that of Harry Liddell, it seems
likely that Carroll's admiration and indeed attempts to win
the boys over, originated in his wish, albeit unconscious, to
please the parents and get closer to the object of his real interest: the Poet Laureate, or the Liddell daughters. And, though
Greville MacDonald was so devoted to "Uncle Dodgson," the
"treats" on which he was taken out were always in company
with his sister. We note, finally, that instances of such praise
given to boys are restricted to the decade 1850–60, in other
words, very early in Carroll's adult life. It is almost as though
these are the exceptions that prove the rule. Though Greville
MacDonald or Harry Liddell may have found favour in Carroll's eyes, it remains that he felt a profound aversion to boys,
not so much instinctive as compulsive. "Face like a pig,"
"black sheep," "porcupine": all these various, and at times
incoherent, images of the animal lying dormant in the body
of every one of them, figures of which Uggug is the paradigm—these are the images Carroll had of little boys, and the
image he claimed to have of himself at their age.

[10] Hatch, *Letters of Lewis Carroll to his Child-Friends*, p. 119.

Victoria

Alice's aggressive attitude to the Queen of Hearts—answering a question from her quite sharply: "How should *I* know? It's no business of *mine*"—hardly prepares us for the few comments Dodgson ever made in writing about Queen Victoria. We read in his diary, in June 1897:

> Jubilee Day: to celebrate the completion of sixty years of the reign of our beloved Queen. . . . The whole day was the perfection of lovely weather, which doubtless they had in London—a blessing which thousands have no doubt been praying for, that the nation's gladness may not be dimmed. (p. 536)

When he was younger, in 1860 for instance when the Queen and Prince Albert made a visit to Oxford, where the Prince of Wales was an undergraduate, Carroll was content to be an avid spectator. But he had an eye to personal publicity, too: when *Alice in Wonderland* first came out, the first copy was sent to Alice Liddell, and the second to the Queen's daughter, Princess Beatrice. And in 1869, when the German version of Alice appeared, Carroll writes in his diary: "On the 31st March I heard from Lady A. Stanley, that the Queen will allow Princess Beatrice to accept a German *Alice*; which accordingly is being bound for her" (p. 280). But the Queen herself had, in fact, deigned to recognize his existence as Dodgson, the photographer:

Heard from Mrs. Read, enclosing a letter from Lady A. Stanley to Lady A. M. Dawson in which she says that she has shown my photographs to the Queen, and is commanded to say that 'Her Majesty admires them very much. They are such as the Prince would have appreciated very highly and taken much pleasure in.' (p. 215)

We may recall here the well-known fable—and Carroll's denial of it—that Queen Victoria, having enjoyed *Alice* so much, made known her wish to receive the author's other books, and was sent one of Dodgson's mathematical works. The story could not have been true, for Carroll took the utmost care never to confuse what was signed by "Carroll" with what was signed by "Dodgson." Nevertheless, he found it necessary to contradict it publicly in 1896, in a short post-script to the second edition of *Symbolic Logic*:

> I take this opportunity of giving what publicity I can to my con-tradiction of a silly story, which has been going the round of the papers, about my having presented certain books to Her Majesty the Queen. It is so constantly repeated, and is such absolute fiction, that I think it worth while to state, once for all, that it is utterly false in every particular: nothing even resembling it has occurred.[1]

For the reasons I have just mentioned, there can be no reason to doubt this denial. On the other hand, it is worth examining it in the context of the date when it was published, with the approaching Diamond Jubilee reawakening all the adulation, however senile or hypocritical, that the English people were at that time encouraged to give their elderly queen; and, above all, to see it in the perspective of Carroll's general wish to "do the right thing." The problem of his pseudonym, futhermore, was becoming more and more troublesome, and the way this denial reaffirms the ban on identifying Carroll with Dodgson is certainly as significant as its purpose of contradicting a story that was by now thirty years old and hardly likely to injure Carroll any more, still less the Queen.

Shortly before *Alice* appeared, in 1865, he wrote in his diary:

> Left for Windsor. Called at the Ellisons, but they are away in

[1] Reproduced in *Diaries*, p. 526.

Yorkshire. Walked in the Park in the afternoon; met the Queen driving in an open carriage, and got a bow from her all to myself. (p. 231)

But his respect of her was by no means sanctimonious. Here is an extract from a letter he wrote in 1868 to one of his little-girl friends, Margaret Cunnynghame, referring to a photograph of himself he had given to her:

> As a great secret (please don't repeat it), the Queen sent to ask for a copy of it, but as it is against my rule to give in in such a case, I was obliged to answer—'Mr. Dodgson presents his compliments to Her Majesty, and regrets to say that his rule is never to give his photograph except to *young* ladies'. I am told she was annoyed about it, and said, 'I'm not so old as all that comes to!' and one doesn't like to annoy Queens. . . .[2]

[2] Hatch, *Letters of Lewis Carroll to his Child-Friends*, pp. 45–46.

Vivisection

Collingwood (p. 166) tells, of his uncle, how

> I was once walking in Oxford with him when a certain well-known professor passed us. 'I am afraid that man vivisects', he said, in his gravest tone.

And he goes on to say:

> Every year he used to get a friend to recommend him a list of suitable charities to which he should subscribe. Once the name of some Lost Dogs' Home appeared in this list. Before Mr. Dodgson sent his guinea he wrote to the secretary to ask whether the manager of the Home was in the habit of sending dogs that had to be killed to physiological laboratories for vivisection. The answer was in the negative, so the institution got the cheque.

Not content with making such individual protests, Carroll resolved in 1875 to send a letter to *The Pall Mall Gazette*, which was published on February 12 of that year—probably only because it was signed "Lewis Carroll." Its heading, "Viv-

isection as a sign of the times,"[1] makes it clear that its author
saw vivisection as closely bound up with the tendencies of the
period toward secularization (especially in the field of education), and supposed progress in learning, especially in medicine and anatomy. He sums up his attitude thus:

> The world has seen and tired of the worship of Nature, of
> Reason, of Humanity; for this nineteenth century has been
> reserved the development of the most refined religion of all—
> the worship of Self. . . . The enslavement of his weaker brethren
> —'the labour of those who do not enjoy, for the enjoyment of
> those who do not labour'—the degradation of woman—the tor-
> ture of the animal world—these are the steps of the ladder by
> which man is ascending to his higher civilisation. . . . This, then,
> is the glorious future to which the advocate of secular education
> may look forward: the dawn that gilds the horizon of his hopes!
> An age when all forms of religious thought shall be things of
> the past; when chemistry and biology shall be the A B C of a
> State education enforced on all; when vivisection shall be prac-
> tised in every college and school; and when the man of science,
> looking forth over a world which will then own no other sway
> than his, shall exult in the thought that he has made of this fair
> green earth, if not a heaven for man, at least a hell for animals.

The letter had some success, for Carroll tells us that a
branch of the Society for the Prevention of Cruelty to Animals asked permission to reprint it as a circular—a permission
he willingly gave (*Diaries*, p. 338). But, three months later,
perhaps fearing that his position might appear too much all
of a piece with a generally reactionary view of the times, and
certainly anxious to carry conviction by careful reasoning
rather than any emotional appeal, he wrote a lengthy article
entitled: "Some popular fallacies about vivisection."[2] He
offered it first to *The Pall Mall Gazette*, which turned it
down, and then more successfully to *The Fortnightly
Review*, where it appeared on June 1, 1875. That month, Carroll had 150 copies of it printed in Oxford at his own
expense.

[1] Collingwood, pp. 167–71.
[2] *Works*, pp. 1189–1201.

This piece, also signed "Lewis Carroll," is interesting, not only because of its effort to present a strictly logical argument, but also because of what it tells us about the writer. Two points seemed vital to Carroll, and they explain why he condemned vivisection: first, "that the chief evil of the practice of vivisection consists in its effect on the moral character of the operator; and that this effect is distinctly demoralizing and brutalizing"; and second, "that the prevention of suffering to a human being does not justify the infliction of a greater amount of suffering on an animal." This second point leads him to defend the idea that animals have a certain degree of sensitivity. He was to return to the charge in *Sylvie and Bruno Concluded*, when he had the Narrator say that

> most religious believers would *now* agree with Bishop Butler . . . and not reject a line of argument, even if it led straight to the conclusion that animals have some kind of *soul*, which survives their bodily death.[3]

And this argument also enables him to use against the Darwinians the very weapons they themselves use against the story of Genesis:

> I have a more serious charge than that of selfishness to bring against the scientific men who make this assumption [That man is infinitely more important than the lower animals]. They use it dishonestly, recognizing it when it tells in their favour, and ignoring it when it tells against them. For does it not pre-suppose the axiom that human and animal suffering differ *in kind*? A strange assertion this, from the lips of people who tell us that man is twin-brother to the monkey! Let them be at least consistent, and when they have proved that the lessening of the *human* suffering is an end so great and glorious as to justify any means that will secure it, let them give the anthropomorphoid ape the benefit of the argument. Further than that I will not ask them to go, but will resign them in confidence to the guidance of an exorable logic.

His other argument is more traditional, but he uses it in an interesting way. His first point relates to the tremendous development of anatomy in the nineteenth century, of which

[3] Chap. XIX.

he was well aware: medical students, he says, when present at demonstrations made on live animals, far from feeling pity for them, sometimes even go so far as to "mimic their cries in derision"! Man has enough of the "wild beast" in him to make him become accustomed to such horrors, then become morbidly interested in them, and finally take positive pleasure in them. This is the argument he was to use against "Sport" —i.e., hunting—in the prefaces to both *Sylvie and Bruno* books, contrasting the *need* to kill (for food, perhaps) with the *pleasure* of killing. But here he goes further, and on a more personal note, he questions the supposedly unemotional detachment of the scientist:

> In other words, society is far too ready to accept the picture of the pale, worn devotee of science giving his days and nights to irksome and thankless toil, spurred on by no other motive than a boundless philanthropy. As one who has himself devoted much time and labour to scientific investigations, I desire to offer the strongest possible protest against this falsely coloured picture. I believe that any branch of science, when taken up by one who has a natural turn for it, will soon become as fascinating as sport to the most ardent sportsman, or as any form of pleasure to the most refined sensualist.

This enables him to conclude his tract in tones that may have sounded somewhat apocalyptic in his own day, but in ours sound like the soberest good sense:

> Surely the easy-going Levites[4] of our own time would take an altogether new interest in this matter, could they only realize the possible advent of a day when anatomy shall claim as legitimate subjects for experiment, first, our condemned criminals, next, perhaps, the inmates of our refuges for incurables—then the hopeless lunatic, the pauper hospital-patient, and generally 'him that hath no helper'—a day when successive generations of students, trained from their earliest years to the repression of all human sympathies, shall have developed a new and more hideous Frankenstein—a soulless human being to whom science shall be all in all. . . .
>
> And when that day shall come, O my brother-man, you who

[4] A reference to the Levite who "passed by on the other side" in the parable to the Good Samaritan.—TRANS.

claim for yourself and for me so proud an ancestry . . . what potent charm have *you* in store to win exemption from the common doom? Will you represent to that grim spectre, as he gloats over you, scalpel in hand, the inalienable rights of man? . . . Will you reproach him with the needless torture he proposes to inflict upon you? He will smilingly assure that the *hyperaesthesia*, which he hopes to induce, is in itself a most interesting phenomenon, deserving much patient study. . . .

Nearer our own time, in 1948, the novelist-theologian C. S. Lewis was to take up the same argument, brought up to date:

If a mere sentiment [of loyalty to one's own species] justifies cruelty, why stop at a sentiment for the whole human race? There is also a sentiment for the white man as against the black, for a *Herrenvolk* against the Non-Aryans, for 'civilised' or 'progressive' peoples against 'savage' or 'backward' peoples'. Finally, for our own country, party, or class against others. Once the old Christian idea of a total difference in kind between man and beast has been abandoned, then no argument for experiments on animals can be found which is not also an argument for experiments on inferior men. . . . Indeed, experiments on men have already begun. We all hear that Nazi scientists have done them. We all suspect that our own scientists may begin to do so, in secret, at any moment.

The alarming thing is that the vivisectors have won the first round. In the nineteenth and eighteenth century a man was not stamped as a 'crank' for protesting against vivisection. Lewis Carroll protested, if I remember his famous letter correctly, on the very same ground which I have just used.[5]

As with other controversial problems, Carroll's position was not, in actual fact, quite as thoroughgoing as one might expect. As Collingwood says (p. 166) : "He did not, however, advocate the total abolition of vivisection—what reasonable man could?—but he would have liked to see it much more carefully restricted by law." Thus, Carroll warns against a *reductio ad absurdum*:

[5] *Vivisection*, a pamphlet published by the National Anti-Vivisection Society, London.

Never may we destroy, for our convenience, some of a litter of puppies—or open a score of oysters when nineteen would have sufficed—or light a candle in a summer evening for mere pleasure, lest some hapless moth should rush to an untimely end! Nay, we must not even take a walk, with the certainty of crushing many an insect in our path, unless for really important business! Surely all this is childish.

But he could show real solicitude where pets were concerned. Hudson (p. 219) gives excerpts from a letter he sent in 1887 to a friend of his who was an eminent surgeon, when one of the Christ Church cats was evidently near death:

> It seems a shame to occupy your time and attention with so trivial a matter as a pet-cat; but all the modes [of killing it] you suggest, except the poisoned meat, would be unsuitable. To shut it up in a cage would produce an agony of terror: and the same may be said of the hypodermic injection (which would have to be done by a stranger, I suppose), and, most of all, of the journey to London. Is there no kind of poison which would *not* involve the risk of being vomited, and which would produce a painless sleep? My own idea would have been to give *laudanum*, (I don't know what quantity, say a drachm) mixed with some meat or fish—Would not this do?

This is a fascinating example both of his fondness for animals, and of the strict logic (whether resulting from that fondness or from his mathematical training) of his determination to prevent the old cat's suffering in any way, even psychologically by receiving an injection from a stranger.

It does not appear that he himself ever owned any pet, but in his letters to little girls, Carroll often sends his love to the cat or dog of the family, and his concern even extended to animals he came across in the street. One of his sisters records how, seeing a kitten that had swallowed a fishhook, he took it himself to the doctor; on another occasion, he begged a young man who was working his horses with bearing-reins to take them off, and his sister wrote that the man "had the satisfaction of seeing his animals work all the better for being allowed the natural use of their necks."[6] She also shows how

[6] *LCPB*, pp. 357–58.

Carroll combined care for animals with his passion for "gadgets":

> To get rid of mice in his rooms, a square live trap was used, and
> he had a wood and wire compartment made which fitted on to
> the trap whose door could then be opened for the mice to run
> into the compartment, a sliding door shut them in, and the compartment could then be taken from the trap and put under water;
> thus all chance of the mice having an agonised struggle on the
> surface of the water was removed.

The death of small animals was always a matter for deep
concern, and Collingwood (p. 174) tells us that, when *Alice*
was first acted in the theatre,

> Mr. Dodgson . . . put his veto on a verse in one of his songs, in
> which the drowning of kittens was treated from the humourous
> point of view, lest the children in the audience might learn to
> think lightly of death in the case of the lower animals.

Cats, however, seem to have merited special treatment,
not only in real life, as the stories above suggest, but also in
his writings, as is clear from Dinah and the Cheshire Cat in
Alice in Wonderland, and the two kittens in *Through the
Looking-Glass*. We must surely link this treatment of cats
with the very special relationship he had with children, particularly girls. These excerpts from letters to little Agnes
Hughes, for instance, illuminate the connection:

> . . . That reminds me of a very curious thing that happened to
> me at half past four yesterday. Three visitors came knocking at
> my door, begging me to let them in. And when I opened the
> door, who do you think they were? You'll never guess. Why,
> they were three cats! . . . However, they all looked so cross and
> disagreeable that I took up the first thing I could lay my hand on
> (which happened to be the rolling pin) and knocked them all
> down as flat as pancakes. . . .
> About the cats, you know. Of course I didn't leave them lying
> flat on the ground like dried flowers! no, I picked them up, and
> I was as kind as I could be to them. I lent them a portfolio for a
> bed—they wouldn't have been comfortable in a real bed you
> know: they were too thin—but they were quite happy between

the sheets of blotting-paper—and each of them had a pen-wiper for a pillow.[7]

In this instance his attentions do not seem to be quite in line with the anecdotes recorded by Collingwood!

On the other hand, he was surprisingly open-minded, and displayed a keen interest in medicine, especially anatomy and surgery. We find an illustration of this in a youthful episode he records in his diary (p. 78):

> Mar. 1 [1856]: S— was seized with a fit this morning in the passage leading from the Anatomical School Quadrangle. I was passing through at the moment and caught him as he fell: having no idea of what the nature of the fit was, I could think of nothing but loosening everything about the neck, and dashing some water in his face. Luckily there was a doctor in the Anatomy School, who was brought by one of the men bringing coals, who happened to be there. He pronounced it to be epilepsy. . . . I am thankful that I was passing at the moment, and so had the opportunity of being of use in an emergency. I felt at the moment how helpless ignorance makes one, and I shall make a point of reading some book on the subject of emergencies, a thing I think everyone should do.

The next day he bought his first book on first aid. It was by no means the last; for that day, a keen interest in medical problems was born in him, with the result that when his library was sold after his death, it included more than thirty medical works—medical dictionaries, textbooks of anatomy, surgery, and so on.[8] And in his diary (pp. 132–33) he gives quite a lengthy account of visiting a London hospital to watch an operation:

> The case was a man with an abscess below the knee-joint, which had to be cut into and examined: this was done under the influence of chloroform. The chloroform took several minutes to act fully, producing first convulsions, and then stupor like that of a man dead drunk. The surgeon found about three inches of bone actually destroyed, and decided on amputation above the knee.

[7] Hatch, *Letters of Lewis Carroll to his Child-Friends*, pp. 65–66.
[8] See *Dodgson Sale Catalogue*, Oxford, 1898.

The whole thing lasted more than an hour: I fully expected to turn ill at the sight, and be forced to go away, and was much surprised to find that I could bear it perfectly well. I doubt if I could have done this had the man been suffering pain all the while, but it was quite evident that he felt nothing.

This is an experiment I have long been anxious to make, in order to know whether I might rely on myself to be of any use in cases of emergency, and I am very glad to believe that I might. Still, I don't think I should enjoy seeing much of it.

This helps perhaps to explain the arithmetical discussion between two characters in Knot X of *A Tangled Tale* about the war-wounded pensioners in the Chelsea Hospital:

Say that 70 per cent. have lost an eye—75 per cent. an ear—80 per cent. an arm—85 per cent. a leg—that'll do it beautifully. Now, my dear, what percentage, *at least*, must have lost all four?

From the excerpts I have quoted it is clear that Carroll's horror of vivisection was not a rejection of medical progress; nor was it due to sentimentality. And it certainly could not have been a horror of the body as such—for among his possessions were a skull and skeletons of a hand and a foot for sculptors' models; indeed, he even tried to sell photographs he had taken of skeletons! It was a strictly moral and rational position, a deliberate refusal to inflict suffering on any living being, together with a fear that people might come, either out of habit or out of instinct, to take pleasure in doing so.

Zeno's Paradox

It was in 1885–86 that Carroll's focus of interest shifted from mathematics to logic. In this, as in other areas, though the seed was sown early, germination was very slow. Thirty years earlier, in fact, he had written in his diary (p. 64): "Wrote part of a treatise on Logic, for the benefit of Margaret and Annie Wilcox"; and, the following day: "Sent off two pages of Logic to Whitburn." This was in the third summer of his Studentship, and the following October he took up his duties as Lecturer at Christ Church. He was probably, therefore, still under the influence of the teaching he had been given, and any logic must have been Aristotelian logic, for the major works by Morgan and Boole only came out in the period 1845–55. However, since none of this youthful work remains, we can only go by what Carroll wrote and published from 1885 onward.

I shall make no attempt here to assess the importance of Carroll's contribution to the development of logic: that has been done in considerable detail by Ernest Coumet.[1] But I would point out the paradox—which indeed fits in with the rest of his contemporaries' reactions to him—that no one at the time was aware that he might have anything new to offer

---

[1] "Lewis Catroll logicien," in *Logique sans peine*, Paris, 1966; and "Jeu de logique, jeux d'univers," in *Cahier Lewis Carroll*, Paris, 1971.

in the field. It was Bertrand Russell, in 1903,[2] who was the
first to show how much logical insight Carroll had.

Methodology and Popularization

But we must make a distinction. Carroll's writings on
logic fall into two parts: an effort to establish a *method*, and
the formulation of a number of *problems* (paradoxes). The
method is almost certainly what figured in 1855 in that first,
unknown, treatise on logic. It was certainly evident by 1884
in work he planned: "In these last few days I have been
working on a Logical Algebra and seem to be getting to a
simpler notation than Boole's" (*Diaries*, p. 430). And, in
1885: "I have occupied myself at Guildford in teaching my
new 'Logic Algebra' to Louisa, Margaret and the two boys"
(p. 431). In March 1885 (p. 433), he mentions, among a list
of "literary projects," "A Symbolical Logic, treated by my
algebraic method," with a reference to the date of the entry
quoted above. That October (p. 439), he writes: "Began
writing out my Logical Treatise, and filled 37 pages!" The
following year he turned again to practical work, for we read
on June 7, 1886 (p. 442): "Went to Lady Margaret Hall and
lectured for about an hour on Logic."

The high point of his work on methodological construction was achieved in the two serious books, *A Game of Logic*,
published in 1887, and *Symbolic Logic, Part I*, published in
1896.[3] In each case, the preface makes it clear what aims he
has in view. The very short preface to *A Game of Logic* concludes:

> A second advantage, possessed by this Game, is that, besides
> being an endless source of amusement (the number of argu-
> ments, that may be worked by it, being infinite), it will give the
> Players a little instruction as well. But is there any great harm in
> *that*, so long as you get plenty of amusement?

And the preface to *Symbolic Logic*, in a tone halfway
between the gnostic and the salesman's patter:

[2] In *Principles of Mathematics*, London, 1903, pp. 18n., 35n.
[3] The two are now available in one volume: New York, Dover, 1958.

If, dear Reader, you will faithfully observe these Rules, and so give my little book a really *fair* trial, I promise you, most confidently, that you will find Symbolic Logic to be one of the most, if not *the* most, fascinating of mental recreations! ...

Once master the machinery of Symbolic Logic, and you have a mental occupation always at hand, of absorbing interest, and one that will be of real *use* to you in *any* subject you may take up. It will give you clearness of thought—the ability to *see your way* through a puzzle—the habit of arranging your ideas in an orderly and get-at-able form—and, more valuable than all, the power to detect fallacies, and to tear to pieces the flimsy illogical arguments which you will so continually encounter in books, in newspapers, in speeches, and even in sermons, and which so easily delude those who have never taken the trouble to master this fascinating Art. *Try it.* That is all I ask of you!

These great hopes remained disappointingly unfulfilled. Yet the presentation was most attractive. Carroll made his publisher insert into every copy of *A Game of Logic* an envelope containing a diagram and nine counters (four red and five grey) so that the reader could play it for himself.[4] (*Symbolic Logic* also required the counters, but this time the reader was invited to write to the publisher for them, enclosing payment.) Though *Symbolic Logic* went through four printings during Carroll's lifetime, it does not appear that young people took to this new pastime. However, though students of logic may not find it delightful, I think students of Carroll must. It is no mean feat to have presented all the logical arguments, all the syllogisms traditionally favoured with such tongue-twisting names (Darapti, Fresison, or Ferio), in so comical a form as to be accessible while retaining their logical validity. What Carroll's logic loses in forbidding solemnity, it gains in universality. Coumet notes, with regard to one

[4] Hudson (p. 278) describes how Carroll "enjoyed himself, and worried Macmillan's" by his fussiness over the colour of the counters, and then by giving them the job of counting the counters once they were made: He wrote to tell them: "I am having a lot more counters sent to you. They are invoiced 21,200 grey and 14,750 red. The former lots were called 1,000 of each, and I retained 120 red and 150 grey. So that you ought to have, now, 15,630 red and 22,050 grey: i.e. enough red for 3,900 copies and enough grey for 4,400 copies."

slightly different example,[5] since it concerns a paradox, that merely by replacing the phrase "who tells two truths" with, "who takes both condiments (salt and mustard)," and "who tells two lies" with "who takes neither," Carroll is able not only to free the famous Paradox of the Liar of its "metaphysical riddles," but also to make it immediately clear that its two premises are incompatible. If this were its only achievement, his "popularizing" would be of value.

Paradoxes

The other element in Carroll's work on logic came later in time than the methodological aspect. In fact, though Carroll had a number of "Papers on Logic" printed (at his own expense) in 1886, both they and the ones printed in 1887 were simply excerpts from A Game of Logic, or drafts of what was to become Symbolic Logic. From 1892 to 1894, however, Carroll began directing his work not to students but actually to logicians, in a series of texts all in various ways concerned with the problem of what are today called "the paradoxes of material implication."[6] One variant, "A Logical Paradox," can be found in the Lewis Carroll Handbook; it is about three barbers—Carr, Allen, and Brown. But in others, he uses the two characters Nemo and Outis (the Latin and Greek, respectively, for "Nobody"). At this stage, interestingly, what was involved was a serious logical debate between Carroll and the then Professor of Logic at Oxford, John Cook Wilson. The debate did not end there. It was still going on in 1896, as is clear from a letter of Carroll's to Cook Wilson,[7] on which the latter wrote these words:

> This letter is a good illustration of the extraordinary illusions Dodgson is liable to, from want of study of anything like real logic or even real process of thinking.

[5] "Jeu de logique, jeux d'univers," p. 27; the example is on page 192 of Symbolic Logic.
[6] See E. Coumet, "Lewis Carroll logicien," p. 273.
[7] Reproduced by W. W. Bartley III in Scientific American, July 1972.

—which seems a little sweeping. Another piece,[8] undated, takes the problem up again, but in a shorter form:

A Disputed Point in Logic: A Concrete Example

This island consists of a Northern and a Southern Division; but I am not sure where the boundary line is.

The Northern Division is Brown's estate: the Southern is mine. Brown is selling his estate to me; but I don't know whether the sale is completed. The following propositions are true.

I. If this field is Brown's, it must be in the Northern Division (for otherwise it would be part of *my* estate).

II. If the sale is completed, then, if this field is Brown's, it cannot be in the Northern Division (for otherwise it would be mine by *purchase*).

Now let 'A is true' = 'This field is Brown's'
'B is true' = 'This field is in the Northern Division'
'C is true' = 'the sale is completed'.

Then Propositions I, II, are equivalent to (A), (B), and the question 'Can C be true?' is equivalent to 'Is it possible that the sale is completed?'

Here the two Propositions, 'If A is true B is true' and 'If A is true B is not true', both contain a logical sequence. Also they are *compatible*; their combined effect being 'A is not true'.

Hence, if C is true, A is not true; and, *vice versa*, if A is true, C is not true; i.e. A and C cannot be true together.

But there is nothing to prevent C *alone* being true, i.e. it is possible, consistently with I and II, that the sale *may* have been completed.

Thanks largely to Bertrand Russell, logicians have come to know Carroll's name even better in relation to Zeno's Paradox of Achilles and the Tortoise than the Paradox of the Liar.[9] An unpublished piece, in Carroll's handwriting,[10] gives us an indication of the kind of debate he engaged in, in this case with a logician friend:

[8] "A Disputed Point in Logic: A Concrete Example," manuscript in the possession of Christ Church, Oxford.

[9] See E. Coumet, "Lewis Carroll logicien," pp. 281–82.

[10] "An Inconceivable Conversation between S. and D. on Indivisibility of Time and Space," manuscript in the possession of Christ Church, Oxford.

S. And thus your favourite paradox, my dear D., is finally disposed of, and Achilles and the Tortoise will walk off hand
in hand. No argument of any sort can be maintained, which
would prove him *not* to overtake it.

D. No *mathematical* argument, you mean; for, if you permit me
a *classical* one, I will contend that the Tortoise was nothing but the *'Testudo'* of the ancients, a machine of common
use in Sieges—that it was at that moment moving against
the walls of Troy—and that the true reason why Achilles
did not overtake it was simply that he was sulking in his
tent and never went near it.

S. I beg to limit this discussion to *mathematical* argument.

D. Be it so. And the mathematical argument you dispose of, as I
understand you, by the assertion that we find ourselves at
last among indivisible distances and indivisible periods of
time, and thus you propose to plunge us, however reluctant
we may be to take the leap, into the dark abyss of the
Inconceivable?

S. That is my solution of the paradox.

D. Granting, for argument's sake, that the paradox is thus finally
disposed of, let me ask you a question or two. These indivisible distances—are they equal, or unequal?

S. Am I bound to choose one or other of these categories?

D. I fear I can offer you no third.

S. Well then, as I do not clearly see what you are aiming at, I
will, for the present, say 'unequal', reserving to myself
however the right of substituting 'equal' should I see reason
to do so.

D. The privilege is an unusual one, but I will not object to your
exercising it. Let them then be: unequal. Now take two of
these unequal distances: lay them side by side, so as to coincide at one end: will they coincide at the other end also?

S. Surely not.

D. There will therefore be a difference between them: and this
difference, being homogeneous with the things differing, will
itself be a distance?

S. I cannot deny it.

D. Divisible, shall we say? Or indivisible?

S. (laughing) Indivisible, of course. You would not wish me to
imagine a divisible distance less than an indivisible one?

D. You shall please yourself in that matter. Let me now add

together these two lesser indivisible distances. Will their sum total be divisible or indivisible, think you?

S. (after a pause) It occurs to me that I would rather take the other horn of your dilemma, and say that these indivisible distances are all equal.

D. With all my heart. They shall now be all equal. And we will suppose that Achilles has just passed over one of these indivisible distances. What time would you say that he occupied in doing so?

S. An indivisible time, clearly.

D. But the Tortoise had previously passed over the same indivisible distance: how long do you suppose *he* took to do it?

S. As he travelled at only half the pace of Achilles, it is evident that he required *two* of our indivisible periods of time.

D. No doubt. But now tell me—at the end of the *first* of these indivisible periods of time, *where had the Tortoise got to?*

S. I will trouble you to pass the wine. I think I should like another half-glass of sherry.

Nov. 22, 1894

Carroll became enthralled by these paradoxes in the final years of his life (1892–97), and tried to bring to bear upon them, too, his efforts at methodology. The second part of *Symbolic Logic*, announced in 1896, and a section of which has recently come to light in proof,[11] was to deal with considerably more difficult points of logic, especially the "classic problems"; these Carroll, not content with trying to formulate them in a way that could be understood by ordinary people, tried to resolve "definitively," also in terms more accessible than those he used in his debates with fellow logicians. I will give three examples:

2

Pseudomenos

This may also be described as '*Mentiens*', or '*The Liar*'.' In its simplest form it runs thus:—

----

[11] Extracts from them were published by W. W. Bartley III in *Scientific American*, July 1972. The manuscript from which the following extracts have been taken is in the possession of Christ Church, Oxford.

If a man says 'I am telling a lie', and speaks truly, he *is* telling a lie, and therefore speaks falsely: but if he speaks falsely, he is *not* telling a lie, and therefore speaks truly.

3
Crocodilus

That is '*The Crocodile*'. This tragical story runs as follows:—A Crocodile had stolen a Baby off the banks of the Nile. The Mother implored him to restore her darling. 'Well', said the Crocodile, 'If you say truly what I shall do, I will restore it: if not, I will devour it'. 'You will devour it?' cried the distracted Mother. 'Now', said the wily Crocodile, 'I *cannot* restore your Baby: for, if I do, I shall make you speak *falsely*, and I warned you that, if you spoke *falsely*, I would *devour* it'. 'On the contrary', said the yet wilier Mother, you cannot *devour* my Baby: for, if you do, you will make me speak *truly,* and you promised me that, if I spoke *truly*, you would *restore* it!' (We assume, of course, that he was a Crocodile of his word; and that his sense of honour outweighed his love of Babies).

5
Achilles

This may be described, more fully, as '*Achilles and the Tortoise*'. The legend runs as follows:—

Achilles and the Tortoise were to run on a circular course, and, as it was known that Achilles could run ten times as fast as the Tortoise, the latter was allowed 100 yards' start. There was no winning-post, but the race was to go on until Achilles either overtook the Tortoise or resigned the contest. Now it is evident that, by the time Achilles had run the 100 yards, the Tortoise would have got 10 yards further; and, by the time he had run those 10 yards, it would have got a yard further; and so on for ever. Hence, in order to overtake the Tortoise he must pass over an *infinite* number of successive distances. Hence Achilles can never overtake the Tortoise.

In discussing Carroll's formulation of the Paradox of the Crocodile, Bartley comments somewhat surprisingly: "I have never seen its full implications so precisely—and movingly—set out." "Movingly" is not an adverb that would have come to my mind, but I think perhaps that it expresses a response to a new element peculiar to Carroll's particular approach to logic: the effort to *make himself understood*. We recall, of course, what he said in the prologue to *Euclid and His Modern Rivals* about scientific language. But is that as far as it goes? Surely it is patent that Carroll, far from introducing something new is in fact *restoring* something lost: his way of talking is not so different from that of Socrates and Protagoras in Plato, nor indeed that of Zeno himself. That is something worth noting quite apart from any contribution Carroll may have made to the enrichment of logic as a study. For it reminds us yet again of the amazing consistency and continuity of the man's work. That consistency was evident enough in the fact that *Symbolic Logic* was published by "Lewis Carroll." Not merely did he always write in the same style; he always had the same approach to language, and basically, the same way of apprehending reality. Certainly there was a considerable move toward disembodiment from Alice's adventures to Zeno's Paradox. But what mattered is that both were told by Carroll, and in telling them, he made them both his own. Indeed, by 1896 or 1897, he got as much emotional excitement out of a single mathematical or logical discovery as he had once had from seeing the body of a little girl. If we are defined by our desires, then for Carroll, Alice and Zeno were one and the same thing.

CODA

In Carroll's fiction, though time plays a major role, it is not exactly respected: starting with its being murdered, in *Alice in Wonderland*—not just by the Mad Hatter, but by the author as well, who turns it into the ghost-time of dreamland —and concluding with *Sylvie and Bruno*, when real time and imaginary time overlap, one turning into the other, interleaving. He seems to lay time out flat, as though it were space.

We may say the same thing of Carroll's life: it is like fragments of a mirror that can be put together again by the eye, *disjecta membra poetae*. It is all there from the first, and yet there is also a certain development during the life, which one has to try and trace.

Two times are of fundamental importance: 1855–56, and 1880–81. Each of these marks a turning point in Carroll's development, a focus for a particular form of change. The first, 1855–56, represents his definitive break with the world of his family and his childhood. Mrs. Dodgson, of course, had died in 1851, the year Charles first went to Oxford; but though this was a grief, it was not a real break. In 1855, Charles actually became *free*: his starting to keep a diary in 1854 is significant, that being a suitable means both of confirming his already established literary beginnings, and of enriching them in a new way by the addition of what is, for a writer, the most subjective of all forms of communication. That writer then went on to *christen himself*; for, though it was Edmund Yates who actually decided upon the pseudonym "Lewis Carroll," it was Charles Dodgson who made the four suggestions from which he had to choose. In doing this, Charles broke with his earlier works—so much so that they had later to be integrated into the Carroll *oeuvre*, though in fact no great changes were necessary. But he also broke with the Dodgsons, from whom he was thenceforth always to see himself as quite distinct. This break was psychologically essential: by replacing his father's name with a pseudonym, Charles was getting rid of his father—and the fact that Archdeacon Dodgson did not die physically until 1868 makes no difference to his son's rejection of him in 1856. The break was also marked by a new financial freedom, for, having completed his studies in 1855, Charles began getting his first regular salary, and chose what was to be his permanent career. The future traced for him (by him?) up to then was thenceforth determined, and no advice from his father was to change it.

But it was also in 1855–56 that Charles—but we must call him Lewis Carroll now—discovered three new interests which were to be vital to him for a long time, though just how vital was not at first apparent. It was, in fact, then that he discovered photography, with his uncle, and bought his first camera; then that the Liddells came to Christ Church, with their daughter Alice; and then that Carroll composed the beginning of Jabberwocky, at Croft. Three revelations: they were to have far-reaching consequences in his life. Photography was enormously to increase the attraction he already felt for the beauty of children, first of all with the little Liddells; Alice herself was to be the occasion for a major encounter between desire and writing; and in his writing language play was to be the outstanding feature.

It was thus a period in which everything was preparing to blossom, the springtime of Carroll's life in its every aspect.

In 1880–81, he was again profoundly shaken, and though not brought back to his original course, which would have been impossible, he did change considerably the direction of much of his life. Two avenues were abruptly closed: photography and his Lectureship; and with the marriage of

Alice Liddell, who on December 15, 1880, became Mrs. Reginald Hargreaves, another episode came to an end. All three had certainly diminished enormously in importance since their beginnings in 1855–56: Alice was no more than a name, lecturing the sheerest routine, and photography simply a means of sustaining the visual image, a means he could quite well replace with drawing. All the same, something was being shut off, some ways were being barred. The shutting off was further expressed in Carroll's everyday life, for it was then that he decided, and announced his decision, that in future he would refuse invitations to dine out; he was going to lead his life to suit his own wishes and not those of other people. This is indeed significant, for, in fact, other people were now to stop mattering altogether. Not that up to then he had ever talked of anyone but himself: but the mirror in which he looked at himself and saw Alice became distorted, and like St. Paul, he was seeing "through a glass darkly" for a time, as his feelings, impulses, and centres of interest shifted and re-formed.

It was in this period that he moved in the direction of *Sylvie and Bruno*: nonsense, in the utterances of Bruno and the Professors, exploded and dissolved into fireworks; having tried to reduce the multiple—or at least the double—to one, Carroll saw desire escaping, and he put it into a cage; and in his effort to deal with the dichotomy between dream and reality, he found no way out except the clichés of a vague metaphysics which suddenly revealed a sense of aloofness utterly at variance with the rest of his books. In *Sylvie and Bruno*—of which the first volume appeared in 1889—all the complications and all the contradictions of the later Carroll found expression. It was like a kind of sieve through which he put himself, like so much polluted water; the result was a clear stream, canalized but thin, in which logic and mathematics were harmoniously combined. The last few years of his life evinced a wholly new balance, ending only with his death, which was in fact the culmination of the process that had begun around 1880: everything, or almost everything, had been abandoned in favour of intellectual work, which was thenceforth in command. The girls became a class to whom

he taught logic; the outside world became restricted to logicians, either established or in the making; and his greatest
delight was to discover some new method of calculating. So
far as Alice, photography, or even writing survived at all,
they were in a nostalgic haze.

Closing In and Shutting Out

This trend in Carroll's life helps to indicate a gradual
shutting out—of other people, the world, personal interests,
one after the other—in which ordinary "reality" was rejected
in favour of a different kind of reality as established solely by
himself. This is the analysis I myself have made of it in the
past.[1] Now, though it still remains valid, it seems to me inad-
equate. For everything in Carroll was actually determined
from the very first; and if he seems to have become increasingly shut in as the years went by, it is because he had shut
himself in on all sides from the start.

We must remember the threefold oppression under
which he laboured: the shadow of his father, the weight of
religion, and the constraints of Victorian society. Of course, he
was not unique in this at the time, but in his case it reached an
extreme of intensity. The yoke of the Victorian ethic, eased
only towards the very end of the century, which was made
not lighter but infinitely heavier by university life; a religion
which, faced with attack from all sides, could only defend
itself in words, clinging to the law since it could find no liberation in life; and finally, a father from whom he only became
emancipated in order to take upon himself the characteristics
and responsibilities of fatherhood: everything combined to
suffocate Carroll beneath the burden of a law that he certainly found more intolerable than most people did.

It became a social obligation to conform, and a psychological necessity to escape. All his life, Carroll was to try to
harmonize these two demands, or at least to enable them to
coexist on two parallel, never-meeting, levels. He chose a profession, accepted a college post, published the results of his

---

[1] In my *Lewis Carroll*, Part III.

work, wrote poems, joined in some of the debates of the day, and took part in the life of his college. Alongside this he established a second, and quite different, life, in which his "colleagues" were children, and his writings a means of trying to destroy the framework and the content of speech. His pseudonym indicated the duality but did not create it; though it gave it a material embodiment, the split was already there, evident in everything he did. One of the most extraordinary indications of it was his attitude to his manuscripts. He described to Ethel Arnold[2]

> the precautions the publisher had had to take to prevent the theft of the priceless little notebook—of how a detective had been engaged to sit in the room all the time the pages were being photographed for reproduction.

And what Furniss tells us is more extraordinary still:[3]

> He was determined no one should read his MS. but he and I; so in the dead of night (he sometimes wrote up to 4 a.m.) he cut his MS. into horizontal strips of four or five lines, then placed the whole of it in a sack and shook it up; taking out piece by piece, he pasted the strips down as they happened to come. . . . These incongruous strips were elaborately and mysteriously marked with numbers and letters and various hieroglyphics, to decipher which would really have turned my assumed eccentricity into positive madness. I therefore sent the whole MS. back to him, and again threatened to strike! This had the desired effect.

This seems to be the heart of the matter. It was not, as one might have expected, his "private life" that Carroll was so anxious to keep from the gaze of the curious. The wall he was trying to erect was personal to the nth degree, the code entirely his own; it was to constitute an impassable barrier— in this case between nonsense and social status; between, if you like, the fiction and the reality; or, most of all perhaps, between *his* writing and the printing, the book, the reading, all of which were other people's.

This escape into writing went hand in hand with his

[2] E. M. Arnold, "Reminiscences of Lewis Carroll."
[3] H. Furniss, *Confessions of a Caricaturist*, vol. I, p. 105.

attempt in his fiction more and more to create another world, a world that could be judged by its own standards alone. It took the form of a "dream world." But with that world, as with the country Alice travelled in her adventures, it was not really another world. Loving parody as he did, he made that his starting point, but it was a false start. You depart from a text only to come safely back to it again. Alice leaves her world, the world of the well-brought-up middle-class Victorian child, but she does not find anything different when she gets through the looking-glass. What could she find but what the mirror reflects? The strange world of which Mein Herr talks in *Sylvie and Bruno* is no more than a reflection of the England familiar to the Narrator and his friends. We keep returning to the inside and the outside, Fortunatus's purse, Moebius's ring, right side out and inside out: the journey takes place on one spot, for there is no break between inside and outside, between here and what is wrongly called elsewhere.

What Carroll was setting out to do, therefore, was impossible; he could not put up a wall and build a fortress behind it. No more than fiction can exist without reality, no more than the written word is separate from the spoken, could Carroll dissociate his two worlds, for they were not dissociable. Though shortly before his death he was still furiously trying to separate them, by refusing to accept letters addressed to "Lewis Carroll," the whole of this last phase of his life shows how aware he was of the hopelessness of the attempt. Though 1855–56 seemed to show flight as a possible solution, indeed *the* solution, the break he made in 1880–81 was an admission of failure. Just as the real hero of *Sylvie and Bruno* is the Narrator, "I," so it was to be thenceforth toward himself and within himself that Lewis Carroll was to look. Whether we think of it as a closing in upon himself or a shutting out of everything else, it was simply a recognition of a closure that had taken place at the very beginning.

Because it is impossible to get away, there is no solution but to burrow into oneself. To do this does not mean giving up living, but living in a different way. Logic, then, comes to play a vital role, for it replaces the world of men with the world of propositions—or, rather, worlds of propositions, for as Carroll says proudly in his preface to *A Game of Logic*, "the number of arguments that may be worked by it [is] infinite." Coumet concludes one of his articles[4] with the forceful rhetorical question: "Does not logic, by devious means, tend, behind a façade of intelligibility, merely to contrive puzzles?" Certainly in Carroll's case the problems of living were converted into problems of words; and by resolving the latter he thought to resolve the former. It was for this purpose that he used them in the last years of his life. Paradoxes of words, paradoxes of life, paradoxes of the prison one must get out of and yet cannot, paradoxes of the inside and the outside. All this we find in the supreme Carrollian paradox—movement combined with immobility, division combined with indivisibility—the way he himself lived. Valéry has summed up the meaning and the possibilities of that paradox in words worthy of Carroll:

> Quelle ombre de tortue pour l'homme,
> Achille immobile à grands pas![5]

[4] "Jeu de logique, jeux d'univers," p. 29.
[5] What tortoise-shadow is to man,
    Achilles striding motionless!

A Selected Carroll Bibliography

----◆----

The Works of Lewis Carroll Available in English

The Complete Works of Lewis Carroll (see p. 6); containing
nearly all the works of fiction.
The Diaries of Lewis Carroll (see p. 6).
The Lewis Carroll Picture Book (see p. 6).
Symbolic Logic and *The Game of Logic*, Dover, New York, 1958.
Pillow Problems and *A Tangled Tale*, Dover, New York, 1958.
The Rectory Umbrella & Mischmasch, Dover, New York, 1971.
The Nursery "Alice," Dover, New York, 1966.
The Complete Letters of Lewis Carroll (edited by Morton Cohen
and Roger Lancelyn Green); in preparation.

Books on Lewis Carroll and his work

COLLINGWOOD, S. D., *The Life and Letters of Lewis Carroll* (see
p. 6).
EMPSON, WILLIAM, "The Child as Swain," in *Some Versions of
Pastoral,* Chatto & Windus, London, 1935; reprinted 1968
GATTEGNO, JEAN, *Lewis Carroll,* José Corti, Paris, 1970.
GERNSHEIM, HELMUT, *Lewis Carroll, Photographer,* London,
Max Parrish, 1949; revised edition, New York, Dover,
1971.

GREEN, ROGER LANCELYN, *Lewis Carroll,* London, Bodley Head, 1960.

HUDSON, DEREK, *Lewis Carroll: An Illustrated Biography,* Constable, London, 1954; new edition, 1976.

HUXLEY, FRANCIS, *The Raven and The Writing Desk,* London, Thames & Hudson, 1976.

LENNON, F. B., *The Life of Lewis Carroll* (revised edition of *Victoria through the Looking-Glass*), Dover, New York, 1973.

PUDNEY, JOHN, *Lewis Carroll and His World,* Thames & Hudson, London, 1976.

Index

White Knight *(cont.)*
  Carroll as, 25, 105, 107
  sexuality of, 254–255, 258
White Queen, 180, 252
White Rabbit, 37–38, 120, 252
  Carroll as, 21–22
Wilcox, William, 213
"Wilhelm von Schmitz," 118
Williams, S. H., 6
Will-o-the-Wisp, The, 118
Wilson, John Cook, 302

"Wonderland Postage-Stamp Case, The," 54–55, 105
Woollcott, Alexander, 6
word games, 107–108, 116
wordplay, 22, 23, 188
Wordsworth, William, 122

Yates, Edmund, 8, 120, 122, 229, 275, 310

Zeno's Paradox, 303–305, 306, 307